THUMBS UP at FIVE

Adventures of a Hitchhiker

1934 - 1948

by Ralph D. "*Corky*" Sutherland

Library of Congress Control Number: 2004104850

ISBN 0-9753784-0-6
First Edition: June 2004

Printed in the USA by
New Life Press
2971 Ninth Avenue
Monroe, WI 53566

This book is a work of non-fiction. All events
happened as stated, per my notes and recollections
though a few names have been changed as prudent.

Thumbs Up at Five copies are available for $25
Mail your request, name, address and check to
Sutherland Enterprises, c/o Ralph D. Sutherland
2724 West Reservoir Blvd – Apt C-205
Peoria, IL 61615   [Ph. (309) 688-0728]
E-mail   corkymarilou@comcast.net

To my family ...
thanks for your support and
encouragement.

This book is dedicated to my parents,
Glenn Clifford Sutherland and Grace
Juliann Ashwood Sutherland, who
trusted me and allowed me to follow
my dream.

Thumbs Up at Five

* * Forward * *

Thumbs Up at Five is a book outlining my hitchhiking travels throughout the entire continental United States plus Alaska and side excursions into Canada and Mexico. It takes place in the 1930s and 1940s when life had a different flavor. The depression hit, World War II was on, the atomic bomb was dropped and there was a marked separation between blacks and whites. It consists of eight adventures, divided by chapters and is 90,000 plus words long. These are the times I lived through, as I traveled throughout the U.S. from one car to the next. I have colorfully described the world and the many people I met along the way. I think it will be fascinating reading for anyone interested in non-fiction or historical type stories.

I am a retired Civil Engineer. I was born in 1928 to a middle class family in a small town in west central Illinois. My father was an insurance agent and my mother took in boarders to make a little extra money. I always worked and funded my own travels. I have traveled to all seven continents by hitchhiking, during my naval career or later with my family. My excellent memory, coupled with detailed diaries, has allowed me to get the particulars down and keep my stories factual. I hope you enjoy the book.

Ralph D. "*Corky*" Sutherland

PROLOGUE

I grew up in Rushville, IL in Schuyler County. When I entered high school I was the biggest kid in my class. The football coach was standing there, grinning and wringing his hands with delight, in anticipation of obtaining a potentially great lineman. Of course, like any red blooded American boy, I wanted to play football. However, my parents were against it. There was a boy in my brother's class who had gotten killed during a routine football practice. So they told me the same thing they had told my brother seven years before... "We prefer that you do not play football." They weren't being mean, insensitive, or obstinate. They always, at least felt, they had a good reason for any decision they ever made, and they were usually right.

So I forgot about football and, like my brother, I took on a variety of jobs after school and on weekends to take up my spare time. I worked hard and saved my money. One job was carrying coal and doing odd jobs for an elderly lady in the west end of town. At varying times I had jobs working in the A&P store, Keeling's Grocery and the Corner Store grocery near home. In the summers I mowed a number of yards in addition to working in the grocery stores. In the height of the season it kept me busy all week.

I could earn up to $600 a year and still be claimed as a dependent on my parent's income tax report. Back in the 1930s and into the early 1940s were the Depression Years. Jobs were scarce and any work a kid could get didn't pay much, so back then $600 was a lot of money. Early on, at least in the summers, yard mowing was my main 'occupation' and source of income. I used my Dad's old

Rio Grande reel-type mower that made a sixteen inch cut. This was long before ordinary power mowers and lawn tractors ever reached Rushville. For example, I mowed the Scripps sisters' (Henrietta and Eliza) yard. It was a quarter of a square city block, which is a little over half an acre, less the house itself. It would take me all morning and much of the mowing I did while running. I got $1 for mowing it with that hand mower. After I earned $600 Dad would not let me work anymore. Of the $600, it was understood that I would put $400 in the bank and the remaining $200 I could spend in any way I wanted... on movies, candy, 10¢ comic books, or whatever.

From an early age on I had been afflicted with a touch of the wanderlust. By that I mean I always wanted to see what was around the bend in the road and over the next hill. I also seemed to thrive on the excitement of adventure, curiosity and venturing into the unknown.

The first chapter, short though it is, unknowingly was a preview as to what was in store for me in future years. This was the only excursion I was actually reprimanded for and then not too seriously because I didn't do it to be bad; I just wanted to go meet my Dad.

That sort of adventure for me went dormant for the next ten years. By my mid-teens I decided to use a portion of my spending money to fund excursions to find out just what really *was* around the bend in the road and over the next hill. That was when my interest in traveling really took off. After that things would never be the same.

However, I am getting ahead of myself because now it is time to go back to a late afternoon in the spring of 1934.

INDEX

Thumbs Up at Five

<u>Trip #1</u>
* * THE BEGINNING * *

1934

Age: 5 years, ±10 months

RUSHVILLE, IL TO NEAR THE LITTLETON JUNCTION and HOME.

It was early spring of 1934. I was still five, but it was only perhaps a couple of months before my sixth birthday. The big depression was on and my parents were busy doing all they could to provide for the family, which beside them, included my brother Keith and me. Back then, Rushville didn't have a kindergarten program that I could attend and my brother, who was older, was in school all day. Donnie Skiles lived across the street from me. Unfortunately, he was the only other kid in my neighborhood that was anywhere near my age.   Many times he wasn't home because he would be playing with his cousin, Jimmy Davis, at the other end of town... and this was one of those days. My brother hadn't gotten home from school yet for me to pester, or more likely the other way around since he was seven years older than me. Therefore, as often was the case, I was relegated to amusing myself in order to pass the time of day. But on this day particularly, I was bored out of my gourd.

Fortunately, my parents had bought a new car a year

or so before... sometime after the first economic downturn, but before the deep depression which was soon to happen. It was a 1932 model Plymouth. I recall the front doors were hinged at the rear, so it opened from the front. That was unusual. It was easy to get in and out of and seemed real modern. Actually, that method of door mounting was dangerous. Back then they didn't have seatbelts, so in an accident people could be thrown from the car. Sometimes the car would roll over and the people would be crushed. In later years they were referred to as the 'suicide doors'.

About a year after they had bought the new car, in fact on March 6, 1933, President Roosevelt ordered all the banks closed due to the depression. A lot of people were out of work, including my Dad, Glenn Clifford Sutherland, who lost his job as a teller at the Rushville State Bank. Dad had been raised on a farm near Brooklyn, IL, which was some sixteen miles northwest of Rushville. For many years it had been ably farmed by John and Ethel Kelly. Since Dad didn't have a job anymore, he would go up and help John on the farm. By having the new car, Dad had reliable transportation to get out to the farm in the morning and back home at night.

One of my favorite past times was going down by the railroad tracks, which were about two blocks west, to wait for Dad to come back into town. When I'd see him coming, I would stand up and wave. He would stop and pick me up and I would ride home with him. Going to meet Dad was something I always looked forward to doing.

On the day of my first adventure, Mom was busy getting supper so it would be ready when Dad got home from the farm. This was one of those especially boring days for a 5 year old kid with no one to play with and I was more than likely in Mom's way. Since I was so bored, I'm guessing it may have been earlier than usual when I asked Mom if I could go down by the tracks to wait for Dad. She said "All right" and was probably glad to get me out of her hair.

Where the railroad tracks crossed US 67 back then, the Rushville Elevator was on the south side of the highway and the Cudahy Packing Company was on the north. For a young kid this was a beehive of activity. I sat and watched the trucks come and go in and out of the elevator across the street, on the south side of the road. That was interesting, but not near as interesting as on the north side. This was where the Cudahy plant was located. There they took in milk and eggs. They manufactured all sorts of cheese and ice cream, and candled, boxed and shipped eggs all over. It was a fun place, especially the ice cream section. John Petermann often had a new batch of ice cream that he needed a 'professional' opinion as to its quality. I was considered a *professional* in this field and was very thorough, as it usually took me a couple of scoops before I could render my final *expert* opinion. It always passed inspection.

On this particular day I had done all the things I usually did... visited John Petermann in the ice cream section... watched the ladies candle and box the eggs... observed those in the cheese processing section... and watched workers load railroad box cars with crates of cheddar cheeses. [This would be a job I would do, for a couple of summers, a few years in the future.] They were used to me being there. I never got in their way, was always cheerful and never stayed too long. I got to know everybody and even the plant manager was friendly.

Completing my routine I went back outside, along side of US 67 (that was locally referred to as the Macomb Road) to wait for Dad. It was hot sitting there in the sun and waiting and waiting. My 5 year old brain was wandering and I got the idea... 'Why not go meet Dad *further* up the road?' I had seen hitchhikers before and I knew how they got rides. I knew I'd be able to spot Dad's car and was aware I'd have to keep a sharp lookout to be able to get out of the vehicle I was riding in, soon enough, to flag him down before he drove by. Admittedly I was pretty young to start my hitchhiking travels but, though I was unaware of it at the time, traveling was in my blood. So I figured, 'By golly I think I'll give it a try'.

It worked like magic! I don't remember how many cars went by but not many and it seems I got in perhaps the second or third car. As I recall there was only the driver in the car and I think he was driving a Model A Ford. Anyway, he asked, "Where're you goin' son?" and I told him "To meet my Dad."... and off we went.

That first ride took me out to Ryan's Corner, maybe three miles away. At that point US 67 junctions with the Camden blacktop county road which goes due west to Camden and US 67 (which, back then actually ran from the SE to NW through Rushville), curved north toward the Littleton Junction and onto Macomb. Since the driver was going west on the Camden blacktop and I needed to continue north, I thanked him and got out.

Dad was still nowhere in sight as I waited alongside the road for my next ride. I didn't have to wait long though. This time the driver was a rather elderly gentleman, driving an old Model T Ford. He pulled up and stopped. After the same exchange of information regarding my destination, I

4

climbed aboard.

There were several things I vividly recall about his car and my ride in it. It was a two-seater and it had three small pointed pedals on the floor. I'm not sure to this day how it worked, but that third pedal somehow was used to change gears. I do know there wasn't any gear shift as such. Also, there were two skinny levers, one on each side of the steering column, just below the wheel. I believe the one on the left was for the gas and the one on the right was for the spark... and the car was *terribly* noisy. Twice I asked a question and each time he had to lower the throttle so he could hear me. After two questions I never asked anymore because it was too much trouble for him to answer.

I kept my eyes glued on the road up ahead. Fortunately, the highway was rather flat and I could see for quite some distance. Finally, when we were still a little south of The Log Cabin (a small rural grocery/gas station), I saw a little speck coming toward us, that I knew was Dad. I pulled on the man's sleeve, pointed up ahead and yelled, "**DAD!**" He promptly pulled off to the side of the road and I jumped out... yelling "Thank you" as I ran around the rear of his car and out to the centerline of the highway, where I began waving my arms over my head.

Never in my life will I *ever* forget the look on Dad's face as he stared at me in sheer disbelief as he zipped by. His eyes were as big as saucers, his jaw hung down... and... he kept *right-on-going* down the road. THEN it sunk in that it *was Corky*. He slammed on the brakes, backed up to where I was and I piled in. He had at least two other men with him, so I got in the back behind the front seat passenger. I don't rightfully recall the conversation on the way home and perhaps that is just as well.

When we drove in the driveway at home, Mom and Keith came running out of the house and Mom was yelling... "Cork is gone!... Cork is gone!" She hadn't seen me yet on the far side in the back seat. Before Dad could get a word in edgewise she said, "I sent Keith down to Cudahy's to check on Cork and he couldn't find him!" She added, "He asked around and one of the drivers said he thought he saw him standing along side the road out by Ryan's Corner." When she came up for air, Dad was able to tell her I was in the back. Once she saw me her emotions turned from near hysteria... to relief... to thankfulness... to anger. I got kissed, hugged and swatted all at the same time. The truth is that sweet woman didn't know whether to cry, laugh, or get mad, though I think she managed to do all three simultaneously. During all this, I pondered my fate which I was sure I would find out about directly.

At the inquisition, which was held very quickly, I really got off easy. They asked why I had taken off and hitchhiked to meet Dad. I explained I felt I had waited an extra long time and just figured I'd go meet him. It was just that simple. It was obvious I hadn't intentionally done anything that I thought was wrong... ok, maybe it was *dumb*... but not mean, spiteful, ornery, or disrespectful. It then was made *perfectly clear* to me, that in the future, I was to go *no farther* than Cudahy's to meet Dad. Actually, for both my brother and me, the worst punishment of all was knowing that, for whatever reason, we had displeased our parents.

I don't know what Mom had made for supper that night. The reason is that I wasn't at the table. After I had cleaned up, I was promptly sent off to bed. As I laid there in bed, thinking back over the high and low points of the day, I realized I should not have done what I did, but *man* **what fun!** It had been exciting and I'd like to do something like that again. However, I knew I would have to lay low for a few years. In fact it was ten years and a few months later before I rekindled my dream, but this time it was with my parent's blessing.

On the Road Again

Trip #2
* * REKINDLING A DREAM * *

1944 - August 15th - August 24th

Age: 16 years, 0 months, 23 days

CHICAGO - DETROIT - CANADA - BUFFALO -
CLEVELAND - SOUTH BEND and HOME.

World War II was beginning to go our way.

On August 15, 1944, a little less than a month after my sixteenth birthday, I went to visit my brother Keith. He was working for Bell Aircraft in Buffalo, NY as a Mechanical Engineer. My parents took me up to Vedder's Drug Store on the northwest corner of the square, in my Schuyler County hometown of Rushville, IL. Vedder's Drug Store was sort of an institution within itself. You could get a prescription filled, buy the Sunday paper, get a malted milk shake good enough to die for and catch the bus, as it also served as the local bus stop. When the bus finally came, I took it to Union Bus Station in the heart of the Chicago Loop. It was shortly after noon by the time the bus arrived.

A few years before, I had traveled by train with my parents to Chicago on the Peoria Rocket. It arrived at the LaSalle Street Station train depot. I recalled it was also in the downtown area, so I asked a policeman how to get there.

9

He pointed me in the right direction. As it was a nice day and the depot wasn't all that far, I decided to walk and save the bus fare my parents had given me. I knew the train I wanted wouldn't be leaving until late afternoon. In fact it would be some time before it even arrived at the station; then it would be a while longer before they would let people go aboard, and still longer before the train pulled out. Therefore, I would have plenty of time. I began to saunter toward the train station. I gawked up at the tall impressive buildings, watched the buses, the people, and was amazed by all the taxis driving by. Now and then I'd stop here and there, to peer in the windows of various shops along the way and maybe step into one or two.

The LaSalle Street Station was a large building with very high ceilings. Everything seemed so massive to me. It was pretty impressive for a kid from a small town in the west central part of the state. Inside, just off the street, there was a large wide open waiting area, with some shops around the periphery. The various sounds seemed to echo in all that openness. The interior of the station was built out of a whitish marble. The trains came in down below and that is where I headed.

The steps, going down from the street level to where the trains were, seemed unusually wide. But I guess that was to handle what, at times, must have been large masses of people. However, it wasn't too busy when I arrived. There was a broad landing about half way down. Ahead of me a lady was trying to get her baby carriage down the steps, bumping one step at a time while dragging a small, rather shabby suitcase and also trying to marshal a young child. She had her hands full. I easily caught up with her and said I'd carry her bag down for her. I guess I didn't look like a crook because she smiled and handed it to me. I put the small suitcase under the arm that I was carrying my bag with and with my other hand I took hold of the front of the stroller and raised it up off the steps. She picked up the back of the stroller and proceeded down much faster and easier to the bottom of the steps. I returned her suitcase, she thanked me and we went our respective ways.

Once below, the first thing I did was to search for the ticket counters. When I located the right window I purchased my round trip ticket to Buffalo, NY and back. After that, the waiting game began. While I waited for my train to be announced, I sat on the very hard oak benches and watched the people. I always found watching people fascinating. The Jesus people were around proclaiming the coming of the end of the world. Some of them claimed that you could find out the details if you'd give them 25¢ for a pamphlet they were selling. Here and there you would see an obvious homeless person wandering aimlessly about, and now and then you could spot a few passed out winos curled up in a corner sleeping. There were the usual moochers wanting to know if you could spare a dime. Naturally, due to the war, there was a wide mix of armed forces personnel of all branches and ranks, but mostly enlisted. They appeared to be continuously on the move. Other people just meandered around gawking at nothing in particular. They were probably killing time, just like I was, until their train was called. Everyone seemed pretty aloof and it was hard to get a conversation going with anyone who might even sit down next to you. However, now and then one would converse with you. I couldn't help but wonder of all the tales these people could have told. You only saw them for a moment and probably never would again.

By now, I was beginning to get a little hungry. I hadn't eaten since breakfast, but then I'd been too busy to think much about that. Fortunately, Mom had packed me a lunch with a couple of sandwiches, an apple, some crackers, candy bar, etc. I broke open my sack and ate most of it, but saved a sandwich and the apple for later.

During my wait, there were announcements of train departures and arrivals to and from points all over the country. The station announcer's voice would reverberate through the cavernous confines of the LaSalle Street Station with a hollow, eerie, echoing sound. It was relatively cool down there and there was always a good breeze from somewhere. I suppose it was due to a battery of huge ventilation fans used primarily to suck out the fumes from the trains, etc. One could detect different smells occasionally, but nothing obnoxious really, just different than what I was accustomed to.

Late in the afternoon, and after what seemed to be an eternity, came the announcement I was waiting for. The station announcer with an authoritative voice called out, "Train #4077 for Gary... Kalamazoo... Ann Arbor... Detroit... and, <u>Buff</u>-a-low... now boarding on Track 9." I got in line. The man at the gate punched my ticket and I boarded the closest car. Before long I heard the conductor call out in a very resonate voice, "All Ab<u>oooo</u>aarrd." With that, the whistle tooted a couple of times, the train lurched and we slowly pulled forward. Soon we were out of the station. The train gently swayed back and forth as we rolled through South Chicago. The clickity-clack, clickity-clack, clickity-clack sound of the car's trucks (wheel assemblies) crossing the rail splices, got closer and closer together as we picked up speed. We headed southeast past tenements, factories, neighborhoods, crossed over the Calumet River along the south end of Lake Michigan, through Hammond and swung through Gary, IN. I fascinatingly watched the scenery as we passed and enjoyed seeing the cars lined up at crossings and the red lights flashing alternately on the cross-buck signals as we passed through. There were small parks with children swinging, sliding and using the overhead bars that look like a horizontal ladder, several feet off the ground. We flashed by small neighborhoods and business areas, where old men would sit in front of the stores to watch the train go by... just as I was watching them. I looked out the window until it was too dark to see. After that I just observed the other passengers on the train. We made short stops at the various cities that had been called out by the station announcer. Gradually I dozed off somewhere between Kalamazoo and Ann Arbor.

We had to make a stop in Detroit where we were going to switch some cars as well as change the crew. The train stopped with a jolt, which woke me up. I looked out and saw several railroad workers passing back and forth carrying lanterns. They were shouting and uncoupling some cars, and as we switched to a side track they were coupling on others. Thus, we jockeyed back and forth for some time. It was fascinating to watch them work. After they had taken out the cars they didn't want and added the ones they wanted to pick up, we continued east, a short distance to and across the Detroit River. This was the international border between the United States and Canada. At some point we had to switch the crew, but I don't know exactly when that took place. With the crossing of the Detroit River, we now had passed into Windsor, Ontario, Canada. It was shortly after midnight and we now had a new conductor. He and an assistant made their rounds through the passenger cars, checking people's ID cards and tickets. I just used my birth certificate for my ID since I didn't have a passport in those days. I had been in Canada once before with my parents when I was six years old. We had crossed into Canada at Sault Ste Marie, Ontario and Upper Michigan however, this was the first time I had actually traveled out of the country by myself and on my own.

I broke out the rest of the lunch Mom had packed and ate it. The train gradually picked up speed, and with our whistle announcing our approach to several small towns along our way, we rolled on east through southern Ontario. I was beginning to get sleepy again. As I drifted off, I was aware of a strange gut feeling that this thrilling adventure, of being on my own, was just the tip of the iceberg... and that there would be a lot more of this sort of thing in store for me.

I vaguely recall stopping at what I presume was London, Ontario, then I drifted back to sleep again. Gradually, the sky grew lighter as we rumbled on through the early morning mist. It was interesting to see the inhabitants of the small villages beginning to go about their chores. Many would look up and wave at the train as we rolled through the land, with our whistle wailing a warning as we approached their crossings. We passed through a light shower a couple of times, but then the weather cleared again as we continued our trek eastward. By now we had nearly traversed the southern tip of the portion of Ontario that lies just above Lake Erie. The next stop I recall was at Hamilton, at the very western tip of Lake Ontario. It was light now. There we switched a few cars that were obviously destined for Toronto. After we left Hamilton, it

14

wasn't long before the train crossed the Niagara River and we were back in the USA. Again, we switched conductors and repeated the ID and ticket check, even though we were very near to our final destination. Shortly after that we pulled into Buffalo, NY. I don't recall the time, but it was probably early to mid-morning by the time we actually arrived at the train station.

Unknown to me, a few hours before he was to meet me Keith had gotten called into work. Since he couldn't be there, he asked his friend, Warren Jefferies, to meet me instead. He gave Warren my description so he'd know who to look for. Warren didn't have too much trouble spotting a tall, lone, 16 year old kid, who obviously was looking for a familiar face in the crowd and was not being too successful.

Warren came over to me and asked if I was Corky. When I told him I was, he explained about Keith being called into work and said we had a few hours to kill before Keith would be off. He then shocked me by asking if I wanted to go flying. '**WOW!** Is the Pope Catholic? Sure I did!' As it turned out, Warren happened to be a test pilot for Bell and, as such, had access to the use of their planes. We got in his car and drove from the depot out to Bell's field. We went through security and he checked out a Taylorcraft. Once we were in and buckled up, he hit the ignition switch. There was a whine, a couple of mild backfires and it started. Warren taxied out and waited in a holding area for an assignment by the control tower, as to what specific runway he was to use. Before long he was assigned one and we taxied over to it. While again waiting for tower clearance, this time for take off, he revved the engine to make sure it purred as smooth as silk. When the tower gave him clearance, he gunned the engine and we hurtled down the runway. A couple of light bounces and we were in the air. After he had pulled up and leveled off, he asked if I had seen Niagara Falls yet. I told him "No." He said, "Well, let's fly over there and *you* fly the plane. *Then* you can say the first time you saw Niagara Falls... you flew a plane over it!"

Niagara Falls and the Maid of the Mist.

So I did! I had read several books about flying, and the handling of a small plane, so *doing it* didn't scare or intimidate me at all. Actually, if I had known what the air speed should be I wouldn't even have minded taking off, or bringing it in for a landing for that matter. Of course I didn't ask and naturally he didn't offer.

He gave me a fast lesson on what to do and how to do it. Actually, he didn't tell me anything I didn't already know however, I kept my mouth shut and attentively listened for any pointers that would help me. Then he told me to go ahead and experiment. I pulled back gently, *always* gently, on the stick which made us rise, then forward to go down at a gradual angle. I banked to the left and right using a light pressure to my rudder pedals, gently leaning the stick in the direction of the bank. I did a full circle or two and even a spiraling ascent and descent. Of course, I kept a sharp lookout at all times for any other aircraft that might be in the area, as I am sure he was doing also. Warren would tell me what compass heading to go back to occasionally. They were all simple maneuvers, nothing dramatic or breathtaking. All told, I imagine I flew for at least forty-five minutes to an hour before we headed back. As we approached the field, Warren took over the controls and brought the plane in for a perfect landing. Certainly this was a day and an experience that I'd never forget.

After turning the plane in, Warren had some minor paperwork to finish after the completion of the flight. He then took me over to the cafeteria at the Bell field and bought my lunch, saying Keith would meet me here at the cafeteria about 2:00 p.m. By now it was after twelve. Since I knew where Keith was going to meet me and when, I told Warren that he didn't have to baby-sit me if he had something else he needed to do. I thanked him for meeting me, taking me flying and for lunch. We shook hands and he left.

I still had a good hour before Keith could meet me, so I went out and just looked at the planes. I decided to take a walk along the fence that separated Bell's airfield from the area I was in. As I was walking along the fence I saw a plane coming in very low... but I didn't hear anything. It just drifted in over me, maybe only thirty to fifty feet, maximum, above my head. I just knew the pilot was in trouble. I couldn't hear the plane's engine and then I noticed IT DIDN'T HAVE ANY PROPELLERS! I figured somehow the pilot lost them and was making an emergency 'dead stick' landing! Just after he had passed over my head, I heard a **"WHOOSSSHHH."** *I had just seen my first jet,* even though I didn't know exactly what I *had* seen at the time. I later learned it was actually the Bell XP-59A, called the Aircomet. It was the first U.S. jet fighter plane ever made and was still rather semisecret; at least there had been no press release that they even existed. The first flight was on October 2, 1942. The Bell Aircomets were far from a great success, but it was the first jet for the U.S. It only flew operationally for about a year and mainly served as a pilot training unit for other jet aircraft being developed. At least it was a beginning. After that I returned to the cafeteria to meet Keith.

I stayed with Keith in his third floor apartment on Delaware Ave. It was about two blocks south of Kingman Ave. which was a main E-W arterial highway in Buffalo. Where he lived was a T intersection with Delaware, which ran N-S as the top of the T, and the E-W side street forming the stem. Keith's apartment house was on the northwest corner. There was a neighborhood delicatessen across the street, at the top of the T, and a small traffic circle with a little park in the middle, a few blocks south of there, called Victoria Park. I didn't know it then, but my vivid memory of this location and area was to keep me out of a jail on the Mexican border less than a year later. But... that's another story.

One of my more memorable experiences occurred the night of August 19th when Keith and I took the Lake Ferry over to Toronto, Canada. There was a storm that night. The ferry was lurching, pitching, yawing and waves were breaking over the rail on the lower deck. Inside, in the ship's parlor, a band was playing the hit tune of the time, over and over. It was named, *You'll Never Walk Alone* and was about a storm, at sea, at night. Certainly that was appropriate that evening. For some unexplainable reason, that setting and those conditions made a very stimulating and indelible impression on me. One I never forgot. In fact, to this day, in my mind I can still hear that music; see the ferry; the waves breaking over the railing; feel the motion of the ship below my feet and know the thrill and exhilaration of that night. I can't and will not even attempt to explain it, but from that night on, there have been many subsequent August 19^{ths} during which some memorable event or special occurrence has taken place. For the most part they have been good. Later I even began a file of events occurring on August, 19th. Now, I don't mean to imply that August 19th is mystical or anymore unique than any other date... but it seems special to me.

The next morning after reaching Toronto, we went sightseeing. We toured many places of interest and I was very impressed with Toronto. One of the highlights was an Army-Navy Club downtown that somehow Keith got us into. In there, on display, they had the wicker seat that belonged to the World War I German flying Ace, Baron Manfred von Richthofen (May 2, 1882 - April 21, 1918). He was often referred to as The Red Baron, because of the red colored three winged (tri-plane), Fokker DR-1 Drideker that he flew. He was the all time leading fighter pilot in World War I, reportedly having downed eighty planes. The cause of his demise is in dispute. Von Richthofen was chasing a British plane at the time. He was very low, only a few feet above some frontline allied trenches in the Somme battlefield in France. Australian soldiers were in the trenches and were firing up at his plane as he passed over. The downing of his plane was credited to a Canadian pilot by the name of Captain

Arthur Brown.   Captain Brown had just gotten on von Richthofen's tail and was shooting at him, in the process of coming to the aid of the British flier that von Richthofen was pursuing. The Baron crashed and when the Allies recovered Von Richthofen's body from his wrecked plane they noticed that the path, of what was very likely the bullet that actually killed him, came from the lower left, up and out the top right of his chest. Therefore, the Australian's claimed only one of their people could have been in the position to have fired that shot so they claimed that they deserved the credit. Nonetheless, his plane was shot down by Captain Brown and the Canadian's have his wicker seat. The British dropped a note at the German air base at Cappy notifying the Germans of Von Richthofen's death. He was buried in France with full military honors. His body was later returned to Germany and resides at the family plot in Wiesbaden, Germany.

Keith and I stayed a couple of nights in Toronto. We did a lot of sightseeing and ate in some nice places. Then we took the ferry back to Buffalo. I stayed with Keith another day or so and then he took me back to the train station.

My trip from Buffalo back to Illinois was by train, just as it was going out. However, this time I passed on the south side of Lake Erie, through Pennsylvania, Ohio, going through Cleveland, Toledo, then across northern Indiana, through South Bend and into Chicago.

After reaching Chicago, I made my way back to the bus station. It was still morning, but already hot with the promise of getting hotter. As I entered the bus station waiting room my nostrils immediately sensed an unpleasant assortment of stale, stagnant, musty odors and some I don't care to further describe. There was the usual din of voices, many of which you couldn't understand.   Big green flies were buzzing around, the floor was filthy and several children were bawling loudly. I couldn't blame them for that because I didn't like it in there either. Then I found I would have to wait several hours to get a bus to take me to my hometown of Rushville. Since it was early in the day and I was the one making the decisions, I decided to hitchhike home. I knew it would be faster and wouldn't cost anything. I'm not sure if I remembered my parent's reactions to my first hitching experience ten years earlier, but if I did... it didn't deter me. After all that was then, this was now and I was... 'well almost' grown up, or so I thought. First, I got out of the downtown area by taking local buses and getting transfers to get to a place where I figured it would be easier to get a more meaningful ride. Actually, I did quite well. I had a few waits along the way, especially after turning off of US 66 (later I-55) at McLean and heading west toward Havana, but not many and overall I made pretty good time.

When I walked in the door at home Dad took his watch out of his pocket, looked at it and said with a not too happy look on his face... "Your bus doesn't leave Chicago for five minutes yet... so what are you doing home?" I explained, "I first went to the bus station but it was crowded, hot and noisy, and I would have had to wait there for at least three full hours with nothing to do but sweat and watch the flies. By hitchhiking home, I could be doing something productive, save my bus fare and be a heck of a lot more comfortable out in the open air." Well, the folks weren't too thrilled that I hitchhiked home, but I *was* standing there, fit as a fiddle. Nothing terrible had happened to me and everything had turned out all right. Therefore, there wasn't too much they could say, except that they were glad I was home safe and sound and were glad that I had had a nice time. This time I

21

didn't have to go to bed without my supper.

It had been a great trip! I had enjoyed the challenge and responsibility of being on my own, making decisions, and in general just plain taking care of myself. It was an exhilarating experience.

There was something else also... I had already begun to have some of those *restless feelings* inside and it wasn't long before I seriously began considering possible future excursions. However, I tactfully kept those ideas to myself for the time being. The time wasn't quite ripe to share those thoughts with anyone else. So, I decided to put them on hold until after the coming winter and see what ideas or possible plans I might conjure up by the following spring.

Route 66

1945 - May 27th - June 13th

Age: 16 years, 10 months, 5 days

ST LOUIS - TULSA - AMARILLO - ALBUQUERQUE - FLAGSTAFF - GRAND CANYON - PHOENIX - MEXICO - SAN DIEGO - LAS VEGAS - SALT LAKE CITY - OMAHA - MOLINE and HOME.

My thoughts had been spinning ever since my August 1944 trip when I traveled to Buffalo, NY to visit my brother. Hitchhiking home wasn't premeditated; it was for expediency's sake. The whole travel experience of being on your own and responsible for one's well being, gave me a great feeling of accomplishment. The hitchhiking part I found especially gratifying because you meet so many interesting people. Now, my parents weren't exactly happy that I had hitchhiked home from Chicago, but the roof didn't cave in on me either.

I spent the next several months thinking privately about the fun I had and how I *might* be able to do more, but with my parent's approval in advance. At some point during that winter I came to the conclusion that I wanted to eventually travel to all of the then 48 states of the Union. Hitchhiking was a lot of fun and a cheap way to go. I would not ask my parents to fund my excursions, or any portion thereof, because: First, it wouldn't be right, or fair to my brother. Second, even as a kid I always had a job and I saved a good portion of my money, therefore, I knew I could swing it financially without borrowing. In those post depression and wartime days, you didn't borrow for *anything* that wasn't *absolutely* necessary and a pleasure trip, to anywhere, certainly didn't qualify. And finally, third and maybe the most important, I wanted to do it *all* by myself. The only real problem was to figure out how to get my parent's blessing to let their youngest and most *precious* son (my brother never agreed with that opinion), to go traipsing around the country by himself. We were a close family and I would not go against my parent's wishes. If they had said NO... then NO it would have been... (well, at least for the time being).

As it turned out, getting their permission was *much easier* that I had imagined. In early spring of 1945, I told Mom and Dad what I wanted to do. I made them a simple, direct and clear proposition. I told them, "If you will let me go hitchhiking, I promise I will mail you a card each day and I will not do anything that would make you ashamed of me." It worked! They said, "Fair enough, we trust you," and we had a bargain. They kept their word and I kept mine. Oh, I suppose now and then I did a few things that they would have preferred I hadn't done or that they would have thought was not too bright, but never anything that would have made them *ashamed* of me.

Back in those times it was a different world. There wasn't too much danger going off alone, at least if you behaved yourself and used common sense. I was a big kid, large for my 16 years of age and could take care of myself. Also, World War II was on and people seemed closer, that is more willing to lend a hand and more friendly. Also, I wore khaki clothes which resembled army clothing. They were durable, comfortable and neat, and didn't show soil too easily. Since they did look like army clothing, I'm sure they helped me get a lot of rides that I might not have gotten otherwise.

For my next trip, I set my sights on the Southwest. I planned to leave as soon as school was out. One of my two first cousins, Loren Ashwood, lived in Phoenix with his wife Helen and Ann, their brand new daughter. So, I decided to head there, via St. Louis, Tulsa, Amarillo, Albuquerque, the Grand Canyon, then down to Phoenix. After visiting with them a couple of days I would go on over into California. I even toyed with the idea of dipping down into Mexico, then to the Pacific Coast at San Diego, up to Los Angeles and then head back via Las Vegas, Salt Lake City, Omaha, Des Moines and Moline.

A hitchhiker soon learns a few good lessons from experience. For example, such things as: 1) Never get into a vehicle without first asking how far the driver is going. You don't want to get a ride for two miles or out into the middle of nowhere. When people have their speed up, they don't like to stop, hence it is harder to get another ride. 2) Always exhale as you open the door of a vehicle stopping to offer you a ride. As you stick your head inside, inhale quickly to see if you detect any booze. If you do, it is a good idea to be looking for a town 180-degrees from your immediate destination. That lets you gracefully get out of a potentially bad situation and you won't offend anyone. 3) Be clean shaven. 4) Act alive and as if you're really glad they stopped to give you a ride. This will make a good impression. Lastly, 5) be talkative and tell about yourself (within reason), if you feel it is appropriate. Usually this puts the person picking you up more at ease and your friendliness might get you an extended ride. However... I would have to wait until I reached Tulsa before I learned my most important lesson of all pertaining to the art of hitchhiking.

My parents drove me to the southwest city limits of Rushville, out by Scripps Park. They pulled into a gas station area a short distance away to wait until I got my first ride. Before long, a car stopped that was going my way. I waved to my folks, got in the car and my trip had begun. It was Tuesday, May 27, 1945.

I don't remember any special occurrences that first day, except that I finally made it to St. Louis late in the afternoon. I picked up US 66, later known as I-44 and attempted to get as far toward the west limits of the city as I could. This way I would eliminate as much of the next day's early morning local traffic as possible. I also needed to find a place to bunk for the night.

Back then your hotels were normally downtown, and as for motels they were pretty non-existent in those days. Oh, there were some around and maybe a decent one here and there. More often, a lot of those you did find were nothing more than junky one room cabins with the paint peeling and a torn screen door hanging from one hinge. They always seemed to come equipped with a weathered, homemade, wooden sign in front on which someone had sloppily printed MOTEL. They left a good deal to be desired by most folks. What I was looking for was a *tourist home*. For those who are not familiar with the term, a tourist home is just what the name implies, a home that takes in tourists. Often times they were a nice large older home, owned by a widow whose family was grown and gone. There would be a small sign, somewhere in front, that usually read Tourist Home... or Room for Rent. The landlady would rent out whatever extra rooms she might have available, in order to take in a little spare cash. Of course, there are other scenarios, but that is probably one of the more common.

At any rate, I found a nice reasonable tourist home right on the route. That night I was her only boarder. We sat on her screened in front porch, watched the traffic and had a nice interesting visit. My adrenalin was still running with the events of that first day, even though nothing special actually had taken place. However, I knew I should get to bed before long as I wanted to get an early start the next day. So I bid my landlady goodnight and retired by 8:30 p.m.

The next morning, on the 28th, I headed west with my thumb in the air. It took a bit before I got my first ride. I would have been better off farther out of town. Eventually I did get a ride and gradually things picked up. For basically the rest of that day nothing of any importance took place, but that was about to change... *dramatically.*

I arrived in Tulsa late in the afternoon. The driver of the vehicle I was riding in was going to his office which was located downtown. That was ok with me because I usually wanted to at least see what the downtown area looked like. This way he was delivering me directly to it and I still had sufficient time to get a bus toward the west end of town so I could look for another tourist home.

I was slowly walking along taking in the sights and sounds and peering into some of the store windows. The shops had closed at 5:00 p.m., maybe fifteen or so minutes before I arrived. There were a few people on the sidewalk, but not too many, as by then most had headed for home. I stopped in front of a large department store and was looking in the window at their display. I have no idea as to where or what the display was, except that it had caught my eye. Therefore, in that position, I had my *back to the street*. All of a sudden I heard the squeal of tires and someone shout **"Hey, Corky!"** In the reflection of the window I saw a car had pulled up to the curb and one of the passengers had jumped out and was headed straight for me. I whirled around and was amazed to see Mr. and Mrs. W.C. Morrow and their two sons. I had known the Morrows when they lived in Rushville. While I knew them reasonably well, and had always been friendly with them, Corky wasn't exactly a household name. Their sons were older than I, so I hadn't played with them growing up. Therefore there was no real, deep seated connection.

Mr. & Mrs. W.C. Morrow at their apartment house in Tulsa, OK.

For years the Morrow's had owned and operated the Five-and-Dime store on the west side of the square in Rushville and I was a pretty frequent customer. They also owned the apartment house they lived in. However, they had sold everything and moved, but I never knew where. Obviously it was to Tulsa, OK. There they bought a large apartment house and were living there and running it at the same time.

Now keep in mind, two or maybe three years had passed since they had last seen me; from fourteen to sixteen I had to have changed some; this was over 400 miles away from Rushville; they were in a moving car at least fifty feet away and probably were conversing among themselves. So for them to recognize me from the back *is just downright spooky!* It would still have been coincidental if I had merely walked around a corner and met them face-to-face, but I didn't. It happened exactly as stated and that is about as weird as you can get. Whoever said truth is stranger than fiction sure knew what they were talking about. The Morrow's were as mystified as I was and couldn't explain how this happened either. Now with luck like that, if there had been a lottery back then I might have gone out and bought my very first ticket.

They asked where I was staying the night. I told them I had just arrived in town and had not gotten a place yet. Well, they took care of that, *including* supper. That meal was a lot better than what I had been eating. However, what made that chance meeting in downtown Tulsa even more important than seeing friendly faces in far away places, having a good meal and a place to stay, was some information that was yet to come. Before the evening was over, I would learn something about hitchhiking that would get me countless rides that I would never have gotten without it.

The Morrows had two boys, John and Jeff, perhaps four and three years older than I, respectively. They were both attending a nearby summer college where they were also enrolled in the ROTC, but both happened to be home that night. After supper, I offered to help with the dishes but my offer was denied. Jeff, the younger of the two sons, and Mrs. Morrow cleared the table and washed the dishes while Mr. Morrow and John, the other son and I were in their living room visiting. Here is where the tip came in. Mr. Morrow asked me if I had any signs. I must have looked rather blank, which answered his question. Mr. Morrow and John looked at each other, smiled and without saying a word got up. They said they'd be back shortly and left. When they returned they had a few remnant rolls of wall paper they had retrieved from the attic. They never said a word the entire time. They unrolled the paper, split it down the middle and then cut them off in twenty-five inch lengths. (Though I am sure there was no significance, I never figured out why twenty-five inch lengths instead of say twenty-four inches, or thirty inches, but twenty-five it was.) After they had cut maybe thirty or so such strips they started rolling them up, one at a time, with the blank side inside. They would roll the second over the first, the third over the second, etc. until all the strips were rolled up. Then Mr. Morrow rummaged through a drawer and came up with a big black carpenters crayon. He slipped it into a small paper sack, folded the top over, rolled that up, then slipped it into the center of the tube formed by the rolled up wallpaper strips. Next they took a piece of cloth, a little wider than the length of the roll and maybe a foot long. He then rolled the tube up in the cloth, tucked the ends into the center, turned to me and spoke for the first time. "There are your signs," he said, "Now, let us show you what to do with them."

They unrolled the cloth, pulled out the crayon, then peeled off the outer strip of paper leaving the rest of the roll in tact. They rolled the strip backwards once so it would lie flat, picked up the crayon and said to me, "Pick the name of a big city that everyone will know the location. Choose one up to 300 miles ahead, even if you are going to turn off before and not even go there at all. People don't like to pick up someone who is just going a mile or so down the road. But this way they know you are going a *long* way, even though they are probably not going that far themselves. Space out the city name on the sign and print it in as large, fat and legible letters as possible. Be sure you darken the letters so it is easy to read from a distance. After you get there, throw the sign away, peel off the next strip and make a new sign for the next well known point some distance ahead." Amarillo, TX was the logical choice for my first sign.

That was a **GREAT** idea! My first sign read **AMARILLO** and I used that method to solicit rides the rest of the time I hitchhiked. I am grateful to the Morrows for teaching me that little trick. I used that the rest of the time I hitchhiked and it always served me well.

I slept very well that night. Mrs. Morrow fixed a large, substantial breakfast the next morning and then they drove me to a good spot to hitchhike from, at the western part of the city. I thanked them, for probably the 'umpteenth' time, for their hospitality and especially for the signs. We all shook hands and my adventure continued. It was the morning of May 29th.

The signs worked quite well. Of course, I still had some long waits between rides, but there was never any doubt in my mind that the signs helped immeasurably. It was early to mid-afternoon before I reached the downtown area of Amarillo, TX. I had been there once before. It was back in the mid 1930s with my parents, brother and Uncle Horace. I have many pleasant memories about that trip, but this is not the time for that... except that one minor part of that story is the basis for a minor part of this story.

Uncle Horace owned three sections of land around Stinnett, in the panhandle of Texas, some 50 miles north-northeast of Amarillo. Every so often he would go to check on his land, see his renters, and then he would go down to Amarillo to see some oil company lawyers about leases they had with him. Since he was getting older his daughter would often drive him down, but if she couldn't for some reason he would ask Mom, or Dad, to take him. Of course, Uncle Horace paid for everything and I'm sure he made it more than worth while for my parents. On this particular occasion, Uncle Horace asked one of my parents to take him and then added, "Why don't you bring the whole family?" So we all went. Back then the skyscrapers in Amarillo seemed, to me, to reach the sky. After Uncle Horace and his lawyer had finished their meeting with the oil company's lawyers, they came out of their office and Uncle Horace introduced them to us. I must have said something about the tall buildings, because one of the lawyers invited me to come in the office and look out of his window. This building seemed taller than most all of the other buildings around because I could see their roofs. I was quite impressed and fascinated at how small the cars and people looked.

So now, some eleven years after that experience, I was standing there on the street, in the heart of the business district, and wondered if I could locate the building where I had looked down from so many years before. I was able to eliminate many, but finally... though I couldn't be totally sure, I think I found the building from which I viewed the city, from one of the top floors, back then.

It was too early to quit hitchhiking and yet really too late to try to go on. But, my luck had been pretty good up to then and after all I did have my signs... so I decided to head on anyway. That turned out to be a mistake. It was perhaps 3:00 or 3:30 p.m. by the time I headed west out of Amarillo proper. I made a new sign that read **ALBUQUERQUE** and optimistically began my westward trek. There are a lot of wide-open spaces in Texas and New Mexico. Rides were few and far between, perhaps anywhere up to an hour wait between actual rides and many of them were short.

It was well after dark by the time I finally reached Tucumcari, NM, which was only about 100 miles west of Amarillo, so I hadn't made very good time. I went down to the bus depot thinking I'd get a bus headed west. I could sleep on the bus while at the same time getting through some desert stretches that were not overly appealing to me. I got hold of a bus schedule and tried to figure out where the bus would be by perhaps 5:00 or 6:00 the next morning. By then it would be getting light and I'd continue west by hitchhiking again.

Unfortunately, my plans were soon dashed. I found out that the next westbound bus was not due until around 3:00 a.m. Since it would be light in a couple more hours I weighed the advantages of taking the 3:00 a.m. bus (even if it was on time), or just waiting until it was light and then head out from Tucumcari. This was the night of May 29th. There were a lot of Indians laying around sleeping, waiting for a bus to somewhere. The station smelled and in general was filthy. Since I was tired after a full day I decided to forget the 3:00

a.m. bus and to join the crowd and get some shut-eye myself. I found an unoccupied niche, placed my bag crosswise in the corner and sat down with my back against it. This way I protected my bag from 'sticky fingers' and gave myself a little back support, thus allowing me to semi recline. It wasn't long before I was fast asleep.

Around 5:00 a.m. I arose, used the bus stop's free facilities to freshen up and then headed out in search of something to eat. I was pretty hungry because I hadn't had any supper the night before. A couple of blocks down the street I came to a clean, decent looking little place. After a satisfying breakfast I headed west, leaving Tucumcari, NM behind me. My Albuquerque sign seemed to have lost its magnetic quality for getting rides. The rides I did get were similar to the day before, few and far between and unfortunately short.

Eventually I covered the 175 or so miles to Albuquerque. I liked what I saw of the city. It was on a plateau with a beautiful backdrop of mountains off in the distance. I probably spent more time looking around there than I should have, but on the other hand I wasn't running any marathons. I didn't have any formal schedule to keep or anyone to answer to. I simply came to see what I could see, so that is just what I did. I saw and visited everything that was of interest to me. And, of course, I wrote my daily card to my parents to keep them up-to-date as I had promised.

It was getting to be late afternoon and... *I did it again.* I made the same decision as I did back in Amarillo. Instead of finding a tourist home and relaxing, I decided to push my luck and head toward Flagstaff, some 300 miles away. That was perhaps too ambitious, but not impossible. Actually Williams, AZ, some thirty-five miles farther west, was really my hoped for destination on this route. Williams is where I would head north to the Grand Canyon.

It was around 5:00 p.m. on Friday, May 30th by the time I got to a good spot near the west edge of Albuquerque. That was not a good time. Most of the salesmen were off the road for the weekend and people were heading home for supper. Besides, I was headed out into the desert which is never very good anytime. I didn't feel my chances were very promising for getting a ride. A few blocks before I got to the point where I would begin hitchhiking in earnest, I noticed a bus stop sign in front of a drugstore. I checked and found that the next bus for Flagstaff and Williams, and other points west, was due in about forty-five minutes. I felt I could try my luck for a half hour, and if I didn't get a ride I'd have fifteen minutes to walk back to the drugstore, buy a ticket and catch the bus. I'd buy the ticket to Williams and sleep on the way while traversing the miles through the desert. I proceeded ahead a few blocks to where I was going to make my stand in my attempt to secure a ride. I wasn't having any luck with my new **FLAGSTAFF** sign, but I wasn't surprised due to the above reasons. I figured I could wait about five more minutes when a black 4-door Ford sedan pulled up and stopped. The driver, who was alone, was a well dressed man in a business suit.

I went through my usual smell routine that was ok. I was half in the car as I asked the driver how far he was going. He didn't answer my question but merely told me to *sit down.* Then he started asking me a lot of questions. That was ok, because I figured anyone picking up a hitchhiker had a right to ask some questions. Then it became obvious that these were not your usual run of the mill type of questions. I started to *get a bit uneasy.* So far I had only planted one cheek in the car and my other half was still on the outside. To satisfy my growing curiosity, I asked, "Why all the detailed questions?" With that he put his hand into his left breast pocket, pulled out a little leather case and flipped it open. It held a detective's badge and an ID card with his picture on it.

With that I said "Ok" and I swung the rest of me in on the seat and asked what he wanted to know. He said, "Let's start with some identification." I took out my birth certificate that I always carried and my brand new driver's license. He looked at them and asked some more questions: Where I came from, when, what I was doing here, my parents name, my mother's maiden name and a lot more. I answered them straight forward and honestly. Then he ticked me off. He said, "Ok son, now let's have the *real* story." That really burned me...**he thought I was lying!** I told him, "Hey Fella that **IS** the real story. You can take it or leave it." *[I thought to myself, Ooops Cork, you'd better watch it; this guy is carrying a badge and probably packing a .38 Special. Also, the thought almost instantly crossed my mind that he might just throw me in the poky and take his sweet time checking me out.]...* I was **mad**. I dug into my billfold and started pulling out cards, looking for anything that would support what I was telling him. I didn't want to waste too much time and miss the bus! With his forefinger he brushed a few cards aside that I had thrown on the seat. He picked one up and then said "Ok, I believe you." I was still ticked off and said, "How come NOW, all of a sudden, you believe me when a second ago you thought I was a doggone liar?" He said, "Because who I am looking for would NOT be a Life Scout." With that he showed me he was holding my Life Scout card. I sort of hung in midair for a bit because for the first time I realized he wasn't just giving me a hard time, but was actually looking for someone. Then he told me to pick up the clip board lying on the seat next to where I was sitting and to turn three sheets back and read. I did and if I hadn't of known better I would have sworn that was me. The description fit me to a T, all the way from my weight and height, color of hair and eyes, to what I was wearing, carrying and the direction I was probably headed. It even matched right down to the scar on my head. I looked at the detective and blurted out, "That's me... No, No, it's **NOT** me, but that description fits me EXACTLY!" I told him I couldn't have blamed him if he had hauled me into the station with a make like that. I apologized for the way I blew up and asked why he hadn't taken me in and sorted out the details later? He said he had a hunch that 'just maybe' I wasn't the guy on the APB (All Points Bulletin). I was so startled reading the description that I didn't even read what the guy was wanted for.

With that out of the way, he informed me that it was illegal to hitchhike in New Mexico, to which I replied in a surprised tone... "It iiis_SSS_???" [Actually, at that time I _could_ have told him it was illegal to hitchhike in 21 of the then 48 states however, I didn't want to impress him with my knowledge on the subject]. I told him I had already checked out the bus schedule and had allowed fifteen minutes to get back to it, which our conversation had now used up. Then I looked back and saw the bus in front of the drugstore. I told him the bus had already arrived and asked if he would give me a ride back to the drug store before the bus left. Of course, he had just told me it was illegal to hitchhike in New Mexico and now I was asking him, a cop, for a ride! Though I think he was a pretty nice guy, he wasn't that nice and told me he couldn't. [Actually, I had asked him that out of orneriness, just to see if he would give me a ride even after he had told me it was illegal.] I knew there would be no problem if the bus pulled out before I got there, because it would be coming my way anyway. Actually, it did pull out about a half block before I got back. All I had to do was simply step out and flag it down. I bought my ticket on board and picked out a seat. It was more comfortable and definitely cleaner than my bus station accommodations the night before. I sat back and watched the scenery. Several times we would be rolling along down the highway and then the bus would stop out in the middle of nowhere. Believe me they have a lot of nowhere out there in New Mexico. One or two Indians would get off or on the bus. I have no idea as to where they were headed or had come from. Sometimes I saw a trail heading off to who knows where and sometimes not even that.

It was in the vicinity of 9:00 p.m. or a little later that I saw the lights of Gallup, NM. We came around a couple of wide curves going into town before we arrived at the Gallup bus station. After Gallup I fell asleep and didn't remember anything until the bus stopped at Holbrook, AZ. I got off the bus and walked around a bit. For some reason the place made a good impression on me. It was dark, but in the lights of the town I recall a particularly tall bluff nearby. Heading west out of Holbrook, it wasn't too long before I drifted off again. I rode the bus across the desert that night of May 30th dozing and sleeping as best I could in the 'not so comfortable' seats. We made a brief stop at Winslow to let someone off and then continued on west. I don't remember a thing until I was aware that the bus had stopped again. Apparently I had been in a deep sleep and when I awoke I had absolutely no idea as to where I was or what I was doing there. That gives you a rather weird feeling. The cabin lights were on and people were talking in normal to loud voices. Some were getting on, others getting off and it was cold. I looked out and it was actually snowing and pretty hard at that! We had arrived in Flagstaff, AZ. They were having a freak storm due to the fairly high altitude. I got off to stretch my legs and even made a couple of snowballs. It wasn't long, maybe fifteen minutes, before the bus pulled out. I stayed awake because I didn't want to go back to sleep and pass through Williams, which was only some thirty-five miles on farther west.

The bus pulled into Williams around 3:00 a.m. on May 31, 1945. It was pretty cool, because Williams is also on a high plateau, but there was no snow as was the case in Flagstaff. The bus station was closed, but not far away I could see the lights of the train depot, so I walked over there. The depot was larger than I would have expected. There were perhaps two or three people sacked out at the far end of the room, in addition to a clerk behind a barred window. It appeared he also was dozing. It was a pretty nice station. It was clean and had lots of heavy lacquered oak benches with massive arms that would easily sit two, maybe even three people between the arms. I found that if I draped my legs over one set of arms, then laid down on the bench proper, my head would j-u-s-t be under the next arm by only a couple of inches. I made myself as comfortable as possible and dropped off to sleep to await dawn's early light. At some point thereafter, a Zephyr went through. A Zephyr was one of the first modern streamlined looking diesel trains and was usually silver colored. When it was evidently right outside the station it let go with its horn... **BBBLLLaaammmm**"!!! That really brought me up fast! I cracked my head on the underside of the arm rest and that <u>almost</u> put me right back to sleep! I don't know if the stars were shining outside that night or not, but they sure were moving around inside my head! After a bit, I did drift off to sleep, headache and all.

The morning dawned bright and cool. As I slowly emerged from my sleep I was aware of the aroma of coffee, freshly baked bread, fried bacon and a host of other tantalizing smells. There was a restaurant in the station which I hadn't even noticed, since it was closed when I arrived. The cooks had apparently come in sometime earlier and started to work. I got up, used their free facilities and then sat down to an excellent breakfast. With my stomach full and myself fairly rested, I left the depot and headed north. I didn't make a sign, because the Grand Canyon was basically the only destination.

On my way from Williams north to the Grand Canyon, which was roughly sixty miles or so, I got lucky. It was about the third vehicle that stopped. It was a young family, a man, his wife and two preschool aged children. They, at least the parents, were excited about going to see the Grand Canyon and apparently wanted to share their excitement with me. As we arrived, they let me out at the visitor's center. I looked around there for a bit and then went over to the Grand Canyon Lodge. It was run by the Fred Harvey Hotel chain. The hotel was large, clean and appeared well maintained. I made arrangements to stay the night; left my bag in my room, grabbed my camera and then went to see the nearby surrounding vistas.

I had a nice lunch at noon and good meal that night and my room was very comfortable. Early the next morning, Sunday June 1st, I made it out to Yavapai Point at sunrise. I looked around the immediate area and in the souvenir shops at all the things I didn't want, and later around 10:00 a.m. I headed back south.

Corky at Yavapai Point lookout.

It wasn't too long before I got a ride all the way back to Williams. From there I headed west; again on the famous US Route 66, some twenty-five miles or so west to Ash Fork. There, I picked up State Route 89 and headed south. It was the one I would take through Prescott and down to Wickenburg. From there I took US 60 on into Phoenix. While I was waiting at the southeast edge of Wickenburg five nice looking girls, a year or two older than I, stopped to give me a ride in the back of a pickup truck. There were two girls in the cab and three in the back. They were laughing, yelling back and forth at each other, squealing and having a good time. They didn't take me too far, but at least to another decent place to get a ride from.

It was mid-to-late afternoon by the time I reached my cousin's place in Phoenix. I stayed there with Loren and Helen Ashwood, and Ann their young daughter, for the rest of that day and the next two. Ann was just a little baby at the time. Loren is my Uncle Paul's eldest son and my Mother's nephew. It was great seeing them again, and good to meet my new second cousin.

Loren and Helen Ashwood with Ann at their home in Phoenix, AZ.

We had a nice visit and I recall one funny incident during my stay. They had a thermometer hanging outside their home. I looked at it and told Loren he needed a new one, because his wasn't any good. It was obviously broken since it showed 120° F. Loren laughed and said it was correct because there was practically no humidity. When the humidity was so low, one didn't notice the heat.

Early in the morning on June 4th, after three nights in Phoenix, I said my goodbyes and Loren took me to a good place to begin hitchhiking. From there I headed west into California where I picked up Route 78. About a third of the way across the state, I came to El Centro. By now it was about 2:00 p.m. From here I would be taking a side trip down into Mexico and would later come back up to El Centro to continue west to San Diego. Therefore, I decided to get a place to stay here first, before I headed south for Mexico. After checking in at a small hotel, I left my bag in the room and was ready for a new adventure. Soon I would have a bit of a surprise and a couple of anxious moments.

I turned due south and traveled about twelve miles to the Mexican border. The town on the U.S. side is called Calexico. It was dusty, dirty, trashy and definitely unappealing, at least back then. The town on the Mexican side of the border is called Mexicali. I would find Mexicali wasn't great by any stretch of the imagination, yet it would be several notches better than Calexico. I passed on through Calexico proper and approached the U.S.-Mexico border itself. My surprise and anxious moments were now only a heartbeat away.

As I started to go into Mexico, I presented my identification, birth certificate, etc. to the border guard. He looked at them and then looked at me. At that point he asked me to step inside where he told me to have a seat at the table. I thought that was a little strange, but I willingly complied and presumed they routinely made some detailed spot checks and that my number had just come up. It wasn't a very large room; maybe twenty square feet with thick adobe type walls. There were some windows on each side of the room, except on the east side where there were three detention jail cells about fifteen feet from where I was sitting. He studied my papers a little more and then, in a firm but not hostile tone, asked what a 16 year old kid from Illinois was doing by himself down on the Mexican border... and that was just for openers. This guy *probably* thought that I was older than my papers indicated and was either AWOL from the service, a draft dodger, or at least a run away; he couldn't figure out which. Obviously he hadn't considered that *just maybe* I was actually telling him the truth in the first place.

There was another border patrolman on the other side of the room checking out a Mexican headed north and it was obvious he was taking a considerable interest in our conversation. He got rid of the Mexican rather quickly and came over to ask me some questions of his own. Neither of them could believe parents would let their kid roam around the country like I was apparently doing. But, they didn't know my parents and the trust and respect that we had for one another. If they had, they wouldn't have had any problem with it! Pretty soon the second patrolman, who apparently was the senior of the two, asked if I had ever done anything like this before. In a manner and tone that one *could* have interpreted as perhaps a little cocky, or at least as a pseudo *voice of experience*, I told him that last year I had gone out to visit my brother in New York. The head patrolman asked, "Where in New York?" I replied... "Buffalo." With that the fellow seemed rather delighted. With a somewhat sinister glint in his eye, that I didn't understand right away, he told me... "Describe where your brother lives." Now, since Buffalo, NY was next to Canada, at the opposite end of the country, and over 2,000 miles from Calexico as the crow files, you could tell this guy thought I was blowing smoke. *Somehow* he felt that here was a chance to nail me. I thought to myself, 'These guys don't believe me and they just might toss me into one of those jail cells and hold me until they can check me out'. It seemed to me that all of a sudden those jail cells were getting one heck of a lot closer to where I was sitting.

I asked in a rather surprised voice, "What do you mean *describe* it?" He told me he wanted street names, landmarks, directions, anything I could remember. Then he added, "**If you've been there... like you say you have... you shouldn't have any trouble describing Buffalo.** I was rather mystified why a border patrolman, on the Mexican border in southern California, was so interested in Buffalo, NY, but I was in no position to argue. There were two of them; they were BOTH wearing side arms; there were three empty holding cells only fifteen feet from where I was sitting; and they only needed one to hold me. Also, I had their undivided attention, so there was no getting away.

It was here that my vivid memory of where my brother Keith lived, in Buffalo, NY, kept me out of a detention cell on the Mexican border. So I told him... "Ok, my brother lives on Delaware Ave" and I even gave him the address. "Delaware runs N-S. Where he lives it is a T intersection, with the side street making the stem of the T. He lives on the top floor of a three story apartment house on the northwest corner. There is a little delicatessen on Delaware, just across the street. About two blocks south there is a traffic circle with a small park in the center called Victoria Park, two or three blocks north there is a main E-W multilane arterial highway called Kingman Avenue."

With that the head patrolman looked a little surprised and said, "Ok, he is telling the truth." Now I figured it was my turn to ask a few questions so I asked him, "Why all the interest in Buffalo, NY?" The head patrolman told me he was raised on Kingman Ave. in Buffalo, NY and if I had been lying, he would have known it. Now the jail cells didn't look *quite as close* as they did a few minutes before. I mentally reminded myself that it is always best to *tell the truth*.

After that we visited a little and I even asked one of the patrolmen to take a picture of me at the border. That done, I went across the border proper and entered Mexico around 4:30 p.m. on June 4th.

Mexican border at the Calexico / Mexicali crossing.

It was an exciting place. There were a lot of stands selling about anything you wanted, a bunch of things you didn't and a lot of things you shouldn't. I made a few minor purchases of gifts for my parents and brother. Though I don't know why, I purchased a hunting type knife with an eight inch fixed blade, which I still have to this day.

Since I had arrived later than I would have liked, I wasn't able to see anywhere near what I wanted to see. I didn't want to linger down there too long because I wanted to be back in El Centro well before dark. After perhaps an hour, I came back across the border into the U.S. and got a ride the twelve miles north to El Centro. While the hotel I was staying at was no *palatial abode*, it was better than anything I saw in either Calexico or Mexicali, especially better than Calexico where I only saw pretty sleazy dumps. I extended my lodging for one more night, ate supper at a decent restaurant and went back to my room to catch up on my trip log before going to bed.

On June 5th, since I was keeping my room at the hotel, I left my gear in my room and headed back down into Mexico. I wanted to savor the different pace of border life and culture than I was used to. When I came to the border, the patrolmen on duty were the same ones I had met the day before. They remembered me and just smiled and waved me through.

I crossed into Mexico for the second time and enjoyed walking around taking in the sights, sounds and smells of this bustling border town. I went into numerous shops and looked at various stands on the sidewalks and in the street. The main roads were generally clear, but on the side streets the stands would actually encroach out into the street itself, leaving vehicles to snake their way through. There were lots of old pickup trucks and quite a few donkey and horse drawn carts, too. Also, there were a few horseback riders. You did well to watch where you stepped. They were bringing in their wares to add to the assortment of chickens, pigs, fruits and vegetables. There were beautiful homemade tablecloths, clothes, blankets, hats and pottery. There was quite a bit of handmade furniture such as tables, chairs, bookcases and hammocks. Of course, everywhere you could see jewelry of every design imaginable. Most of it, bracelets, earrings, necklaces, etc. were made by local artisans using silver from the nearby silver mines. Many of the pieces incorporated beautiful polished stones. The local color included a good deal of horn honking, shouting, clattering and various other noises.

There seemed to be a lot of police, but they just strolled around and didn't appear to care if the vendors that were in the street impeded traffic or not. In fact, they didn't seem to pay any attention, or care about much of anything. Most of the vendors, even the smallest ones, had some kind of a cloth awning over them to shield them from the sun. The older people, who were often by themselves, would sit on a dirty blanket with their hodge-podge of wares spread out before them. Some would call you to come and buy, others just sat in a rather forlorn and pitiful manner hoping you would come over and buy something from them. Of course, there were the ever present *young entrepreneurs* running up to hopefully would be customers, shoving their items for sale in their faces and asking outlandish prices. They didn't bother me too much, because it was rather obvious I didn't have deep pockets and therefore wasn't a good prospect. Today I was strictly just looking around and watching the people. I had made my limited purchases the day before.

Practically all the shop owners, and particularly the street vendors, expected you to haggle the price with them. If you didn't, they didn't respect you. To them selling was sort of a game. As long as you were sharp enough to haggle until arriving at a fair price, then they respected you. I recall seeing a rather pompous lady in a red dress, approached by a perhaps 12 year old kid, who had a whole fist full of *supposedly* top quality sterling silver necklaces. I don't recall the details of the prices, or the exact conversation, but it went something like this: He told her about the necklaces that his uncle had made. He said they were $75 each, *however*, as a special offer, his uncle had told him he could sell the first five for $50 each. He said he had already sold four and only had one left at this *special* price. Hardly without hesitating, the woman picked out one then turned to her husband and said, "Pay him $50." The man was apparently a bit of a henpecked, spineless type of individual and without uttering a word he shelled out the money. Then I continued moseying along just looking and listening to all that was going on around me.

About an hour later I happened to come across this same 12 year old kid, still selling necklaces. He had cornered another lady and was obviously giving her the same sales pitch, so I moved closer so I could better hear their conversation. I chuckled when I heard how the conversation was going. This time the kid had met his match. He didn't have a ringer with this lady. They were haggling back and forth and in the end the lady bought the necklace for $12. It was a nice looking necklace, but, of course, I don't know how good the quality was and if it would turn green in six months or not. Obviously the kid made something on the deal, or he would never have agreed to the $12. I've always wondered how many more gullible customers, such as the lady in the red dress, he ran into that day and during his career.

I had spent the better part of the day in Mexicali just looking at the little shops, street vendors and the people in general. It was after 3:00 p.m. when I felt I had enough for the day and headed back for the border crossing point. As I crossed back into the good ole US of A, I ended my excursion to 'South of the Border, down Mexico way'.

The next morning I took a bus from El Centro to San Diego instead of hitchhiking. I was the last person to get on the bus which was hot and very crowded. There were no seats left and people were standing in the aisle. I think it was against the rules to have more people than seats and that when the seats were full no one else was supposed to be allowed on. The driver appeared to be a real grouch. But the war was on and transportation was often limited, so he was kind enough to let more on than technically he should have. We pulled out of the bus station. Since I was the last one to board, I was standing in the well, which is the area just inside the bus door and a couple of steps below the upper aisle. After the driver had shifted through all his gears and we were rolling down the highway, he pointed to a little door in the front wall of the bus and motioned for me to open it. There was a fold down jump seat in there. He told me to pull it out so I could sit. I suggested that I should switch positions with the elderly lady standing two or three people behind him. He said, "No, because if there is some kind of an emergency you could get out of the way quick, where as she couldn't." So I lucked out and had a seat for the rest of the ride. Shortly, I struck up a conversation with him. Though on the surface he came across as grumpy and unfriendly, he was actually a pretty nice guy.

During our run to San Diego, he pointed out many interesting sights as we rolled along. Later we started up into the mountains. It began to get cooler, which was fine with me. After a bit we actually drove up into the clouds themselves. Now, I had never been in clouds before while being on the ground at the same time. It was nothing more than being in fog, with some areas being denser than others.

Once or twice we actually were above some low clouds, which seemed even stranger to me. Looking out of the window, I could see the tops of these clouds that we had actually climbed above. Another thing that I'll never forget was that when we were near the summit of the mountain range there were no clouds around at the moment; he told me to look out the window behind him and I could see Death Valley. It was a bit over 200 miles away. It really impressed me that it was so clear and that I could see so far. There were numerous other things of interest that he pointed out, most of which I would never have noticed otherwise. After we crossed the crest of the Coastal Mountain Range we started down, we left all of the clouds above us now and the temperature began to rise.

Coming down out of the mountains, I saw the Pacific Ocean for the first time. I could also see the San Diego Naval Base. It was June 6, 1945, one year after D day. There were an awful lot of ships in the harbor at the naval base. I arrived at the bus station around noon and took a city bus up through town. After looking around San Diego, I worked my way north along the coastal highway US 101. I had several short rides, but that was ok because it was beautiful scenery and I had plenty of time to enjoy it. I went through well known places such as Del Mar; Oceanside; San Clemente; Anaheim; to Los Angeles proper. This was the horizontal apogee of my trip, or my farthest point from home. From here I would gradually be making my way back.

I found fairly inexpensive lodging at a YMCA in downtown Los Angeles. There would be a lot to see here, so I booked my room for two nights. I did what sightseeing I could do in the remaining part of the day. I ate supper at a small restaurant nearby and then went back to my room at the

Y. I brought my log book up-to-date, wrote my daily card back home and hit the sack.

The next morning I was up early and out on the road. I had a lot to cram into one day. As on my jaunt down into Mexico, I left my bag in my room so I would not have to carry it around. From downtown Los Angeles I went up to the Hollywood area. I took in as many of the sights as time would allow. In Hollywood, I went along the famous Sunset Strip and saw the sidewalk with all of the handprints and footprints of the movie stars in front of Grumman's Chinese theater. I took a short tour of the Homes of the Stars, saw Rodeo Drive and went to the famous intersection of Hollywood and Vine, just to say I had been there. Naturally along the way I saw the renowned sign up in the mountains that simply read... **HOLLYWOOD**. After my full day of exploring I returned to the Y for the night and got a decent meal followed by a good nights sleep. On the 8th of June, after a whirlwind tour of the final sights that I wanted to see, I went to, but was unable to get in to visit, the movie sets at 20th Century Fox, MGM, etc. On my way out of the area, I passed through Pasadena where I saw the Rose Bowl, but only from the outside.

By now it was getting to be late afternoon and the evening rush hour traffic was beginning to pick up. However, out there *every hour* seemed to be rush hour. From a hitchhiking standpoint that is not good. Most of the people on the road are on their way home; they are tired from working all day; they usually aren't going very far and therefore they don't normally pick up hitchhikers. I wanted to get away from the metropolitan area as soon as I could. My immediate goal was to at least reach the north side of San Bernardino. Better yet, I would really like to get to Barstow, some sixty miles further northeast of there. In the particular area of the universe I was in, when you did get to the city limits of one city you were smack up against the city limits of the next. There was no 'open air green space' from one city to another where people might actually notice you. It was just one big end-to-end traffic jam. I walked along, backwards most of the time and held up my sign which now read **BARSTOW**. There was way too much traffic to get good rides. That may sound strange, but as the volume of traffic rises you actually get fewer rides based on the percentage of vehicles going by. More often than not, you have to wait longer as well. My rides were few and far between and the ones that did stop weren't going to either San Bernardino or Barstow for that matter. They were either going to Arcadia, Glendora, Ontario, or some such place. Finally, a ride came along that was going into San Bernardino.

I had been on the move all day and had only grabbed a sandwich earlier, so I was getting rather hungry. By now it was early evening, maybe 6:30 or 7:00 p.m. For a variety of reasons I decided not to try and hitchhike to Barstow. I made my way to the San Bernardino bus station and inquired about the next bus to Salt Lake. As I recall the next one wasn't until around 10:00 p.m. That was ok with me because it gave me time to search for a decent meal that I could eat at leisure and relax without having to hurry to catch the bus.

The bus was on time. I bought my ticket, boarded the bus, picked out a seat on the left side, stowed my bag overhead and settled down for the ride that would take me east, then north to Salt Lake City. Why did I choose the left side of the bus? Simple, when you are basically headed north the early morning sun rising in the east would be on the right side of the bus. I wanted to be in the shade so I sat on the left side. We pulled out heading for Salt Lake City. We made brief stops along the way to drop off and pick up passengers. During the ride from San Bernardino to Barstow, I just looked out the bus window. I noticed how the urban-ness of the area was gradually diminishing from the built up areas of wall-to-wall shopping centers, stores, car dealerships and bumper-to-bumper traffic, and turning into areas of orange groves and such. The bus arrived in Barstow after 11 p.m. and was back on the road after a fifteen minute stop. It was dark and there was nothing interesting to observe out the window, so within a matter of minutes I nodded off to sleep.

I woke up briefly when we hit Las Vegas. Back in 1945 it was just a sleepy little town in the desert. The next year, 1946, would see the construction of the Flamingo gambling casino. This would be the first of many to come and little old Las Vegas would never be the same again.

Nothing of any consequence took place on the way from San Bernardino to Salt Lake City. We made good time and it was around 1:30 p.m. when I reached Salt Lake City proper. First, I wanted to see the Great Salt Lake and then I would look around the city. I found the route to go west to the lake. Since the traffic wasn't 'bumper-to-bumper bedlam' as in Los Angeles, I began hitchhiking right away instead of taking a city bus to the west limits. Surprisingly, I didn't have any trouble with getting rides even though I was in town. I didn't have a sign made since I wasn't going far. I just relied on my thumb as I had before I met the Morrows back in Tulsa.

I was let off at a place called Saltaire, some fifteen miles west of downtown. It was a resort area and I went for a short swim at a nearby public beach which was fairly crowded.

There were a lot of people swimming there at the time. The water is definitely more buoyant in the Salt Lake than in fresh water. So much so in fact that people could possibly become injured if diving into the water, therefore one normally walks into the water at the Great Salt Lake.

Corky standing in the Great Salt Lake.

They had freshwater showers so you could rinse off when you got out of the lake. If you don't, the salt will dry into a light crust all over you and it will make you itch. I didn't stay in the lake long, but long enough to say I legitimately went swimming in it. To me, the most striking object in the area near the beach where I went swimming was a big beautiful glass pavilion. It was built out in the water and had a fairly wide, perhaps 150 feet to 200 feet long, wooden wharf-like walkway from the shore out to it. I made my way to the pavilion to look around. There were fancy restaurants, a lot of greenery in large planters on the floor and a great many hanging pots with ferns and colorful plants in them. There were at least two, but I think actually there were three, decent sized ball rooms for dancing. Big name bands would come to play there such as Tommy Dorsey, Guy Lombardo, Sammy Kaye and that caliber. However, nothing was going on at the time I was there. By mid-afternoon I caught a ride back into Salt Lake City. I saw all, of what I was allowed to, of the Mormon Temple and then in the interest of expediency I took a local bus tour of the immediate area.

Having visited the main highlights, I headed east via US 40. I had around six fairly rapid rides taking me about 125 miles from downtown Salt Lake to Vernal, UT. My path took me into the mountains, through Heber City, across Daniels Pass at some 8,000 feet and eventually down into Vernal where I stayed the night at a decent motel. There was nothing of particular to note during that portion of my trip.

The next morning on June 9th, perhaps ten miles east of Vernal, I left US 40 and took a road north to the Dinosaur National Monument. This was a very interesting place. It displayed literally thousands of well preserved dinosaur skeletons, some almost completely intact. It appeared that there were a lot more to be unearthed, but that it had been postponed due to World War II. What they had unearthed was quite impressive. There supposedly had been a river that had flowed there *eons* ago. The excavation sight was where there was a sharp bend in an old river bed. The dinosaurs, which had died upstream, were washed downstream and had gotten hung up in the tight bend in the river; so they just piled up one on top of another over the years.

After a half hour or so I caught a ride back down to US 40 and headed east again. The rest of the trip back home was more or less uneventful. I hitchhiked east on US 40 into Colorado, through Steamboat Springs and down to Denver. I found a tourist home for the night and was on my way early the next morning. In Denver I left US 40 and picked up US 6 which I would follow to my Aunt and Uncle's home in Moline. US 6 took me northeast to Sterling, CO, then shifted east and continued across southern Nebraska through such cities as McCook, until I was somewhere east of Hastings. It was getting late and there was no good place to stay. It was a nice evening and I was beginning to consider sleeping out under the stars which I had done before. I'm not clear on what exactly happened next, or where I was specifically, but a trucker stopped to give me a ride. He was going to Des Moines, then would head somewhere other than east, which was the direction I needed to go. A ride that far was great, I provided him with some company and I had a place where I could doze a bit while still covering miles at the same time. Plus, it was cheaper than a bus. The next few hours passed quickly. The driver reached his terminal in Des Moines around 4:00 a.m. or a little after. As luck would have it there was an all night gas station across the street with an attached diner. I first got cleaned up and then ate a good breakfast for a change. By that time it was probably around 5:30 or 6:00 a.m. I asked the service station attendant if he would ask anyone who stopped for gas if they were going as far as Davenport and, if so, if they would give me a ride. I didn't say Moline because Davenport would have been the better known of the two. Asking the attendant was just a little extra insurance because then I went across to the south side of the road with my new sign **DAVENPORT** and held it up for the eastbound traffic to see.

By this time I was getting anxious to get back home. Nothing of note occurred between there and Moline. When I got to Moline, I went to my Uncle Paul and Aunt Myrt's house. Aunt Myrt's name was Myrtle, but she didn't particularly care for that, so we always called her Aunt Myrt.

She was a real character and loads of fun. One could easily write a book about her. When I arrived I rang the door bell and Aunt Myrt opened the door. Uncle Paul was an engineer for the John Deere company, and was still at work. Aunt Myrt was glad to see me and the first thing she did was to give me a hug. The second thing she did was to hand me the phone to call my parents. They seemed every bit as glad to hear my voice, as I was to hear theirs, maybe even more so. The third thing Aunt Myrt did was to get me a clean towel and washcloth, and to draw bath water for me. By now I had talked to Mom and Dad. Both were home because Dad was now an insurance agent and he worked out of our home. They started immediately for the two and a half hour drive from Rushville to Moline. By now my bath was ready and Aunt Myrt was in the kitchen putting together one of her great meals. After I had gotten cleaned up, I went in to eat what Aunt Myrt had fixed. I don't remember what it was, but it was good. Aunt Myrt and I sat and talked until Uncle Paul got home and my parents arrived an hour or so later. We all visited a while, then Mom, Dad and I headed south for Rushville.

Thus, this fascinating and interesting adventure had come to an end. It was June 13, 1945 and already my mind was at work on where to go next.

The Big Bang

Trip #4
* * THE WINDY CITY * *

1945 - August 2nd - August 6th

Age: 17 years, 0 months, 10 days

WEEKEND TRIP TO CHICAGO - THE FIRST ATOMIC BOMB WAS DROPPED.

I decided to take a trip to the windy city. Normally I didn't take anyone along on one of my hitchhiking trips, but this time I made an exception. Don Corbridge was a friend of mine all through grade school and high school, so I asked if he would want to come along. Don jumped at the chance. Your chances of getting a ride are greater if there is only one of you But on this trip we didn't have all that far to go therefore, we didn't care if the waits were a bit longer in between. Any inconvenience was off set by the fact we had each other to talk to and share the experience with. After all, it would only be up to Chicago and back and it would be nice to have the company of a friend. Don and I left Rushville around 7:30 in the morning on Monday, August 2nd and hitchhiked to Chicago. We went for no particular reason other than for the excitement and thrill of travel. Rides actually weren't too bad considering there were two of us.

We took US 24 up to US 136, west of Havana, which was called Illinois Route 10 back then. We headed east to McLean and picked up what is now called I-55. We turned

59

left and headed directly for Chicago. However, the Interstate System was still many years into the future so what we call I-55 today, back then, was called US Route 66. This is the route that would be propelled into fame in both story and song, and even a movie would be made about it. Route 66 ran all the way from Chicago to Los Angeles, CA.

We had numerous rides. To Don's surprise, I would turn down a ride offer now and then... after thanking them for stopping, of course. I had made a sign that said **CHICAGO**, so there was no question as to where we were headed, though I still always asked the driver of the vehicle, "How far are you going"? If they would be going to another town or junction on up ahead... fine. However, as well meaning as they were, every now and then they would be only going a mile or two which would usually be out in the middle of the country. Yes, we would be a little closer to our destination, but we'd be stuck out in the wide open spaces. It is a lot harder to get a ride when you are out in the middle of nowhere because people have their speed up. Therefore, I'd tell them, "Thanks for stopping, but I think our chances will be better here." If at all possible I would try to hang around an intersection, truck stop, or some place where people weren't going quite as fast. That way they could read my sign easier and decide if they wanted to offer us a ride or not. If they didn't have a chance to see the sign or to visually check us out first, more often than not they'd go right on by and we'd be waiting for the next vehicle to see if our luck improved.

When we hit the outskirts of Chicago, I changed signs. The new one merely said **LOOP**, but that close to Chicago, everyone understood we wanted to get downtown. A fellow stopped and told us, "Hey, Buddy, I'm not going all the way, but a lot closer than you are now." That worked fine for us because we would still be in the city. We finally managed to get near downtown and it was still fairly early in the afternoon. We found a cheap hotel room, checked in, freshened up and then we went sightseeing.

We hadn't eaten yet, so one of the first things we did was to visit a White Castle hamburger place that I knew about. This White Castle was under the 'El' on the east side of Wabash, not far from Marshall Fields. The décor of the White Castle was just that, it was constructed to look like a White Castle. It had a limited menu of shakes, fries, onion rings and baked beans in a small pot like Steak & Shake, but their hamburgers, called sliders, were the main event and best of all back then only sold for a nickel! They were a decent size, maybe four inches in diameter and darn good, too. I suppose our mother's would not have considered this a well balanced meal for their growing boys, but they weren't around to tell us and besides we were on vacation. I remembered the White Castle chain from when I went to the Cub-Cardinal baseball games in St. Louis. Back when I was a 7 or 8 year old kid, the American Legion from World War I sponsored an excursion every year for a bunch of local kids, maybe twenty or so of us. We were called The Knot Hole Gang. They'd rent a school bus and treat us all to a ball game. Before we left St. Louis to come home, we always ate at a White Castle. White Castle was a forerunner to McDonalds and Hardees. While even today you may still run across one, they are becoming a vanishing breed of the culinary trade.

We mused through various large department stores in the Loop looking at all the things we didn't want, had no use for and couldn't afford. There was a good deal of all three. We did a lot of plain goofing off while walking along the streets and around Buckingham Fountain, which is in the middle of Grant Park. We sat in the park and just watched this cosmopolitan mixture of humanity going this way and that. Most people seemed to be in a hurry. There were a lot of business men in suits and professional women decked out like the Queen of Sheba, still others plain, but tastefully dressed. Then there were the visitors and sightseers. They, like us I suppose, were rather easy to spot. Many were dragging kids along who were rubber-necking at the tall buildings. Mothers were pushing strollers, telling the kids to stick close and a lot of people were either waiting for a bus or trying to flag a taxi. There were several groups of kids, many wearing what were obviously school uniforms and carrying satchels or back packs. I thought 'what a bummer' to have to go to school in the summer. Then there were several homeless people who just shuffled along because they had no place to go and had all the time in the world to get there. Most had their heads down and were probably looking on the ground hoping to find a quarter, or even a penny for that matter. Some were going through trash cans and others were lying on park benches with a newspaper over their face to keep the sun out of their eyes.

Later we looked in some of the smaller shops along Michigan Avenue. It had been a pretty full day for us so we stopped at a little hole in the wall, but decent looking restaurant, and got a little something to eat before we headed back to our hotel to play some cards, take a shower and hit the sack.

It had been an interesting day. I laid in bed and listened to the sounds of the city; horns honking and sirens. You could always hear sirens wailing somewhere. It also sounded like the sanitation crews were working right outside tossing the dumpsters around. Then there was the babbling of incoherent people noise, but that was tapering off by that time. Finally, I drifted off into a deep sleep.

The next day, Tuesday August 3rd, we took a bus south on the outer drive, along the lake front to the Shedd Aquarium. We spent a good deal of time in there just watching the wide variety of marine life. Another good reason for spending so much time in there was that it was a lot cooler inside compared to the hot August day outside. By noon we left the Shedd Aquarium and walked over to the Museum of Science and Industry. One could easily spend two or three days in there and still not see it all. There were not only many exhibits to see and displays to marvel at, but there were numerous interactive exhibits. By late afternoon, we hadn't anywhere near covered all we wanted to see, nor stayed as long as we would have liked, however, Don and I left around 4:30 p.m. We crossed to the west side of Michigan Avenue, which was in the shade and casually walked north. Along the way we browsed through a few more stores. We went past Meigs Field to our far right and on up to the Loop proper. Back in the Loop we again revisited our favorite haunt which was the White Castle hamburger place. After scarfing down several hamburgers, a shake and fries, we went back over to the north end of Grant Park and people watched some more. Finally, we made our way back to the hotel. It had been another long and interesting day. I don't know about Don, but I must have been acclimated to the sounds of the city, because it didn't take me very long at all to get to sleep that night.

Wednesday, August 4th: After we had eaten breakfast, around 9:00 a.m., we got on a bus and headed south on Halsted. We were headed down to the famed Maxwell Street Market. Now that was an area unique unto itself. Maxwell

Street ran east and west and was four blocks south of Roosevelt Road. It ran from Union Street on the east, west one block across Halsted and continued west seven or eight blocks to Blue Island Road. The Maxwell Street Market itself was a sort of overgrown flea market or garage sale. You could buy anything you wanted such as, a dining room table and chairs, clothes, the services of a prostitute, canned hams and commodes, etc. While there were regular shops along the street there was a lot of selling going on, rather suspiciously, from the trunks of cars and the backs of trucks out in the open air. There were even guys in the alleyways and on street corners wearing trench coats with bulging pockets and arms adorned with wrist watches and bracelets. Everyone claimed to have the best price in town for just about anything you wanted. If they didn't have what you were looking for, they would tell you they could get it for you by the next day.

I had heard of this Maxwell Street Market before and had always wondered what it was really like. The area gave me an uneasy feeling. It was dingy and dirty. We sure weren't planning to make a day of it, yet I wanted to stay long enough and see as much as I could to satisfy my curiosity. Some of the items for sale were new and some were used. Nearly everything was at what appeared to be a very good price. It was like a discounted Five and Dime, which was a popular store of that era, or better yet, similar to a shopping expedition at a border town on the Mexican border. However, it was expected that one would haggle the price with them. They always set their price considerably higher than they would actually sell it to you for so if you didn't haggle, they would consider you a sucker.

I am sure a lot of the items offered for sale were legitimate. That is, they had been purchased by the vendors at a special sale price from some store, or manufacturer. In some instances, I am sure some of the people were down on their luck and were selling at least some of their possessions for food or other necessities. On the other hand, I am sure a great many of the items were 'too hot to hold' and I am not speaking of the fact this was a warm day in August. That is, hot as in just plain stolen, anywhere from high jacking a truck, to cracking a business or breaking and entering private homes. As an example, besides the overall suspicious atmosphere, I observed a rather shabbily dressed, rough looking middle aged man with a scowl on his face and at least a three day outgrowth of gray stubble, selling some *really* nice looking jewelry. It at least appeared to me to be very expensive. In my mind there was *no way* this guy or his wife, if he had one, would ever have been able to legitimately afford those kinds of necklaces, rings, bracelets, earrings and assorted trinkets.

While there, I did want to buy something. So I chose a pocket knife from some vendor who I felt was legit. I didn't think it was a bad idea to have such an item handy in that area. I don't recall if Don bought anything or not. Actually, we weren't really looking for anything. We didn't linger around too long, because this wasn't the kind of neighborhood I particularly cared to hang around in. It was fun to go there though because I had always heard of the colorful Maxwell Street and now I had experienced it.

Thursday, August 5th: Don and I went to the Chicago Art Museum for about three hours and then went back down to the Museum of Science and Industry to look at exhibits we had not gotten to see before. After spending the better part of the afternoon there, and while on our way back to the Loop, we decided to add a somewhat different dimension to our search for culture. We went to the theater. This particular theater was called Minsky's Burlesque and we were just in time for the late afternoon matinee. This was an on stage type of theater, with real live warm bodies, and definitely not your run of the mill movie theater. Actually, they were running shows continually, with a fifteen minute intermission and about a half hour between shows. Now, no one below 21 was supposed to be able to attend. At least that was what the sign by the box office said. However, both of us at 17 were big for our age and besides the color of our money was the same as everyone else's.

The ticket seller looked at us a little skeptically, or so we thought, but we just stretched ourselves as tall as we could and in a voice about an octave lower than normal said, "One please." We hadn't eaten since having a rather sparse lunch, so we picked up a large box of popcorn and a candy bar. For a drink we opted for the water fountains because they were a lot cheaper than their sodas. We went up into the balcony which was nearly empty, but which offered a pretty good view of everything. It was rather dark up there even when the house lights were up. We settled down, made ourselves comfortable and waited for the stage show to begin.

Whooeee! We never saw anything like that back in Rushville! In fact even the traveling shows that would come to town for a couple of nights didn't have anything like this! Now those ladies were lovely. You could tell it was mid-August and that it was hot out because none of them had much of anything on. They were dancing, strutting and prancing around while fanning themselves with huge feather like fans. They all were tall, willowy and there wasn't one of them below a ten in the lot. Actually, they put on a pretty good show, at least we were impressed. In fact, we were so impressed that we slouched down out of sight in the dark balcony, thus we managed to hang around for the next performance. Of course, it was *just in case* we had napped and missed any part of the first show.

This was our last night in Chicago. We went back to our hotel, got cleaned up and put on our best clothes, even a white shirt and tie. I wore a green plaid sport coat that I really liked and both of us cleaned up pretty good. We went to a decent night club called The Latin Quarter, ate supper and watched their floor show. It was a bit higher-class than the show we had seen earlier that afternoon. During the evening, one of the night club photographers took our picture, which I had for a good many years and maybe still do, somewhere. All in all, we had a good time.

Friday, August 6th: Now it was time to go home. It was August 6, 1945. As we left the hotel to catch a city bus to take us to the end of the line... to get us as far out of town as we could before we started hitchhiking, I remember the newsboys shouting the headlines..."Atom Bomb dropped on Hiroshima." I recall thinking, "So what's the Big Deal throwing little bombs at them?" I didn't even bother to buy a paper to read about those little bombs.

Don and I hitchhiked home that afternoon. There was nothing of particular note about the trip home. It was just a routine matter of getting a ride... getting out... and picking up another one.

It wasn't until the next day that I learned the little bomb the news boys were yelling about had ushered in what we would come to know as *The Atomic Era*. The world would never be the same again.

Crossing the Line

Trip #5
* * THE SOUTHEAST * *

1945 - August 21st - September 2nd

Age: 17 years, 0 months, 29 days

ST LOUIS - JACKSON - NEW ORLEANS - MOBILE - TAMPA - JACKSONVILLE
COLUMBIA - MEMPHIS and HOME.

Up to now, I had mixed my travel between paid transportation and riding my thumb. This trip I was going to do two things. One... hitchhike between major destinations 100 percent of the time and two... see how economically, within reason, that I could make the trip.

Everyone in my hometown of Rushville, IL seemed to have a nickname and there was usually a semi logical explanation behind each. Some nicknames were straight-forward and the origin of others was more complex. For example, sometime in the early 1920s there had been a popular comic strip in the Chicago Tribune called Gasoline Alley. At that time US 24 and US 67 intersected a couple of blocks north of the square, or business district, in Rushville. Surprisingly, there was a gasoline station on all four corners. Now back then that was highly unusual and almost a tourist attraction. It was like a little town having its first traffic signal; it was a source of local pride and attracted a lot of attention. Gasoline stations were not all that common in those years. My father had a 5-gallon gas can with a long flexible neck on it that he carried whenever we went on a trip, just in case he ran out of gas before he found a gas station. In fact, I still have that gas can to this day. So everyone called that intersection of US routes, Gasoline Alley, after the comic strip. In the comic strip, Walt and Phyllis Wallet were the principal characters. They didn't have any children. However, one morning in early April of 1921 someone left a baby boy in a basket on their doorstep. They named the little boy Skeezix.

My brother, Edwin Keith Sutherland, was born to my parents on April 6, 1921, and was the first baby born in Rushville after Skeezix arrived in the comic strip. Therefore, people nicknamed him Skeezix and he was called that by everyone in town for years.

Seven years elapsed and on July 20, 1928, Walt and Phyllis Wallet had a boy of their own. They named him Corky. Two days later I was the first baby born in town. Since the town already had a Gasoline Alley and I had a brother everyone called Skeezix, when they found out I was a boy I automatically was nicknamed Corky. A great many people to this day still don't know my real name.

You could talk about the origin of some of the other nicknames around town and then some were best left unexplained. I had a good friend by the name of Wayne Tomlinson. Back then he went by the nickname of 'Dummer'. Now 'Dummer' was *not* dumb. He later became a successful real estate broker, who owned his own business, but back then everyone called him Dummer and it was he that gave me my first ride on this particular trip.

Dummer's dad owned a small trucking company. Dummer had been driving a truck for his dad ever since he had a license and I imagine well before that, too. During school breaks he would often take a load of cattle to the stock yards in St. Louis. Many a time I would ride along with him on a weekend run just for the fun of it. We always had a good time. The war was on and many things were rationed. We'd scrounge up some unused ration tokens and take them with us. They were red and blue hard cardboard discs, the same size and thickness of dimes. They worked quite well in the dime slot machines. We knew about several slot machines in the back of a trucker's hotel where we would stay, near the stock yards. But this time it would be different. I would only be going one-way. I arranged for a ride from Rushville to St. Louis with Dummer on one of his cattle runs. On August 21st, he came by my parent's home early in the morning to pick me up. I bid my folks goodbye then ran out carrying my small twelve by twenty-four by twelve inch bag that held all my worldly possessions for the trip.

On the way down we had a great time as always. It was around 10:00 a.m. when Dummer dropped me at a good place to hitchhike from, on my way south out of St. Louis. It was somewhat out of his way, but he said he didn't mind. We shook hands, he bid me good luck and I headed south. I had made a sign that read **LITTLE ROCK** and it worked like a charm.

I had several fairly rapid rides for some distance each and by around 7:00 p.m. I was in Little Rock, AR. I grabbed a quick bite at a diner and headed out again. Just for the adventure of it I decided to rough it and hitchhike all night. Up until then everything had been *textbook*, but that was about to change, though I didn't know it. I made a new sign reading **VICKSBURG**. At dusk it was of limited value and would be even less as night came on, unless I was standing under a light. It took a bit, but after a ride or two I got a ride that would take me to near the south limits of Pine Bluff, AR. Then the unforeseeable took place shortly before I arrived in Pine Bluff. It started to rain, nay... **POUR!** I mean it came down in buckets! It wasn't even starting to wane by the time my ride came to an end. The driver was going to turn west and I had to go south. So I had to get out and step into the downpour. Across the street I saw a low end, run-of-the-mill, tavern. There were several cars parked in front, loud music emanating from inside and it had the usual beer signs. One lighted sign was hanging over the doorway and another in the window alongside a red neon open sign. I figured any old port in a storm, so I headed for it.

Lucky's, a road house tavern was a real dive, but it was dry and it was lucky for me that it was there. Inside, the layers of smoke could almost be cut with a knife. There was the usual smell of stale beer and it was real dim. I had to use the bathroom which I could just make out across the room in the far corner. I waited my turn and as soon as it was vacant I went in. I noticed it had a partially opened single window that helped air out the small room, which it needed badly. I am glad I had taken note of that window because I would see it again shortly.

After leaving the bathroom, I found a seat nearby in a corner where I sat keeping as low a profile as I could. I was under the legal age to be in a tavern, even in Arkansas, and I didn't want to get tossed out in the rain. I remember smiling inwardly and thinking, 'I wonder what my parents would think if they could see me now'. In the opposite corner of the place I could see a bunch of slot machines. There probably were a few poker tables also, but I'm not sure about that. You could hear the slots chunking away, the endless babble and loud guffaws of the patrons, see the lightning flash through the windows, hear the wind and "CRACK" of the thunder, and, of course, the unrelenting beating of the rain on the roof outside. I don't know which was making the most noise.

It was maybe a half hour later, no more, before it happened. All of a sudden I heard several police whistles and in poured at least a half dozen or more State Police. The leader was yelling, "Everyone freeze, **nobody** move." I assume they were raiding the gambling that was going on, however, I didn't stick around to find out. With being underage I sure didn't want to get caught in there, so I grabbed my bag and ducked into the bathroom. I opened the window the rest of the way, threw my bag through it and then dove through the window myself; following my bag out into the dark, rainy, stormy night. I picked up my bag and ran, slipping and sliding in the mud and falling down at least once. Lucky's was near the south limits of town, so I headed on south which was the way I wanted to go anyway.

Not too far away I found a small, old broken down, barn. It wasn't locked because anyone or anything could have walked, or at least squeezed through the cracks where boards were missing. The roof wasn't much better. It leaked a good deal however; it wasn't too bad and was a heck of a lot better than being outside. I could make out some kind of machinery in there and several bales of hay, some of which were broken. Because of the darkness, I had to wait until the lightning would flash before I could see much of anything at all. That wasn't a problem tonight because there was plenty of thunder and lightning going on. I fixed a place in the hay, where the roof wasn't leaking, curled up, pulled some of the dry hay over my wet clothes as a cover and also to partially hide me. As I stretched out and contemplated the day's events, I came to the conclusion that it had NOT been one of my better days... or nights for that matter, but it sure had been exciting and full of adventure. Best of all I was ok. Surprisingly, I soon went to sleep there in the hay for the rest of the night.

On August 22nd, the morning dawned clear, warm and bright. I woke up early and scraped some of the caked mud off my shoes and pants due to my fall the night before. Upon exiting the barn I noticed a large arched pipe culvert under highway US 65. I went off the road, underneath the highway and inside the pipe culvert. It was about eight feet high inside. The culvert allowed about a five foot wide stream of seemingly clean water to pass beneath the highway. It was also secluded with nothing but open country to be seen from either end.

I took my shoes and socks off and stripped down, washed the mud out of my pants and shirt first, then washed the rest of my clothes. I wrung them out as best I could and laid them on the bank in the sun. After that I took a rather cold bath in the stream and then put on a set of clean clothes from my bag.

With my semi dry freshly washed pants draped over my shoulders and my now clean but damp shirt tied to my bag, I climbed back up the bank to the highway and held up my **VICKSBURG** sign facing the southbound traffic.

Headed south out of Eudora, AR.

I made it to Vicksburg in only three rides by the way of Eudora, AR and Tallulah, LA, then east across the Mississippi River into Vicksburg. I did some sightseeing in Vicksburg by taking a local tour to the various historic locations including the ramparts and more formal fortifications where the long past river battle of Vicksburg had taken place. Then I headed east to Jackson, MS to see where the Confederate Capitol was located at one time during the Civil War. In Jackson I did some sightseeing around the city, visited the old Confederate Capitol inside and out, as well as paid a visit to the current State Capitol. It was getting late in the afternoon. I had walked a good deal, it was hot, I was tired and my feet hurt. I caught a city bus to get out to the west edge of the city to begin hitchhiking again. I had to head west to get back to US 61 which was the Mississippi River Road that led south to Natchez, MS. Though ambitious, Natchez was my hoped for destination for the night.

My southern trip was made long before the great human rights movement. Selma was a nearly unheard of town in Alabama, Martin Luther King was just a kid beginning to think about shaving and Lyndon Johnson was only an aspiring politician in Texas. Up north you didn't notice it much, but from Arkansas on south, sadly, the color line was quite apparent. For example you would see not one, but two water fountains, one marked 'White' and the other 'Colored'. It was the same way with toilets. Also, on the city buses in Jackson, there were two holes on top of the seat backs and there was a sign with two pegs that fit into the holes, one for each side of the aisle. One side of the sign read 'White Patrons' and the other read 'Colored Patrons'. Each time the bus would stop there was a clamor to move the signs forward or back to give the white's or colored's more seats. As I boarded the bus to get out to the west side of Jackson, I was to have an interesting and rather humorous experience, even though no one else found it the *least bit funny* at all.

Negro shacks in northern Mississippi.

I was tired as I caught the bus and it was jammed with people. At that particular stop the coloreds had won the battle of placing the signs, establishing the line which no one *dared* cross. There were a bunch of whites standing up in the front, their ties loose, collars open, grumbling, sweating, and mopping their brows.

Now there were at least two empty seats *just across* the mythical line formed by the seat signs. I thought, 'Heck that doesn't bother me any... I paid my fare... I'm hot... my feet hurt... I'm tired... and I'm sitting down'. Then I did the unthinkable of unthinkables and *crossed the line.* I sat beside a black woman who was next to the window. She looked very shocked, rather irritated and reared back against the side of the bus. I just smiled and said, "Pretty hot isn't it?" She just glared at me. I don't recall getting any comment out of her, but I sure got some grumbling and angry looks from both the whites and coloreds. However, what I found rather amusing was a comment made by a rather large colored woman directly behind me. She apparently leaned over to her friend beside her and whispered rather loudly... "Damned Yankee," while no doubt pointing her finger at my back. I couldn't help getting a chuckle out of that, but it was rather obvious that I was the only one who did. And so I rode, sitting down all the way.

After reaching the end of the bus line a second memorable event was about to take place. It was still pretty congested so I walked along, backwards some of the time, showing my new sign which now read **NATCHEZ**. I had to get out to the Mississippi River some forty miles further west. There I would junction with US 61 and head south to Natchez. Before long a sharp looking, red, two-door, late model car slowed and pulled over as it passed me. It was probably a 1942, which was the last model year before the start of World War II. Naturally, thinking I had a ride I started to run up to it, however, the driver was just pulling into a gas station. The driver, a very attractive blonde barely in her 20s, glanced at me and realized I thought she was going to give me a ride. She was obviously somewhat embarrassed as she sheepishly smiled and muttered, "Sorry." I sort of laughed, smiled and said, "Hey, ok... no problem." *But* since we were now on speaking terms, limited as it was, and since it was a good bet she felt she owed me one, I asked if she would mind giving me a lift out to as far as the river. That didn't sound too far, though it was actually over forty miles. She hesitated a bit and then agreed. As it would turn out it was a good decision on her part, as well as a lucky one for me.

She paid for the gas and we headed west. She told me she was from the East Coast, her name was Kathy Ferguson and she was married to a soldier in Texas, which was where she was headed. She also had a little boy named Jimmy, who was about two. He instantly took a liking to me. Jimmy and I had a pretty good jabbering session which, of course, made her feel a little better. She told me she had quite a fright at a motel the night before. There had been a wild party nearby and she had left in the middle of the night with only an hour of sleep. She had driven in and out of rain storms following the tail lights of a semi. She said that normally she wouldn't have picked me up, but she knew I thought she was stopping for me and besides she was so sleepy she needed someone to carry on a conversation with to help her stay awake. I asked her where she was trying to get to that night. She said Natchez, then in the morning she was going to head west across the river. Well now, I had only asked her for a ride as far as the river, but *maybe* I could extend this ride all the way to Natchez. Once or twice, she asked "Just how much farther is the river anyway?" I would tell her, "Not far" and then switch back to our general conversation so we would get better acquainted.

After she had gotten to know me better, but before we got to the River Road where I was to get out, I brought up the possibility of extending my ride. I told her that though I had only asked her for a ride to the river, I too was going to Natchez. I reminded her it would be dark before long, that it looked like a storm was coming up and ended by adding I'd sure appreciate going to Natchez with her. I also told her that I used to drive for a doctor back home and that it was strictly up to her, but if she wanted, I'd drive. I suggested she curl up in the back seat and sleep while Jimmy and I visited on the way to Natchez. She took me up on my offer, crawled in back and in a second was sound asleep. After a bit it started to rain; with lightning flashing all around, accompanied by claps of thunder. Also, it was quite windy. I was glad to be in a car and dry this time. So Jimmy wouldn't get scared of the storm, I made up a game about the lightning flashing and the thunder crashing and even put together a little song. Jimmy thought it was great fun and so we rolled on through the night.

Then problems! Shortly before Natchez we had a flat tire. I coasted off to a level spot on the shoulder. As I started to get out to change the tire, Mrs. Ferguson woke up. She asked what the problem was and I told her. She began to get out, but I told her to stay in the car with Jimmy. Then she told me to stay in the car, because she said it was her car. We compromised and both of us ended up getting out. She held the flashlight and I changed the tire.

We reached Natchez around 9:30 p.m. The rain had stopped by then. We drove around looking for a place to stay and finally found a tourist home. When we checked in we asked for two separate rooms. The landlady looked startled, for she naturally assumed we were married and we didn't act as if we had been fighting. She assigned us two rooms next to each other. She probably rationalized the odd arrangement by assuming I had driven all day, was tired and didn't want the baby disturbing me. I don't know what went through her mind when we paid separately for our rooms. However, neither of us offered any explanation.

We went to our individual rooms. I laid out my clothes to dry and then brought my diary up to date. I always kept a fairly detailed diary and that, coupled with a good memory, is how I was able to put all these details into stories later. Next I made a new sign. Even though my next destination was Baton Rogue, I made a sign for **NEW ORLEANS**. Now neither of us had any idea where we were with respect to the roads that we needed to take to get out of town. Before going to bed I wrote a note to Mrs. Ferguson that stated if she hadn't left by the time I got up in the morning, I'd like a ride with her to the bridge. From there I would be headed south and she west. Then I slipped the note under her door.

The next morning I looked out into the parking area and her car was still there, so I went out and checked the tires. The spare was still holding up. Then I heard a little squeal and I turned around in time to see Jimmy running toward me with his arms outstretched, wanting me to pick him up. Behind Jimmy came the landlady and Mrs. Ferguson who was refreshed after a good nights sleep. She was wearing a red blouse and white shorts and appeared more like a teenager than a mother in her early twenties. I picked Jimmy up and swung him over my head while he was jabbering a blue streak. Now it is always nice to say something about the little one, so the landlady told Mrs. Ferguson, "You know I believe the little boy looks more like his father than he does you." Mrs. Ferguson turned about as red as her blouse. I cleared my throat, grinned and said "Thank you."

The landlady gave us good directions to the bridge. We bid her goodbye and headed for the river with Mrs. Ferguson driving now. On the way to the bridge we both chuckled over the events of the day before. She laughingly said she didn't know if she should tell her husband about picking me up or not. Then with an impish glint in her eye said she would, and added "a little jealousy would do him good." When we reached the bridge she pulled over and stopped. I got out and reminded her to get her tire repaired soon.

We said goodbye, Jimmy gave me a hug and they headed west across the Mississippi River bridge. I continued south for Baton Rouge and later to New Orleans itself. On the way I visited several old southern mansions, I became acquainted with their Spanish moss and saw many other interesting regional sights.

Southern mansion with Spanish moss in trees.

It was the start of a hot muggy day. After a few rides, I caught one that took me to Baton Rogue, LA and arrived two hours later. I went to the State Capitol where I took a free tour and heard lectures regarding the history of the state. A lot of the stories were colorful tales of the Huey Long era that were related by the guides. After spending two hours or so, I headed on south to New Orleans.

Through connections back home in Rushville, I had lodging arrangements in New Orleans. Dr. Howard H. Hamman, who lived next door just east of my parents, contacted a Dr. George Upton, who lived in New Orleans. They had been dental classmates. Dr. Upton wrote offering me lodging for as long as I wished. As soon as I reached New Orleans I headed directly for Dr. Upton's house. The Uptons greeted me as though I was a favorite nephew. I was offered refreshments of lemonade and cookies and after a visit I was shown to my bedroom to freshen up. It was on the second floor. I even had my own bathroom and a huge screened in porch. When I went back downstairs they gave me a key and said I was welcome to come and go as I liked. Since it was getting toward late afternoon they suggested I just relax, have supper with them, get a good night's sleep and start my explorations in the morning. That sounded good to me. With that, Mrs. Upton picked up a small bell on a table and rang it. Almost instantly a maid came into the room. She was a rather tall, medium build, pleasant looking colored lady in her 50s. I rose. Mrs. Upton said, "Millie, I would like you to meet Corky Sutherland. He is a neighbor of some friends of ours, in Illinois." Then she added, "Please set another place at the table tonight as he will be having dinner with us." Millie beamed and curtsied, then she left the room and I sat down. We had pot roast for supper, along with sweet potatoes, corn, southern greens plus some other things. For dessert, Millie served what they called sweet potato pie. The pie was delicious and tasted a lot like pecan pie. Everything was good and though I ate a little of all of it, I'm not a big fan of sweet potatoes as such and the greens were definitely my smallest portion.

After supper, Millie cleared the table. Dr. and Mrs. Upton and I sat and visited till around 8:30 p.m. until Mrs. Upton told her husband, "George, stop your questions and let the boy go to bed so he can get a decent night's sleep. After all he has done today he has to be tired and he has big plans for tomorrow." Though I was enjoying our visit, I was glad for the opportunity to get up stairs, bring my log book up-to-date and check out that bed waiting for me.

I went sightseeing each day, and came back to the Upton's at night for the next three full days, though I stayed there four nights.

Nothing of particular note occurred while I was in New Orleans. I took my time and did the usual tourist things. At one time, I managed to get inside of what was then called the Sugar Bowl and naturally everyone goes to the French Quarter.

Downtown New Orleans

You can easily spend a whole day there. I visited the famous Bourbon Street and saw many above ground cemeteries. I took a buggy ride tour of the inner area, seeing some of the cathedrals, statues and parks. Since I always had a fascination for the waterfront, I spent a good deal of time down on the docks watching the ships come and go, and barges being loaded and unloaded. One sight I remember very clearly was a large barge filled with bales of cotton, being unloaded by black workers who were manhandling the bales and working the unloading equipment. I also observed fishing boats bringing in their catch. After unloading, most of the fish was trucked away to a processing plant however; there was a dockside market where some of the catch was sorted out on tables of crushed ice under an open air covering. Small, insulated, local delivery vans were also loaded and would pull out, obviously for area markets. Also, many housewives, as well as I presume smaller shop owners, would come down and haggle with the fish market managers for on-the-spot sales. While down on the docks, I also had my first espresso coffee... Yuck!

New Orleans is often referred to as the City of Levees because the elevation of much of the city is below that of the Mississippi River, especially in flood time, hence the reasons for the network of levees.

Monday, August 27th, I was ready to leave New Orleans. I said good-bye and thank you to Dr. and Mrs. Upton. They would not let me pay for anything, but I did leave a small box of candy in my room for them, when I left.

My next destination was Mobile, AL. I made my way to the east side of New Orleans proper and began hitchhiking.

New Orleans - French Quarter

Two unforgettable things would happen, before the day was over. One, I would wait for what eventually would be my second longest wait for a ride and two, when that ride came, it would be my most *unforgettable* ride *ever*, and the one I would most VIVIDLY remember the details of for the rest of my life.

It was hot and where I was standing there wasn't any shade in sight. I was on a 4-lane highway in front of the Henry J. Kaiser Ship Yards, where they built the famous liberty (cargo) ships for the Navy. The liberty ships were prefabricated merchant ships, and were mass produced during the war to offset the sinking of merchant ships by the German U-boats. They made it possible for the timely delivery of war goods and materials to our troops during World War II. They got their name from Patrick Henry, who said "Give me liberty, or give me death."

There was lots of traffic but, even with my sign reading **MOBILE**, no one stopped to give me a ride. There was a rather strong breeze, which on one hand was good since it was so hot, however, on the other hand there was a lot of grit blowing in the air. The grit was like pulverized cinders. The wind blew it all around and it would get it in my eyes, even if I squinted, and also in my mouth. It seemed I was always going ppfffttttt trying to spit grit out of my mouth. I waited, standing in the sun in that sweltering heat, for two hours and twenty-nine minutes. [This wait was only surpassed once, when I waited for two hours thirty minutes outside Butte, MT two years later.] It was so hot, uncomfortable and miserable, that I think I would've taken a ride from the devil himself... and I'm not to sure but what *I did just that!*

F i n a l l y, a car stopped. It was a big black LaSalle, or Packard... sort of a limo type. There were three men in it, two in the front and one in the back. They passed my sniff test to see if they had been drinking. I asked how far they were going and they said Pascagoula, MS. I got in the right rear. As soon as I sat down there was a squeal of tires and we were off and running at *well* above any minimum speed. The two guys in the front were pretty good sized. The one in back with me was rather small, sharp faced and sort of reminded me of a weasel. The fellow driving seemed to be in charge and I noticed they all talked funny. That is funny as in *strange*, not funny as in *ha-ha*. It sounded like Brooklynese, but with a southern drawl. All three were probably in their mid 40s and very well dressed. Later it would seem, perhaps fit to kill might have been a more appropriate analogy. They were dressed identically, which I thought was a little odd because they sure weren't triplets. Each wore a wide brimmed fedora type straw hat, identical light weight cream colored suits with a pale blue pinstripe and ties, which I felt was even more peculiar. It was hot, I was sweating my tail off and here these guys were wearing suits! The suits were made from a light weight material, but they were still suits. Now why would anyone wear a suit coat in weather like this, unless *maybe* they had something to *hide*? I didn't actually see any hardware, but I did notice what appeared to be a slight bulge under the left arm of the suit coat of the little fellow in the back with me. He was so skinny he shouldn't have had any natural bulges anywhere. Years later these fellows reminded me of portrayals of the gangster goons of the Al Capone and Frank Nitty era, like in the TV shows of The Untouchables. But then those shows were a long way into the future and this was ***now***... and I was sitting with them, in their car!

These guys were tough as nails, not too swift and probably collectively had an IQ of somewhere between an amoeba and a rock. However, they were the type you'd like for a friend, if you were going to get in a serious fight. I'm not really sure why they picked me up in the first place. For the most part they simply ignored me as if I wasn't around. I presume it was a sort of a knee jerk reaction on their part. They saw a kid alongside the road with a sign reading Mobile who was obviously wanting a ride in the direction they were headed, so it was probably a, *'Ok, we'll give him a ride... screech, stop, jump in and off we go'* type of impulse.

Shortly after I got into the car the little fellow in the back turned to me and said, "You got any money on ya kid?" A rather unusual question I thought, but I was sure he was just trying to be friendly and make a little dialogue. He just lacked the social graces of how to institute an intelligent conversation. He appeared curious if hitchhikers even had any money at all and maybe was inquisitive as to how they lived. I didn't for a moment think these guys were going to roll a hitchhiker; that I was sure of. They were driving this big limo, were dressed like peacocks and probably had a roll of $100 bills in their pocket that would choke a horse. I told him I only had a few bucks and that I usually worked for my supper, or got a job for a few days if I needed some clothes. I probably did only have a few bucks in my pocket, but I had a money belt with maybe $150 in it. I noticed this little guy had his right hand all bandaged up. After rapidly assessing their probable line of work and with my imagination running rampant, I could just imagine that the little fellow had gotten shot in the hand. More realistically, if the truth be known, he had more than likely cut it on a beer can.

Now this ride was only a little more than 100 miles long, but was the longest 100 miles I ever traveled. These fellows were in a *mean* and *nasty mood*, especially the driver and the other fellow in front. It had nothing to do with me, but apparently it had *not* been a good day for them. I tried to keep a low profile and not to listen to any of their conversation, but that is a very difficult thing to do. These three had apparently been sent up to Baton Rouge by their superiors to see someone about permission to take a shortcut with a fleet of shrimp boats between that fellow's island and the mainland, or something. Whatever it was, it would have saved them three hours running time with their boats. I never was quite sure of the exact details and I definitely <u>wasn't</u> going to ask! Whoever they had gone to see, for whatever reason, would not give them the permission they wanted and they were *most unhappy.* Now they had to go back and tell their boss they hadn't gotten the job done. It was apparent they didn't feel he would be too happy about it either. They had probably already considered various ways to *scare* the fellow up in Baton Rogue before I got in, but now they were discussing different ways to do away with the guy and who might do it as well. It didn't sound like they were personally planning to do it themselves. It was obvious from their conversation and degree of sophistication that they were just errand boys and not high enough in the organization to make the final decision. Certainly it was conceivable to assume they were *capable* of doing the job, but on someone else's orders. After this glimpse into the way the conversation was headed, I got *terribly sleepy.* I curled up in the right rear, shut my eyes and fell into a *very* **deep** pseudo type of sleep!... or so I hoped my hosts would think if their attention ever turned to me. I even softly snorted once or twice, and emitted a little whine now and then, to underscore how *deeply* I was sleeping, in case they ever considered my state of consciousness.

Never once did I ever feel all this was a ploy to impress or scare a kid. But they were sure doing a good job of it. These guys were anything but a bunch of jokers trying to have a little fun. Besides, they couldn't think fast enough, or have communicated between themselves to pull it off. These guys were *dead* serious, (pun intended) which made it even scarier!

I could hardly believe my ears and it definitely bothered

me that they were really SERIOUS about wanting to murder the guy, or getting someone to do it, and that they would openly discuss such a delicate matter in front of me. It was also of concern to me that during this discussion they were actually naming names. It made me wonder when they might come to the conclusion that I had heard too much! Yes, Mrs. Sutherland's youngest son was definitely between a rock and a hard place and it certainly crossed my mind that I might be headed for a whole bunch of hurt. By now I didn't think it could get any worse. I felt I had heard it all. ...*WRONG!*... the most *disturbing* part was yet to come!

Every now and then they would realize I was in the car and they would abruptly change the conversation. This happened maybe three times. Once the driver said, "Look at dat pretty boid," in their Brooklynese twang with the southern drawl. I popped my right eye open, the one they couldn't see even if they were looking at me. Apparently he was referring to a flamingo that was standing on one leg in the Gulf of Mexico, which we were driving beside. Another time they made a remark about some pretty flowers beside the road. Believe me none of these guys could give a hoot about the birds, bees, flora and fauna around them. It sure wasn't natural how all of a sudden they changed the conversation from 'Murder and Mayhem', to something of 'Beauty and Grace'. HOWEVER, it sure spiked my heart rate and each time that happened, it sent a *Red Alert* danger signal to my brain. To me it meant that they were again aware of my presence and that they realized that their conversation was not appropriate for outsiders to be privy to. THAT *really* concerned me because I felt at some point they *might* feel they had said too much and then decide, to be on the safe side, to just do away with me so I couldn't talk. After all, who would

89

miss a lone hitchhiker? If they decided to do something to me, I considered my chances of surviving a one-way trip to some remote backwater Louisiana bayou as being somewhere from slim to none.

There was nothing I could do to physically remove myself from their presence without arousing their suspicions. I had already asked if they were going to Mobile, which was some distance beyond their destination of Pascagoula, so, if all of a sudden I asked to be let out at the next intersection, even these guys were smart enough to figure that one out. Quietly I began to consider various potential plans of escape and to assess my odds of success. I considered:

A) Jumping from the car: *No good, we were going around 70 mph and I'd never survive the jump.*

B) Running from the car at the next stop: *May work for a bit but, if they didn't get me, with the connections these guys probably had, I'd never make it out of the county.*

C) Do nothing and see what happens: *So far they had not made any hostile moves, or any remarks about me. That was at least somewhat encouraging. So perhaps I should just wait it out and let them make the first move. Then I'd have to play it by ear.*

I discarded Plans A and B as too risky. So far there had been no hostile actions or insinuations directed toward me, so I chose Plan C. Therefore, I would just continue what I had been doing so far, which was to consciously remove myself from their presence by apparently going to sleep. I hoped they would figure that if I were asleep I couldn't hear their discussions about murder and mayhem! I sure didn't want them to come to the conclusion of thinking that perhaps I had heard too much.

On occasions their conversation did switch to some humane subjects. One was who won yesterday's baseball game and who their team would be playing this afternoon etc. When they did, I'd rouse and say something to hopefully keep the conversation on a more civilized plain. But they were so distraught about failing their mission in Baton Rouge, and what the boss was going to say about it, that it didn't last long. Someone would invariably say something and they'd be back talking about that blankity blank blank-blank in Baton Rogue. So, *nap time*! I'd get awfully sleepy *real* quick... as in quicker than you could say Bang-Bang. I'd curled up and plunged into a fake, but wakeful sleep, with my eyes closed but ears open listening for any unhealthy remarks, or plans, regarding Mrs. Sutherland's youngest son.

For someone to say they'd LIKE to... or OUGHT to, commit murder is ONE thing, but actually there is no crime until the act has been done. Uncomfortable as it was for me to be privy to their apparent heartfelt honest desires regarding the future of the gentleman in Baton Rogue, it was like being at a Sunday School picnic for what I was **now** about to hear.

In discussing various ways they might shorten this fellow's days on earth, the driver nostalgically remembered one of the best hits he knew of. It was the way Vic Corzino took care of Al Blazzi. [Those aren't the real names, but are similar. I'm using them only to relate the details of the conversation, which are still *very* clear in my mind.]

Though my eyes were closed, I could sense the fellow in the back had leaned forward and asked, "Did Vic do dat? I knew Al got done in, but didn't know nuttin' about *who* done it." NOW!... this was a horse of a different color! This act had apparently already been committed and I was probably hearing some pretty darn reliable information on the subject. But then it even got worse, because the driver proceeded to VIVIDLY describe the exact details of Al Blazzi's demise to my weasel faced friend in the back. It would have made a great Alfred Hitchcock movie, but I'd rather have seen it on the screen... instead of hearing the script first hand.

It seemed that Al Blazzi lived by the Gulf. Every afternoon he would go fishing alone, in an outboard motorboat some distance out in the Gulf. Vic Corzino, who was in charge of the hit, had got in touch with a tight-lipped friend of his who had a small pontoon plane. So they wouldn't attract any attention, they would practice takeoffs and landings some distance away from where Al Blazzi was fishing, yet where they could keep an eye on him.

The first day Blazzi would look at the plane now and then, but it was always pretty far off so it didn't seem to bother him. After that, he ignored it. The day Vic and the pilot were going to make their move, there was another fishing boat in the area, so they continued to practice takeoffs and landings. On the next day there were water skiers nearby, so again Vic and the pilot kept on taking off, flying around a little, then landing and doing it all over again. At some point, on the third day conditions were right. No one was in sight. Al was fishing with his back to the sun and the little pontoon plane practicing takeoffs and landings had ceased to be a curiosity to him. Vic and the pilot gained altitude, got between Al and the sun, cut their engine and glided down toward Al. The pilot picked him off, striking Al in the back of the head with the left pontoon, crushing his skull and knocking him out of the boat. Al Blazzi was a dead man before he ever hit the water. With that, the pilot turned the ignition back on, the wind from the forward motion of the plane turned the prop, the engine started up and the plane flew off. Mission accomplished! The murder had never been solved.

The revelation of the activities concerning Mr. Blazzi made it all the more likely that something unpleasant would likely befall the gentleman in Baton Rogue. After that my weasel faced friend's curiosity had been satisfied and the conversation drifted to more civil subjects.

By now, I had gotten more than my normal daily allotment of thrills, anxiety and sheer inward terror from the surreal situation I found myself in. Nonetheless, there was one last shoe to drop, however, that wouldn't occur until near the end of this portion of my story.

Even though the general conversation had taken a 180-degree turn, I continued my snooze for several minutes after the driver had finished his detailed and colorful tale, to be sure it stayed on more normal subjects. Then I sat up, stretched, yawned, asked what time it was and where we were. That was a *logical thing* for one who had been *sound asleep* to ask, or at least I hoped they'd think so. They told me, in a voice that at least sounded friendly, that they were going to stop up ahead to eat. *Red Alert* I thought! They are going to take me in *someplace* and plug me, so they won't mess up their car! Besides it was 2:00 p.m., which is too late for dinner and too early for supper, so that within itself was another reason to be concerned.

They pulled up in front of a bar and grill type of roadhouse on the Gulf side of the road. From the outside I had seen worse, such as Lucky's back in Pine Bluff, but I had seen a lot better, too. They got out, but I didn't move. The three of them came over and opened my door. They said, "Come on in kid. Let's get something to eat." Personally I figured I had a lot better chance of surviving in the open, alongside a busy highway, than I had inside some dumpy tavern, so I told them, "No thanks, I'm not hungry." Indeed I didn't have a stomach for anything at all then, not even a last meal. The little guy who had been in back with me smiled a rather crooked, but friendly smile and said, "Aw, its ok kid, com'on in... it's on us." With that he began to withdraw his hand from his pocket. When his hand was all the way out, I was relieved to note that he didn't have a gun in it. What he did have was a *very* large roll of bills and they weren't just ones either. I said, "Thanks... you guys are the greatest, but I hardly got any sleep at all last night. I ate some bad fish and got sick as a horse. I'm really not hungry, but awfully tired, so think I'll just grab a little more shut-eye." They told me ok, to suit myself and then all three turned and went into the tavern, leaving me alone. It is hard to relate how relieved I was. For the first time I felt I might weather this storm... and live to tell about it.

I thought about cutting and running. No, it was still a dumb idea. Even with a head start, and even if they weren't watching, I was still in their backyard. It is doubtful if I'd ever clear the area. Maybe they didn't realize the implications of all they had said, or they thought I really was asleep and didn't hear anything. If they were worried about me, I don't think they would have left me alone.

On the other hand, if they were a *little* suspicious that maybe I had heard too much, they might watch me from inside... but back from the windows where they could see me, but I couldn't see them. If I panicked and bolted, they would have no recourse but to catch me, and no doubt I'd become another notch on their gun. However, if I didn't run, I was hoping they'd think I didn't hear enough of their conversation to make any difference.

I stayed slumped over as if I was sleeping like I said I was going to do in case they were looking out a window. Around thirty to forty-five minutes they came sauntering back, picking their teeth and got in the car. Now, since they had eaten, they were a bit more docile. They had pretty well covered the dismal future of the gentleman in Baton Rouge. I didn't feel I could fend any more sleep for the rest of the trip, so I went on the premise that the best defense is a good offense. I started talking about this and that and, from then on, I more or less dominated the conversation all the rest of the way to Pascagoula. I talked about nearly everything... except violent deaths, murder, mayhem and airplanes with pontoons.

I actually felt relaxed for the remaining miles I spent with them. They never seemed hostile or even unfriendly to me. If they were going to do anything to me, I figured they would have done it by now. As we approached Pascagoula, which was as far as they were going, the driver told me he'd take me across the river to the highway junction which would take me directly to Mobile. He said, "You'll have a better chance of getting a ride from there." Everything he said made sense, and from my map I could see he was probably right. Then he added, "But first, we have to swing by the docks to let the boys know we're back." Now I won't say I wasn't at least a *little* bit concerned about being taken down to the waterfront, but his explanation seemed logical. Then too, I seemed to have a good rapport with them, so again I decided to play it by ear.

We drove out onto a rather high wharf. It was a commercial fishing setting, complete with nets, dingy fishing scows that needed scrapping and a coat of paint, buoys, coils of line, lobster pots and all the associated smells. The tide was obviously out because all you could see of the adjacent fishing boats was the tops of their masts. A third of the way down the wharf the driver stopped beside the mast of a certain fishing boat and honked three times. Pretty soon a tall and slender, very dirty and smelly guy came trotting up a ladder from I assume a shrimp boat. He looked to be in his mid 40s and he had a good deal of oil or grease on his hands and face. He was wearing a watch cap and a khaki skivvy shirt and pants that probably had been another color at one time. He came directly over to the car, leaned his arm on the driver's window, ducked his head down and said, "What did he say?" Even though he looked like a scumbag, it was apparent this guy out ranked all of those in the car. "He wouldn't go for it," the driver said. The guy got real mad, clenched his fist and shook it, saying "We'll kill that S.O.B." and then he glanced in the back and saw me sitting there. "Who's **THAT** GUY!!!" he shouted, pointing his finger and looking straight at me! Red Alert!... Here we go again I thought. Then the driver quickly said "Oh he's just a kid we picked up. We're going to take him across the river and get rid of him. But first, I just wanted to let you know we got back." Ouch...Red Flag again! I didn't like his choice of words about *getting rid of me*, but I at least THOUGHT I knew what he meant and, fortunately, I was right.

As good as his word, the driver turned the car around, took me over the bridge to the junction he had mentioned and they let me out. We all four smiled and shook hands all the way around. I'm sure they NEVER KNEW how relieved I was to be able to shake theirs and to part as FRIENDS! Of course, they did not hand me a business card, but if they had, five will get you ten if it *didn't* say…

MAFIA

All three of them were nice to me during the entire time I spent with them. In hindsight I do not believe it ever entered their minds to do me any harm, though certainly I didn't know that until the very end.

I have had some very interesting and exciting rides, with some interesting and exciting people, but beyond any shadow of a doubt this was the most memorable ride of my life!

I got a ride out of Pascagoula in the back of a pickup truck. Soon a misty rain began and I ended up getting a little wet before reaching Mobile, AL. I didn't really care though, at least I was alive! I spent the night at the YMCA in Mobile. It was a hole, at a cost of 25¢ for a cot. There is an expression… two-bit flop house. It denotes a lack of desirable accommodations and is something you won't see listed in the AAA books. I have stayed in a total of three of these. This was my first two-bit flop house and strangely, number two would be the next night in Tampa and the third would be a year later in Quebec. World War II had only been over for two weeks and there were a lot of transient service personnel passing through who often slept there. There were also the usual drunks and, no doubt, a few perverts lurking around. Not exactly a family orientated atmosphere. This place appeared to be a gymnasium that had been turned into a dormitory. I slipped all my money into my billfold and put it in my skivvies. I also slept with an open switchblade knife under my pillow. This was a routine procedure that I followed in unsavory situations such as this, when for one reason or another they could not be easily avoided.

The next morning, August 28th, again dawned bright and fair and I worked my way east into Tallahassee, FL where I visited the State Capitol, etc, and then headed for Tampa. I didn't make very good time after leaving Tallahassee and night came on long before I ever saw the city limits of Tampa. I was hitchhiking at night and I soon found myself in a very unpleasant situation. Down there in the swampy areas, at certain times of the year, they have what they call mayflies. They are fairly large and black and look something like a mosquito, only about ten times larger. I am not sure what their life span is, but I was told it was very short... they hatch, mature rapidly, reproduce and then die. Thank heavens for that. They are pesky critters. They don't bite or didn't bite me, but they swarm all around you by the thousands and get into your hair, even your eyes and you sure want to keep your mouth closed. I got a ride that let me out on the south side of the Suwannee River Bridge. With those mayflies swarming around, I thought I'd go berserk. Fortunately, I didn't have to wait too long before something nice happened.

An older gentleman, in a nice expensive sports car stopped and gave me a ride. His name was Leland J. Cobb. He was the president of the Cobb Construction Company of Florida. He told me he had four brothers and that each was the president of his own construction company in surrounding states. There was one in Georgia, South Carolina, North Carolina and Mississippi. He was very interesting to talk to. He said his company had just rebuilt the press box for the Boston Red Sox stadium. It was probably around 8:30 p.m. when he picked me up. We drove along with his wipers on high to clear the mayflies that kept splattering all over his

98

windshield. After a bit, even using his windshield washer's full force, it was still getting difficult for him to see. At least twice he got out and used a towel to wipe the bugs off. As I recall, it was around 11:30 p.m. when we got to Tampa. He asked where I wanted to go and I told him the YMCA. Usually they were pretty good, reasonably clean and cheap. I didn't know it, but this was going to be another of those two-bit flop houses. I was led into a large area, similar to the type of place I stayed in the night before. I was assigned a steel frame cot with a thin cotton mattress, an apparently clean sheet and a pillow. I washed up, went through my routine of stashing my money in my skivvies and went to bed, again with the open switchblade under my pillow. I was tired. It had been a slow, tiring and unpleasant day, due in part to the bugs, rain and several long waits between rides. However, tomorrow was to be the beginning of a different type of odyssey.

It was Wednesday, August 29, 1945, and a beautiful day. The YMCA was close to the waterfront, so I decided to go down to the docks and look at the ships. There was a nice, clean looking restaurant at the waters edge. I hadn't eaten much the day before, so I was particularly hungry. Though I didn't usually eat breakfast, I had a big one that morning, just about as much as one could waddle away with. It was a good thing I did, because as it would turn out, it'd be nearly eight hundred miles, several states and a few days later before I'd eat a full meal like that again.

As a small boy, I always had a love for the sea. Now that didn't make much sense when you think of it, growing up inland as I did, but after breakfast I went right down to where the ships were moored. Though what I was about to do was not premeditated, my parents, especially Dad, probably would have thought I had a stupid pill for dessert that morning. While wandering around, a shipping officer with a chalkboard out in front, stating 'Deck Hands Wanted' caught my eye. My next actions were probably due to a gene or something I must have inherited from my Great Great Grandfather Harding. He owned and was the captain of a three mast schooner that plied the Atlantic in mercantile trade between Europe and America.

I went over to the shipping company office and asked the clerk about their shipping schedule. I wanted to know what they had going out... when it was leaving... and when it was getting back. I don't recall any more details, or even asking what they paid. One of the ships that needed deck hands was a banana boat going to Cuba. It was going to load up, then turn around and come back. I felt I could spare that much time. The man behind the desk was delighted because, due to the war, help was hard to get. I filled out the application papers and slid them through the window. He asked me for identification, so I gave him my birth certificate. He looked at it, then sadly shook his head, gave my certificate back to me and began tearing up my application. I said, "Hey, what are you doing that for?" He said, "You're only 17!" I told him, "Yeah, well so what?" He replied, "You have to be at least 18 to ship out. If I signed you up and someone found out, it would be your a__ and mine both."

Well, that was that. No sea voyage for me this trip. Little did I know at the time, but in less than ten years I would get my wish to go to sea. I would join the Navy and travel around the world serving in the 2nd, 6th, 7th, 5th and 1st Fleets. Those adventures are covered in my book *Sea Tales*.

I didn't leave Tampa until around noon and then headed for Daytona Beach via Orlando. The rides weren't very good at all, so it was late when I even got to Lakeland. Guy and Helen Pickenpaugh, some friends of my parents back in Rushville, had some relatives in Lakeland and they wanted me to stop and say hello for them if I had a chance. I stopped, but no one was home and a neighbor said they were on vacation. I went back down to the highway that led to Orlando. I saw a small hotel and, since it was getting dark and I didn't want to be heading out through swampy areas at night, especially if the mayflies were still active, I checked in. They didn't have a dining room and there was no restaurant around, but there was a small grocery store next door. I bought a quart of apple juice and two nickel Cheese Nabs. Each package contained four double cheese crackers, with peanut butter between them. Not exactly a gourmet meal but they tasted good and by now I was getting a little hungry because I hadn't eaten since breakfast that morning in Tampa. At least they helped fill me up some. I went back to my room, brought my log book up-to-date and then I decided to shave because I wanted to get an early start the next morning.

It was hot and my window was up. I was shaving when the light went on in the room directly across a four foot wide ventilation shaft, between building wings that separated our rooms. A very attractive unclad young woman, with dark hair below her shoulders came into the room. I glanced over, but kept on shaving. In a bit I noticed some movement out of the corner of my eye and looked over. She had obviously decided to do some aerobic exercises before retiring. I was only half shaved however, with the main attraction of the evening beginning across the vent, I would have cut my throat if I had continued. Therefore, I went over and turned off my light, pulled up a chair, propped my feet up on the windowsill, sat back, relaxed and took in the show. It was nearly as good as

Minsky's Burlesque in Chicago.

Then the show was over. She slipped on a robe and a shower cap, and left the room to go down the hall to the shower. That was common back in those days for ordinary hotel accommodations. Most rooms didn't have a shower or toilet facilities in the room. A lot of them just had a lavatory, as mine did. The other facilities were normally down at the end of the hall and were shared with the other guests.

I got up, put the chair back, turned on the light, washed the dry lather off the unshaven side of my face, lathered back up and finished the job I was doing when I was so *pleasantly* interrupted!

The next morning I was up and out early. I got a ride in an old pickup from a driver that had brought some produce into town. I was working my way northeast toward Daytona Beach. I was not getting good rides, even around Orlando, which surprised me. Most were short rides with a bit of a wait between them. However, this was going to change dramatically beginning at 8:00 the next morning, but that was still a day off.

I was looking forward to seeing the Atlantic Ocean for the first time and I saw it at Daytona Beach at 2:29 p.m. on Thursday, August 30th, which was my Dad's 56th birthday. There were some portable bathhouses on the beach where one could change, so I did and went swimming in the Ocean. Similar to the Great Salt Lake, there were freshwater showers at intervals along the beach, where one could rinse the salt off.

My first view of Atlantic Ocean at Daytona Beach.

After rinsing, I got back into my regular clothes. I was getting rather hungry by now, especially after swimming in the ocean. I hadn't had anything to eat all day because I had left Lakeland real early and was never near any place to eat when I wasn't riding in a car or truck.

I got a ride fairly quickly and shortly the driver stopped for gas. As he was paying, he yelled out and asked if I wanted a Pepsi. "Sure," I said. Besides being hungry with nothing to eat all day, after swimming in the ocean I was also rather thirsty. I offered to pay him for it, but he said it was on the house. I made it north to St. Augustine in two rides.

At St. Augustine I stopped to see the Fountain of Youth. Years later I figured out I made a major mistake while I was there. I took TWO drinks at the Fountain of Youth and apparently the second must have counteracted the first because I have continued to get older ever since. After leaving there I went into Jacksonville, where I looked around some, then worked my way toward the north end of town and found a nice tourist home. After I settled in my room and freshened up a bit, I was ready to go out to look for a restaurant to fill up the growing void in my stomach. By now it had been two full days since I had eaten a regular meal, which was the morning before last in Tampa. I asked the landlady where a nice restaurant was. She shook her head and said there weren't any nearby and I'd have to go back downtown to find one. I was sure disappointed because any satisfaction from the quart of apple juice and the two Cheese Nabs in Lakeland and the soda in Daytona was long gone. By then I could've eaten a horse. However, I was tired and I just didn't feel like going all the way back downtown. I brought my log up to date, made a new sign for **SAVANNAH**, drank several glasses of water, tightened my belt around my stomach to feel full and then went to bed.

The next morning I left the tourist home shortly before 8:00 a.m. on August 31st. I figured I'd get a ride up the road to a truck stop somewhere and chow down. I went out, set my bag down and noted the time I began hitchhiking in my diary as I always did. It was 8:00 a.m. I immediately heard a roar and something flashed by me nearly sucking my new Savannah sign out of my hands. It was a car. The driver stopped about a block away. Then with a squeal of his tires, he came roaring backward to me, stopped and shouted, "I'm going to Savannah, get in." I still don't know why I got in... most drunks would've been safer to have ridden with, than him.

The big change in my length of waits between rides had just occurred. From here to Cairo, IL, I would be getting out of one vehicle and into another. My longest wait for any one single ride would only be twelve minutes, and that would be in the middle of nowhere, outside of Memphis, TN, at 4:00 in the morning! One ride would take me around 650 out of the 1,100 miles from Jacksonville, FL to Cairo, IL. This was back long before the days of interstates and most of the roads were only two lanes and winding. In the mountains they were also steep and if you got stuck behind someone it was hard to pass.

I only remember *two* things on my fast trek from Jacksonville to Savannah, GA. One, we only came to a complete stop once, and that was at a bridge where the state or county had prisoners literally chained to the east side of the bridge. This caused one-way traffic. The prisoners were scraping, priming and painting the bridge. Just as we stopped, the southbound traffic cleared and we were waved ahead. And, two, I remember *remembering nothing much else.* You see, I had my head down, my eyes closed and I was praying as hard as I could that we'd get to Savannah in one piece.

Yes, the Lord does answer prayers because only by the grace of God did we make it. He dropped me off and as he pulled away I glanced at his tires. They were as bald as a cue ball. Checking the map I figured the mileage and divided it by the time and found that we had AVERAGED an even 90 miles per hour! I don't recall if there were any restaurants where he let me out, but my stomach was too full of butterflies to have eaten anyway. I made a new sign, this time for **COLUMBIA**, SC.

Almost instantly I got a ride, then another, then another. Most of these were not too far, but I was moving progressively toward Columbia, which was where I figured I'd probably spend the night. Shortly, I recovered from my wild ride and my appetite was returning real fast. Around noon I rode into some town. About a block before that particular ride came to an end, I noticed a restaurant out of the corner of my eye. After thanking my driver, I headed back for the restaurant. As I approached, I noticed a long line, clear back out onto the sidewalk and down the block, of people waiting to eat. Most were soldiers apparently on leave from a nearby Army base. These guys were used to standing in lines and probably had nothing else to do. I had a long way to go and was on a roll of getting a bunch of quick rides. Besides, if I had of gotten in that line, the restaurant probably would have been out of food by the time I made it to the counter. So, I pushed on.

Based on the frequency of my rides, it was soon obvious that I was going to be in Columbia by the middle of the afternoon if it kept up. It would be too early to quit hitchhiking so I made another sign that said **GREENVILLE**. That was too far to expect to reach that night, but at least it would take me in the general direction.

By the time I got to a logical place to hitchhike I must admit I didn't assess my chances as too good. In fact, they were downright terrible. As far as the eye could see there were soldiers hitchhiking, all in the same direction I wanted to go. I expect there were well over a hundred soldiers with their thumbs up. Now, even though I looked like a soldier, I wasn't one. I didn't figure my chances of being singled out and offered a ride, in the middle of that line of bona fide soldiers was very good even with the most optimistic outlook I could muster. It is an unwritten law among hitchhikers that the new man on the scene goes to the far end of the line, but in this situation who knew WHERE the end of the line was? You couldn't even see it. So I slid in an open gap and held up my sign. At least there was a good deal of traffic.

I was there maybe three or four minutes, max, when a

car, which had passed me, backed up past no less than five soldiers and stopped in front of me. The driver leaned over, opened the door and said, "Hop in, I saw your sign and I'm going through Greenville." He was an army captain who later mentioned he was being transferred to the 5th Army Headquarters in Memphis, TN. 'Hmmmmm Memphis' I thought, I'm going through Memphis, but I didn't want to lay that fact on him until he got to know me a little better. He was a pretty big guy, rather heavy set and jovial. We got along real well. By now it was around 6:00 p.m. He asked me if I had eaten. Instead of answering his question I asked if he had, and he said yes that he'd eaten at the base just before he left. I didn't say anything more, but after a bit he asked me again if I had eaten. I told him, "yes." Since he had already eaten, I didn't want him to stop just so I could feed my face.

After a while I brought up the subject of Memphis again. I told him I was going to be passing through there myself and if he didn't mind I'd like to ride along. He said great because he was planning on driving on through and, with someone to keep him company it would help him stay awake.

Sometime around 2:00 a.m. we were somewhere deep in the Smokey Mountains and both of us were getting sleepy. We pulled over to the side of the road and slept a bit. After about an hour we woke up cold, so we started on. For some reason, I still remember the warm, rather musty smell of the car's heater as it came on. Dawn was breaking shortly after we left South Carolina and pulled into the little town of Franklin, NC. There wasn't much to the town that I could see, but maybe we were just at the edge or around the corner. The captain saw a restaurant on the side of a hill, up some steps from a little parking area. He let out a big yawn, stretched and said, "I'm getting kind of hungry... how about you?" I allowed that, "Yes, I *could* eat." So we parked and climbed the steps up to the restaurant and went in.

It was around 5:30 the morning of September 1st. We were apparently the first customers. The coffee was on and oh did it smell good! There was a big, middle aged, burly hillbilly fellow with a full beard standing in front of a large grill behind the counter. "Hi there!" said the captain in friendly salutation, as we each climbed up on a stool at the counter. The cook greeted us with a deep sort of rumble, "Howdy ...what'll you boys have?" as he slipped a menu to each of us. The captain mentioned he was *really* hungry. After glancing at the menu briefly, he ordered the biggest breakfast platter that was listed. It was called The Mountaineer's Breakfast. It consisted of a thick slice of country ham, a big stack of pancakes, grits and two eggs, with hash browns on the side, toast, jelly and coffee. Then the cook turned to me. I said, "I'll have the same... but make it two," holding up two fingers. I don't think mountaineers normally change expression much, but this one looked down right flabbergasted. He muttered... "TWO"?, holding up two of his fingers. "Two" I replied, again holding up two fingers. The captain spun around and looked at me as if I was some sideshow freak and with a disbelieving look on his face, he also held up two fingers and said, "TWO?" and I showed him my two fingers and repeated, "TWO" once again. The captain just turned back around on his stool... shaking his head. The cook, still in a state of disbelief as to the conversation, wagged his head, poured our coffee, then turned around and started cooking. Before long, he slipped each of us one of the most beautiful and tasty breakfasts that had ever been prepared. As the captain said, he was hungry so he dove right in. The cook was watching me, and when I was well into mine he started cooking my second one. As I finished, he had it ready and brought it over. The captain, who was only about half through his platter, glanced over as I started on the second one. As the cook walked back, he and the captain exchanged a look, not really believing I was actually putting away two of those Mountaineer's Breakfast platters.

When the captain finished his plate, he swiveled around and hunched over. He put his left hand on his knee, and with his right elbow on the counter, looked at me with a rather incredulous expression on his face. At the time I was making a final pass across my plate with my last bite of toast. The captain with some dismay asked, "Do you ALWAYS eat like that?" I told him "No sir, but you see, I haven't eaten for three days."

'*Whooeeee*' did he ever explode! "YOU LIED TO ME!" he yelled. I told him, "No sir, I didn't." He said, "YES YOU DID, because I asked you last night if you had eaten, and you said you had." I told him, "Yes sir I did, but I didn't tell you which day." With a bewildered look on his face, he asked, "Now WHY did you do a dumb thing like that?" I told him last night he had told me he had just eaten, and since he was kind enough to give me a ride I didn't want him to stop just so I could feed my face. I don't rightly recall what he said in response to that, but it probably shouldn't be repeated anyway. He wasn't really mad at me personally, but rather frustrated.

We proceeded west now for the rest of the trip, but did not arrive in Memphis until the middle of the night. Fortunately, his destination was near the west side of the city. It was too late to look for a room and it was a nice night, so I decided to continue hitchhiking. The captain let me out at a bus stop and I caught the last city bus that was still running. It went out west of town to a road that led back to a naval communications base. This was the last bus for the night and it was leaving shortly, at 3:30 a.m. There were perhaps a half dozen sailors on the bus. At the final stop, we all got off and the sailors walked down the intersecting road toward their base. The bus turned around and headed back to town. So now it was just me and one lone street light on a power pole at the intersection. I looked at my watch. It was 4:00 on Sunday morning, September 2nd; I made the appropriate notation in my diary. The stars were out and it was a nice evening. I figured my luck of quick rides had just run out. So far the longest I had waited for a ride had been ten minutes. However, if I couldn't get a ride shortly, I'd go over into a field across the road and sleep there for the night. That way I would be in position to get an early start in the morning. However, my luck was still holding. The very next car that came long picked me up. It was a family that was headed for Cairo, IL. The time was 4:12 a.m. The twelve minutes to get that ride was the longest single wait I had for any one ride all the way from Jacksonville, FL to Cairo, IL!

It was 7:00 a.m. when we reached Cairo. Normally Sunday is not a good day to hitchhike, and this Sunday would be no exception. Salesmen are home with their families, or at least off the road; business travel is nearly non-existent; and most of the traffic involves families going for a Sunday drive, to see Grandma, Aunt Martha or whoever. This was a typical Sunday, because from there on hitchhiking was extremely poor. I had long waits between short rides. The longest wait of this segment was at Virginia, IL. I didn't get home for another seven and a half hours, until 2:30 p.m. Sunday September 2, 1945.

One of the things I wanted to do was to see how economically I could make the trip. When I subtracted the cash I brought back, from what I had when I left, I had spent only $32. I had bought a little something for Mom, Dad, Keith and myself; there were a few city bus fares; a sightseeing admission or two; a small but nice box of candy for Dr. and Mrs. Upton where I stayed four nights for free; and I had paid for lodging five nights, but two were only 25¢ per night. The rest of the time I was moving all night except the one night I slept in a small barn in Pine Bluff, AR, after diving out of the bathroom window of Lucky's after the police raid. The rest was for food. At approximately 3,600 miles traveled, that figures out to less than nine tenths of a cent per mile. I felt fine, even though I'd lost approximately thirty-two pounds ...BUT WHAT A TRIP ! !

Home from the Southeast.

111

A Lesson In Living

1946 - August 10th - August 28th

Age: 18 years, 0 months, 28 days

CHICAGO - BENTON HARBOR - TORONTO - OTTAWA - MONTREAL - QUEBEC - MAINE - BOSTON - NEW YORK - PHILADELPHIA - WASHINGTON - RICHMOND - LOUISVILLE - and HOME.

I didn't like hitchhiking with anyone. The main reason was, I figured your chances of getting a ride were reduced by about the square of the number of people hitchhiking. With two people it would be roughly four times as hard to get a ride, with three maybe nine times as hard, etc. Also, I liked to go where I wanted, by the route I preferred, to do what I wished, and to stay as long as I liked; without having to placate or satisfy any poorly thought out whims of a fellow traveler. You might say I was sort of a loner. However, the year before I had gone to Chicago with a friend by the name of Don Corbridge. It was only a short trip and we had basically agreed upon our plans in advance. Though getting rides are not as good when you have someone with you, there are some advantages. It *is* nice to have some companionship and it's nice to have someone to share your experiences with later.

By the time I was planning this trip I had gained a reputation around town with my travels and hitchhiking. A

113

friend of mine named Jack Burns had heard about several of my adventures and he wanted to go with me. I liked Jack, but I preferred to go it alone and told him no. He still kept after me. Finally, I told him ok, I was going to make up the itinerary and select the routes, and I made it very clear to him ahead of time that it was my plan we were going to follow and I didn't want ANY misunderstandings.

We started out fairly early the morning of August 10, 1946. I had made a sign that read **CHICAGO**. Actually, we went the same route Don Corbridge and I had taken the year before, going through Havana, heading for McLean. At McLean we picked up US Route 66 (now I-55) and headed northeast toward Chicago. When we reached Joliet, I made a new sign reading **DETROIT** and we headed east. We bypassed the main Chicago area, went though Hammond, IN, then curving north we went up to Benton Harbor, MI. From there we headed east to visit the capitol at Lansing. That done, we went on to Detroit. So far it was pretty routine and nothing exciting happened between home and Detroit. By now it was late afternoon and it was time for us to shut down.

We went downtown to see what that part of the city looked like and we registered at an old, cheap, hotel. Our room was on the third floor. As we looked out our window we noticed a movie theater a few doors to the right, showing *The Outlaw* with Jane Russell. People were lined up for blocks to see it. Back then this was considered a rather racy film; in fact, it had been banned for a long time by the Catholic Church. We went down to the lobby to see if they had a restaurant. They didn't, so we went out to look for something to eat. A few doors to the left of the hotel was a small grocery store. We bought a quart of milk and a few items to take back to our room for our supper. We also asked the grocery clerk for a dozen or so small brown paper bags, about three by four by six inches in size.

Back in our room we ate our grocery store supper and then had a little fun. We turned out the lights in the room. We could still see quite well from the light filtering in from the outside. For starters, we each filled a couple of the bags half full of water and then played 'bombardier' on the people three floors below standing in line to see The Outlaw. We only went for near misses. We never even tried for any direct hits, and we got pretty good, too. The women would scream and the men would swear. They would look all around, but, though some did, surprisingly few actually looked up. When they did, however, they never saw us because we never hung out of the window. That would have been too easy for them to have spotted us. We'd just peer out, from the side of the window casement of our darkened room, to watch the confusion going on below. After we had our fun we decided to go to bed, but just for the heck of it we dropped only three of our shoes on the floor and wondered if there was someone below and how long they may have waited for the other shoe to drop.

The next morning we made our way to the international border between the United States and Canada. After showing our identification and answering a few basic questions we crossed the Detroit River and entered Canada at Windsor, Ontario. Just beyond the immigration check point we held up our sign for **TORONTO** and almost immediately we got a ride as far as London, Ontario. Then two or three more fairly quick rides after that, we found ourselves fast approaching Toronto. Up to now Jack was pretty impressed and seemingly enjoying himself, but after we crossed the border into another country, even though it was only Canada, he began asking how far I thought we were from home now. I didn't think much of it at first, but later, thinking back I should have seen there might be a problem looming on the horizon.

By mid-afternoon we were finally in Toronto, which was our first real destination. I had a pen pal there named Jeannie Carson, who I had been writing to since I was in the 5th grade. I had already written to her letting her know we were coming. Jack and I located a tourist home first. It wasn't easy because it seemed nearly everything was filled. Actually, we rented a couple blankets, a pillow and space on the floor in a room with several others. That was it! It seems we paid 50¢ each for our meager accommodations. Then I called Jeannie. She gave us instructions how to get to her parents place.

We took a street car (some call it a trolley) to the end of the line and then walked a ways until we got to her parent's home. When we arrived we found they had a very nice home, complete with a maid, in what was obviously a rather exclusive section in the north end of the city. That wasn't surprising since, as it turned out, her father was an executive with General Electric. We met Jeannie's parents. They were very nice and hospitable. Jeannie had invited Cindy Cook, a friend of hers, as a date for Jack. Cindy was a tall, slender, and a strikingly good looking girl with long dark hair.

By now it was late afternoon, so we just stayed at the house and in general got acquainted. Jeannie's parents asked us and Cindy to stay for supper and we spent a very pleasant evening visiting. Jeannie and Cindy suggested we go on a picnic the next day, then later that evening the girls walked us back to the north end of the trolley stop and from there we returned to our lodgings at the tourist home.

The next day we went out to the Carson's fairly early.

Jeannie's dad tossed me the keys to their big Buick limo and said that as long as I drove, not Jeannie, we could take it to Lake Simcoe for our picnic. The girls had the picnic basket all packed, so we jumped in the limo and drove about 50 miles north of Toronto to Lake Simcoe. It was quite a large lake and had all sorts of recreational facilities around such as boating, water skiing, fishing, etc. We had a nice picnic and then went swimming. It was a little cool but not bad. As I was in the process of diving into the lake, and was in midair, I realized I had my wrist watch on. There was sure no turning back. I hit the water and immediately came up sticking my arm out. It was too late. The water had leaked in and, by the time I got back to Rushville, it had started to lose time. As we visited, I noticed Jeannie and Cindy were asking me all sorts of questions that took a certain amount of explanation. After a bit I began to get a little suspicious that something was going on... so I asked Jeannie, "Why all the questions?" She sort of laughed, and said she and Cindy enjoyed my southern drawl. I told her, "Honey, if you think I have a southern drawl, just take a trip south of the Mason-Dixon Line. After a full and tiring day at Lake Simcoe, we drove back to Toronto. I gave the keys back to Mr. Carson, grinned, and told him, "Jeannie didn't drive, and there are no scratches."

We stayed in Toronto three days. The girls had taken us sightseeing all over town, we had the trip to the Lake for the picnic, and Jeannie's folks had us for supper at least twice. They all showed us a very nice time, all of which we appreciated. The last evening Jack and I were at the house, we left a small gift for Mr. and Mrs. Carson to show our appreciation for their hospitality. We didn't stay too late because we wanted to get an early start the next day.

The next morning, August 14th, as we were getting ready to leave, I could tell something was troubling Jack. When I asked him what the problem was Jack said he had enjoyed the trip but wanted us to head back home. [He was getting a little "homesick."]

I told him, "No sir, that wasn't our deal." I told him that I wasn't going back. "If you want to," I said pointing in a west-southwest direction, "home is that-a-way." As for me, I was going to head for Montreal and points beyond. So, somewhat reluctantly, Jack decided to head for home. We did part friends. He turned back while I continued on east-northeast as free as a bird, which was what I had wanted in the first place.

Something else took place that last morning in Toronto. A little *insignificant thing* happened that was the catalyst to what would eventually blossom into a profound friendship that would last for nearly half a century. The tourist home where Jack and I had stayed was bursting at the seams with transients. Many of them were servicemen, still in uniform, who had been discharged and were headed home. There was only one washroom downstairs and there were a lot of people that used it. As I was exiting from the lavatory, after my turn, there was an American Naval Ltjg (lieutenant junior grade) waiting to go in. I nodded and said "Good Morning," he responded likewise, and that was that. I picked up my bag, said goodbye to Jack and left for Ottawa, the Canadian capitol.

Later that day I reached Ottawa. As I was walking up the long walk to the parliament buildings, which were located quite some distance back from the street; I noticed I was in stride with a short, semi-formally attired, dapper looking gentleman wearing a black bowler hat.

Parliament buildings in Ottawa.

While making our approach to the buildings, I asked him what the rather impressive looking building was, over on the right. I was instantly treated to a long and eloquent dissertation on not only what that building was, but nearly every other building in sight. I was quite impressed. I thanked the gentleman and asked him how he knew so much about all the buildings and their history. He said, "Oh, I work here; I am the Minister of Agriculture."

I went through most of the main buildings, and up to the gallery on top of their impressive clock tower. From there I had an awesome view of the entire parliament grounds and beyond. After that I left.

Parliament clock tower.

As I was walking back across the street that ran in front of the parliament buildings, I saw and recognized the same American Naval Ltjg I had spoken to, ever so briefly, at the tourist home earlier in the day. He was coming toward me, crossing the street in the opposite direction, headed toward the parliament buildings. He recognized me at the same time, so we went back to the south side of the street and got acquainted. After talking a bit we found that we were both doing the same thing, sightseeing by hitchhiking around. We exchanged names and addresses. His name was Doug Waugh and at that time he lived in New Haven, CT.

That chance meeting was the start of a very long friendship spanning nearly five decades. Doug had just been discharged from the Navy and was hitchhiking home, the long way, and sightseeing as he went, thus saving his travel allowance. It was obvious we had a common bond.

Doug Waugh

Though we didn't know it then, in two years we would travel to Alaska together where we would end up working on the Alaskan Railroad. Douglas V. Waugh would become the most traveled, unusual, unforgettable, clandestine, and mysterious man I would ever meet... but that's another story.

From Ottawa I pushed onto Montreal. I remember at least one of the rides was in the back of a pickup truck with two men and a girl. None of them spoke English, only French. We tried to talk by sign language etc., but not with much success. Pretty soon, in jest I said, "...and a hinky dinky-par-le-vou-to-you, too." That puzzled them and they jabbered back and forth trying to figure out what I had said. Then I thought I'd better stick to English, because as far as I knew I might be cussing them out. After that we continued along, pretty much in silence, other than the conversation that they shared among themselves.

Since I had spent the morning in Ottawa, it was mid-afternoon by now. It was a gloomy day and after a bit it began to sprinkle some off and on. Not hard, but enough to be annoying. Since I was still in the back of the pickup, I was beginning to get a bit damp. By the time I arrived in Montreal, the weather didn't appear that it would get any better, so I worked my way to the east side of town and located a place to stay for the night.

The next morning, August 15th, I ate breakfast at a nearby diner and then got a ride that took me through Trois-Rivières. [About five months later a big four lane bridge, which I had passed over, collapsed killing four people]. Two quick rides, one after the other came along and I was soon approaching Quebec.

Arriving in Quebec (the locals call it by its Indian name of Kebec [K-beck]) around noon, I headed down into the heart of the lower city. First off, I decided to find a place to stay the night. I had planned to remain in Quebec until the afternoon of the following day because there were so many things to see. However, I found normal decent lodging was pretty expensive even in that area of town. I felt my pocketbook would have a hard time adjusting to the economic realities of the surroundings, so I decided to downgrade my lodging and ended up getting a cot behind a curtain in another, literal, two-bit (25¢/night) flophouse. It was sort of like a walk-in closet, but without a regular door. This was my third, and would be my last, two-bit flophouse during my hitchhiking days. There was a shabby dresser in this cubby hole. On top if it was an ash tray with 25¢ in it.

The doughty, semi-toothless old woman with tousled hair, terrible breath, and bad complexion, showed me my cot and said in her best English, "OOoooh, someone left me a tip!" I thought, "Yeah, in a pig's eye!" When I left that dumpy hole in the wall the next day, I turned the ash tray upside down.

Lower Quebec City. My third and last two-bit flophouse in circle.

From the entrance of where I stayed that night, one could look up the steep cobblestone street and see the impressively large and majestic Chateau Frontenac hotel. It looked like a huge castle, which I guess it actually was, and it was beautiful. I vowed if I ever returned to Quebec, I would stay up there. That would come to pass nine years later, accompanied by my wife, Marilou.

All told, I spent the rest of my first day, that night, and the better part of the next day, August 16th, in Quebec. I saw the changing of the guard, visited the impressive citadel, an interesting nearby museum, as well as Battlefield Park. I viewed the St. Lawrence River from the area overlooking The Narrows. The location of which is what made Quebec such an important fortress in guarding access to Lake Ontario and points beyond via the St. Lawrence River. I also looked around at a few other points of interest and wandered through many shops, including inside the stately Chateau Frontenac.

By mid-afternoon it was time to go. I crossed the St. Lawrence on a ferry to Levis and set a southerly course on Quebec Route 173 for the state of Maine. I reached either Linere or perhaps Armstrong, before I stopped for the night. Shortly after dawn the following morning, August 17th, I crossed back into the U.S. at the border crossing located between Armstrong and Jackman. Now I was on US Route 201. It was rather cool, foggy and a little misty. I soon passed into and through an area that was one of the most eerie and depressing places I've ever been. There was a large asbestos plant there. It was gray all around from the dust of the pulverized limestone used to make the asbestos fibers. The houses, cars, trees and even the grass were gray. The scene looked like a landscape portrait drawn using a dark gray pen on a dirty white canvas. Years later asbestos was deemed very unhealthy.

I continued south-southeast passing through Waterville, and then curving to the south-southwest where I visited the capitol of Maine at Augusta. Nothing of particular note occurred, other than my visit to the state capitol building.

My next objective was to visit the capitol of Vermont at Montpelier. But there was a problem, namely the White Mountains were in my way. There was no direct access as such to Montpelier from Augusta. I had to get to Fryeburg, Maine first. To get to Fryeburg I continued southwest on US Route 201 from Augusta, picked up US Route 1 at Brunswick, then on down to Portland. From there I went up to Fryeburg.

In looking at a map, going through Portland seemed to be an around about way of getting from Augusta to Fryeburg. It was sort of like traveling the two sides of a right triangle instead of taking the hypotenuse. However, the map indicated the road from Portland to Fryeburg was a bit straighter and a higher service class highway (indicating more traffic) than the highway network between Augusta and Fryeburg. Hence, going via Portland was a better choice.

I took US 302 out of Portland, which was good for a couple of reasons. First, it was a US Route indicating that it probably carried more traffic than other roads in the area and second, it went all the way to Montpelier, which meant I wouldn't have to remember to change routes along the way. My first ride was to Fosters Corners, the second to Bridgton and the third to Fryeburg. Fortunately, the rides came fairly quickly. It was supper time by now, so I ate and then looked for a place to stay. They didn't have any tourist homes or hotels, or at least I didn't see any, therefore, the only remaining option was to hitchhike all night. Now up there in the mountains with more forests, rocks and yes, even bears than there are cars, it isn't the best place to hitchhike at night, especially since it appeared there *might* be a storm headed my way. However, I didn't have a choice, so you just do what you have to do.

I headed west from Fryeburg, following US 302. In a mile or less I would leave Maine behind and enter New Hampshire. I didn't like what I saw to the northwest. It was starting to lightning, and thunder could be heard. I just hoped I'd get a ride before the storm hit. About fifteen or so minutes later a nice family saw my Montpelier sign and picked me up. They were well intentioned people and explained they weren't going to Montpelier, but to Intervale just north of North Conway. Well here I fouled up. I didn't recognize the name, and I didn't check my map to see *just _where_* Intervale was. As it turned out, Intervale was just north of North Conway all right, but it was also off of US 302 maybe a mile or so. Had I realized that I would have respectfully declined the ride, or would have gotten out in North Conway. As it turned out, I was let off out in the middle of a forest at night... with not a light showing in any direction... and with a storm fast approaching. That was the bad news. The good news, if you can call it that, was across the highway there was a school bus shelter for kids to keep out of bad weather while waiting for the bus. During the next half hour only two cars drove past, but neither stopped. Then a short time later, I felt some big heavy drops that soon got closer and closer together, and fast turned into a full fledged rain.

Now let me tell you, that shelter and I became intimately acquainted real fast. Actually, it wasn't very funny at all, but I still get a chuckle out of thinking this was what a lidless vertical coffin must be like. There was no door, but the rain was from the back, so other than some minor blowing in, it wasn't all that bad. It did have a seat to sit down on. It probably would only have held three grade school kids, four if they were skinny, or two adults like me.

Whenever a vehicle approached heading west, I would run out and just use my thumb. They couldn't see my sign anyway, and maybe not even me, because who would expect to come across a hitchhiker at night, in the rain, in the middle of a forest? Anyone out there must be out of their mind, and who would want to give a ride to someone like that? After a few attempts, I resigned myself that I wasn't going anywhere for the rest of the night, so I tried to make myself as comfortable as I could in my vertical coffin. It was a long... damp... and cold night.

By dawn's early light on August 18th, I was one stiff, damp, and hungry hitchhiker who needed to shave and clean up. Fortunately, I was able to get a ride shortly after daybreak that took me to Bethlehem, some sixty miles further. I stopped at a gas station and used their free facilities, then looked for something to eat. After eating, and making it about thirty miles farther, I crossed the Connecticut River leaving New Hampshire and entering Vermont. This added another state to my growing list. In another fifty miles I entered Montpelier. After visiting the capitol building, checking out a cultural feature or two, and taking a few pictures, I set out again.

This time I headed southeast; which eventually took me back into New Hampshire and to its capitol at Concord. Today the highway is called I-89 and passes through Lebanon. I arrived in Concord in the mid-afternoon of the 18th. As always I visited the capitol building, but I didn't see much else of interest to me, or perhaps I just missed it.

By late afternoon, around 5:00 p.m., I was walking south down a fairly steep hill. I was headed toward, I hoped, a better place to begin a hitchhiking in earnest. I didn't really expect a ride, but I would still turn around now and then as I walked, and flash my new sign that now read **BOSTON**. About half way down the hill a six wheeled truck pulled over. I ran up and asked the driver how far he was going. "Boston" he said, but then added, "However, I have a bunch of stops to make along the way, but they won't take long if you don't mind." Heck no I didn't mind because a little earlier I had seen some dark storm clouds coming together back to the west. With last night's school bus shelter still fresh in my mind, I was wondering when I should hang it up for the night and find a place to sleep. I just now found it and it happened to have six wheels. I asked the driver what he was hauling and he told me a refrigerator truck full of frozen fish.

The rain began sooner than I had expected and had this ride not have come along when it did I probably would not have had time to have found a place to stay before it started. However, now I was dry and in the presence of a friendly, middle aged, medium built though rather stocky fellow with a pleasant New England twang to his voice, which I enjoyed hearing. He seemed happy to have someone to pass the coming night hours with. He was right, he made a lot of stops, usually around fifteen minutes, but once or twice up to a half hour. He delivered frozen fish to numerous restaurants. Some of the places would still be open, others were closed, but he had a key to those that let him get in at least as far as a locker where he could deposit the fish. Once or twice I helped him, but he usually just told me to stay in the cab as there wasn't that much to deliver at most places.

We passed the time by visiting and getting acquainted. At one point I pulled out a pack of Old Gold cigarettes, which I had purchased some time back, and offered him one. He said, "Sure," and then added, "Here... try one of mine," and tossed me his pack. His was a Black Cat brand, which I had never heard of before. He told me it was a Canadian brand. I lit one up and boy *was it ever strong*! I had to roll the window down a bit to help clear the air and my head. I never had another Black Cat after that.

By now it was getting pretty late or early as the case probably was, and I was getting sleepy. That was no surprise after the rather restless sleep I had endured the night before. It wasn't long before I dropped off to sleep in the cab.

Now it is only sixty to seventy miles maximum from Concord to Boston. If we were driving straight on through it should have taken us about one and a half hours getting us there between 6:30 or 7:00 p.m. However, we didn't go straight through but, in fact, had taken a very circuitous route with many stops of varying durations. Hence, we didn't get into Boston until around dawn. That was great for me. I was dry, had been going in the direction I wanted to go and had managed a certain amount of rest. Best of all, by the time we reached the end of the line it was starting to get light. Luck had owed me one for the night before and it had paid off.

I found a decent tourist home and made arrangements to stay there the nights of August 19th and 20th. This would give me time to take a bath two nights in a row, give me an opportunity to wash out my dirty clothes (which were beginning to accumulate), and give them ample time to dry before I hit the road again. In the meantime, I put on my clean spare set of clothing, left my bag in my room, and set out on an aggressive sightseeing tour of the area. One of the first places I went to was to the state capitol building. I don't recall the order in which I visited the various historic sites, but between walking, local city buses, actual bus tours, and yes even some hitchhiking in the area, I managed to see a great deal of the historic sites over the next two days. I climbed

Bunker and Breeds Hill; followed along the Charles River, past Harvard University, and to Concord and Lexington to see the Lexington Green battlefield; I stopped at The North Bridge, which was the site of the first major battle of the Revolutionary War, and is often referred to as where the shot was fired that 'was heard around the world'; I saw Paul Revere's lantern that he supposedly carried on the night of his famous ride; the Old North Church from where the signal lanterns (one if by land, and two if by sea) were hung to let Paul Revere, and doubtless other unknown sentinels, know how the British would be approaching Boston so they could alert the various communities; I visited Paul Revere's home where he had his silversmith shop; went to the site of the Boston Tea Party; saw Old Ironsides... etc. There were many other sites, equally important and impressive, that I visited on my whirlwind tour of Boston.

After checking out of my tourist home, I headed on down the coast to Plymouth to see Plymouth Rock where the Pilgrims landed, then out to the very end of Cape Cod and back. Next I headed for New York City, via Providence, Rhode Island and Hartford, Connecticut, visiting both capitol buildings.

My next stop would include visiting some former neighbors. Back home we lived next door to the Houston's. They had four children; the two older were twin girls. The twins were grown, working in New York City, and living in Upper Manhattan. My mother happened to mention to Mrs. Houston that I was going to go hitchhiking in the northeast later that summer and was planning to go down through New York. Mrs. Houston mentioned it to her daughters and they in turn graciously extended me an invitation to come stay with them a few days. That was great. They were friendly, I knew both of them well, and I felt comfortable around them.

When I arrived in New York, I went to Sally and Minerva's apartment building and took the elevator up to their floor. It was only about three in the afternoon and too early for them to be home from work, however, I thought that since they knew I was coming maybe they might come home early, so I went up to check. As expected there was no one at the apartment so I went back down and crossed the street to a square block city park. I put my bag down and sat on a park bench under a line of shade trees where I decided to spend the next hour or so until the girls got home pursuing my favorite pastime of people watching. There were four distinctive unrelated occurrences that took place while I was sitting there, that I felt were rather philosophical.

The **first** occurrence involved two rather large middle aged ladies on possibly the sixth floor of an apartment house. They were a half block south of me and across the street from the park where I was sitting. There were possibly three or four windows between them, which was a good thing considering their obvious demeanor. They were leaning out their windows and screaming naughty innuendos and other unpleasant things at the top of their lungs, as well as shaking their fists at one another. They were talking in some foreign language, I think Italian, but anyway I couldn't make out what their problem was. Maybe the daughter of one woman was seeing the son of the other and one didn't liked it... or one lady had slipped some of her garbage in the can of the other. Who knows, but whatever it was they were pretty bent out of shape about it. This tirade probably went on for a good ten minutes.

The **second** occurrence involved an enclosed white delivery van that was headed east in front of the building where the women had been screaming at each other. When

131

the driver came to the intersection, I saw him turn right without hesitating. He wasn't speeding, but obviously never even thought about stopping or even slowing for that matter. Though I couldn't see his signal, I could see the southbound signal was green so the delivery van just plain blew a red light. At the same time there was a little blue car headed south toward Lower Manhattan. It had just gone past me and was at the intersection when the van pulled out in front of him. The driver of the blue car laid on his horn, swerved to the left, and slammed on his brakes all at the same time. Fortunately, he missed hitting the van which nonchalantly continued on south. In addition to hearing his horn and the squeal of his tires, the air was soon filled with a considerable amount of blasphemous expletives emitting from the blue car. The driver was not a happy camper and rightfully so.

The **third** occurrence involved a well groomed, rather sophisticated looking lady, perhaps in her early 40s, who appeared to be a professional woman. She came out of the same mid-block apartment complex that Sally and Minerva lived in. Let me tell you, she was dressed fit to kill. She had on an attractive, well tailored, dark brown ladies business suit, matching high heels, a metallic looking gold scarf and a rather high crowned broad brimmed brown hat with a sweeping feather in it. She also carried a normal size, matching leather briefcase. I had a real good look at her since she was right in front of me, though across the street from where I was sitting in the park.

The traffic wasn't too heavy at that time. She looked to her right, spotted a cab, and hailed it. I noticed that a half block further south a man had stepped out and also hailed the cab. The cab driver apparently saw the man, but not the woman, because he passed her and slowed down for the man.

The woman, thinking he had just overshot her, began to run to catch *her* cab. The cab driver picked up the man and pulled away, leaving behind a very disgruntled woman who was swinging her briefcase in a hot, but losing pursuit. As she ran, yelling unladylike utterances, one of her high heels broke off thus ending the pursuit. She skipped on her other foot two or three times while she leaned over and finally got the shoe with the broken heel off her foot. In an expression of her frustration, she threw the shoe at the taxi cab which by now was half a block away. Of course, she didn't even come close. I heard several more choice words that were very similar to the general content of what I had heard on the two previous observations a bit earlier.

Then she turned around and walked... no, *stomped* back up the middle of the lane she was in, with one shoe on and one shoe gone. She was pumping her arms up and down *sideways* for some reason, rather than swinging them back and forth which would have seemed more normal. What southbound traffic there was gave her a wide berth as no driver had the nerve to tangle with a woman in her obvious state of mind. Though it was a pleasant day, it still was August. I could see she had gotten a good sweat up and no doubt could use a bath. Her hat was askew, her suit was in disarray, and her neatly coiffured hair was in dire need of some serious damage control, she needed a new pair of shoes, probably had broke a nail or two, and she undoubtedly would miss her appointment. It appeared the only thing that survived without blemish was her briefcase.

The **fourth** and final noteworthy occurrence of my people watching experience, that 21st of August came along shortly thereafter. It was in sharp contrast to the previous three. It emerged in the form of a very laid back, easy going, unperturbed human being who was obviously a homeless person. I noticed him some distance away, slowly and calmly walking down the sidewalk in my direction. He was clearly oblivious to anyone or anything around him. As I was studying his persona, I could see he was somewhere between his mid 40s to early 50s. Even though it was not a hot day, it sure wasn't cold either, and this fellow was wearing a long, heavy, dirty, gray overcoat. In lieu of any buttons, his coat was held together near the top by a large oversized safety pin that we used to call a horse blanket pin. He was hatless, had wavy graying black hair and a short salt and pepper stubble on his somewhat smudged face. As he came sauntering along toward me, by now only twenty feet or so away, I noticed he was smiling... at no one in particular. It was a relaxed, at peace with the world type of a smile. In his hand he was holding what back then was called a 'poor boy' sandwich, which today we call a 'sub'. It was obviously the remainder of a sandwich had been liberated from a trash barrel somewhere; and he was chomping with some difficulty on his feast. When he got to around fifteen feet or so from me he took another bite. I noticed he was missing several teeth which was why he had trouble eating his sandwich. I could also see some drool that was trickling down one corner of his mouth.

It wasn't until he got to within about ten or so feet of me that he even noticed me sitting there. He stopped, looked at me, then looked at my bag on the ground, and looked back at me again. Apparently he thought I was like him... homeless. He gave me the most sincere, warm and friendly smile I have ever received. Then he stretched out his hand and offered me a bite of his sandwich. He never said a word the entire time. I returned his well intentioned smile and told him, "Thanks, but I just ate." With that he gave me a shrug as if to say... "Ok friend, but you would have been welcome," and I am sure I would have been. Then he ambled on down the street. Actually, I was quite touched by his willingness to share what little he had.

This was a mind provoking experience for me. He had so little, but was willing to share it. I have thought of him many times in the ensuing years and feel this was truly *A Lesson in Living.*

I said at the beginning of this portion of my story that there were four occurrences that I felt were rather philosophical. In #1... The two women were obviously unhappy and distraught. Too bad, but it is doubtful their problem was life threatening. #2... The driver of the little blue car was very upset and rightfully so, and no doubt had some unpleasant feelings about the driver of the van. But, after all, there was no damage and no one got hurt. #3 The professional woman chasing the cab... well her demeanor was a disaster. But it was really her fault for getting so flustered. What was the problem anyway? Another cab would have been going by in a minute or so and besides, it was a nice day. Then there was the fellow in #4. He had nothing going for him, except perhaps a full tummy for the next few hours. He didn't have an apartment like the two women. He didn't have a car like the fellow in the blue car. He didn't have a job like the well dressed woman had. Yet, which of the four was the **happiest** and the one with the fewest cares?

My homeless friend made a lasting impression on me. His demeanor and outlook on life is well represented in Luke 12:22-26 of the Holy Bible.

And He said to his disciples, "Therefore I tell you, do not be anxious about your life, what you shall eat, nor about your body, what you shall put on. For life is more than food, and the body more than clothing. Consider the ravens: They neither sow nor reap, they have neither storehouse nor barn, and yet God feeds them. Of how much more value are you than the birds! And which of you by being anxious can add a cubit to his span of life? If then you are not able to do as small a thing as that, why are you anxious about the rest?"

Thought provoking isn't it? Yes, we can learn a good deal by quietly people watching.

Sally and Minerva got home shortly after 5:00 p.m. They had, earlier in the day, put together an excellent meal for supper that night. We spent the evening catching up on the news back home and on what each of us had been doing over the past several years.

The next morning they gave me a key and they went to work. I started out, to get in as much sightseeing as I could. In no particular order I went down to the foot of Manhattan and took a ferry to see the Statue of Liberty and Ellis Island. I climbed up inside the Statue itself, but not all the way up because it was too crowded. On Ellis Island, I walked around the grounds and through the reception area where the arriving immigrants assembled. If you tried to filter out the jumble of conversations taking place all around, you could almost imagine the babble of foreign tongues that must have taken place here as new immigrants arrived from overseas. I couldn't help but notice a few, rather touching instances of some older couples with their arms around their now grown children, and in some cases also around their grandchildren, pointing to this and that. I assume the older people had been immigrants and had come back to show their children and grandchildren where they had arrived in this country and started a new life. After all, it was part of their children's heritage, too. I wasn't close enough to hear their voices or what they were saying, but I assume many spoke in broken English or perhaps still in their native tongues. Yet it didn't take too much imagination to figure out what they were probably talking about. Strangely it gave me a warm feeling, because it was people like these, from all over the world that gave America her unique character.

I took the ferry back to Manhattan from Ellis Island. Since I was still down by the waterfront, I decided to go on an excursion up the Hudson River. It was a nice day so I chose the upper deck at the stern. While wandering around the deck, looking at this and that, I struck up a conversation with two friendly girls that were a little older than me. After their first few words, I detected a Brooklyn accent which was as *long as your arm*. Jokingly, I told them I bet I could tell them where they were from. They replied, "...aw go on, you can't either." So I told them to stand sideways... then turn their backs to me... to look up... and to look down. All the time I was going "Hmmm... yep... Uh huh... that figures." They kept asking why I was making them do all that and what that had to do with my figuring out where they were from. I told them "just be patient" because I just about had the answer. Then shortly I announced, "Ok! You're both from Brooklyn!" They were amazed at my perception and asked me, "How on 'oith' did ya figure that out? I told them, "Well, it was actually just a lucky guess." On the way up the Hudson we passed both Sing-Sing Prison and West Point located on the west bank. Eventually we went as far north as President Roosevelt's home at Hyde

Park. There I visited his grave and went through his home. Then the steamer turned around, re-boarded the passengers, and returned to Manhattan. It was a nice, interesting, enlightening and enjoyable trip.

While touring New York City, I went to the top of the Empire State Building; visited Times Square; rode on the subway to Brooklyn and back, just to say I had done it; visited Rockefeller Center; attended a performance of the Rockettes at the Radio City Music Hall; walked in Central Park, and took in a host of other sights and attractions.

I stayed in New York for three nights, and spent two full days sightseeing. Sally and Minerva were perfect hostesses. They would not let me take them out for supper. They seemed to love to cook, so we always ate in. That was a lot better than diner food anyway.

The morning of August 24th, I left New York behind and headed west across the George Washington Bridge. It was a toll bridge, so I purposely managed to get a ride *before* I got to the toll gates, so I went across for free. My next stop was Trenton, the capitol of New Jersey. From there I headed to Philadelphia, PA to visit the capitol and many of the numerous historical landmarks and objects in the Cradle of Liberty such as Independence Hall and the Liberty Bell.

Next I swung down to Dover, the capitol of Delaware, then west to Annapolis, the capitol of Maryland. While in Annapolis I went to the U.S. Naval Academy to see Bill Mills, a friend of mine from Rushville. He was out on a training cruise at the time, so I missed him. Rides continued to be good as I headed for Washington, DC, which was my goal for the day. Everything was routine and nothing of any particular note took place. I arrived in Washington, DC in mid to late afternoon of the 24th, and found a tourist home where I planned to stay for that night and the next night of the 25th, as well. I took a bath and cleaned up. It had been a full day, so I got something to eat for supper, brought my diary up to date, and went to bed early.

The morning of August 25th, I left my bag in my room and headed out on a marathon sightseeing tour of all I could see that day. I used a combination of local buses, walking, and some minor in town hitchhiking in order to get to many of the historical and other points of interest. Whether I had to extend my stay would be determined by how much I could fit in. Again, I do not recall the order in which I visited the following, though I first went to our Capitol building. I mingled in with various guided tour groups, listening to their guides. As most took more time than I wished, I would go on and join a group up ahead. I did the same thing later at the White House. I visited the Library of Congress, Ford's Theater where Abraham Lincoln was shot and, of course, the Lincoln and Jefferson Memorials, and the Washington Monument. I also spent some time, but far too little, at the Smithsonian Institute. One could easily spend at least two days there and still not see it all.

The morning of Aug. 26th, I finished the last of my sightseeing in Washington, DC and then headed across the Arlington Memorial Bridge, over the Potomac River, thus entering the State of Virginia. Here I stopped at the Arlington National Cemetery. This was truly something to behold. Everything, the grounds and all, was extremely well cared for. The simple, neat, white crosses, symmetrically laid out in all directions, were truly awe-inspiring. I waited to view the ceremony of the changing of the guard, at the Tomb of the Unknown Soldier. I also took a buggy ride around at least a portion of this vast cemetery. During the ride, we passed

General Robert E. Lee's home which is situated within the grounds.

After leaving Arlington National Cemetery I headed for Richmond, going by the way of George Washington's home at Mount Vernon overlooking the Potomac, then west to the Civil War battlefield at Manassas, then south to the battlefields at Fredericksburg and Spotsylvania. From there I continued on south to Richmond, where I briefly visited the Virginia State Capitol building. Afterwards I went a few blocks northeast to visit the Museum of the Confederacy and the White House of the Confederacy, which was next door to it and was used by the Confederate President Jefferson Davis.

By now it was time to head toward home in earnest. However, on the way I stopped briefly at the Appomattox Court House where Generals Grant and Lee signed the surrender of the South to the North, thus ending the Civil War. Charleston, WV was my next intended destination, though I knew it was much too late to reach there before nightfall. I got as far as Covington, VA where I secured a place for the night. I was getting rather hungry since I had skipped lunch and had been on the go all day having only had a roll and a glass of juice for breakfast. I cleaned up and then went out in search of something to eat. Upon returning to my room, I brought my diary up-to-date and turned in. Laying there in bed, I mulled over the day's occurrences and thanked God for a rewarding and safe journey. While nothing out of the ordinary had occurred, it still had been a good day. I had covered a lot of ground, thanks to getting good rides all along, and I had seen a great many things of historical and general interest this 26th of August. I asked God for his protective arm for the morrow... and fell asleep.

August 27th was a bit gloomy, but not really

threatening, though you can never tell what the weather will be from one minute to the next up in the mountains. I pulled out the **CHARLESTON** sign I had made before leaving Richmond. The rides were not as good today as yesterday, but I couldn't complain. They can't be good all the time. I skipped breakfast since I had really chowed down last night; therefore I wasn't too hungry this morning, and besides, I wanted to get moving. I hoped to make it to Frankfort, KY by nightfall. I was on the road before 8:00 a.m. and my first ride came along fairly soon, but after that there was a bit of a wait between rides. I reached Charleston during the noon hour. I made a fast visit to the capitol, grabbed a bite to eat, and made a new sign for **LOUISVILLE** even though I was headed for Frankfort, the capitol of Kentucky.

It was around 6:30 p.m. by the time I reached the capitol building at Frankfort. As it was after hours there was no more tourist access, so my visit was limited to just looking around the outside. Afterwards I caught a ride from inside the city that took me to the outskirts of town. I really lucked out when I got there. I came across a good sized truck stop, with a decent looking trucker hotel. I figured that would be a darn good place to stay for the night as they usually have decent bunks and good food. Besides, where better to catch a ride from than at a truck stop, where you can go up and talk to the drivers face to face.

At first it seemed like there was going to be a problem. The not-to-bright desk clerk at the truck stop hotel wouldn't rent me a room and when I asked him why he said, "Because you're not a trucker." I politely argued with him a bit, and then asked if his hotel was full. He said "No," so then I pointed out to him that... 1] my money was a good as any trucker's... 2] I needed a place to sleep... 3] I wasn't a drunk, or a trouble maker... 4] I was paying cash... and 5] he'd have one less empty bunk. It took a bit for the logic of that to sink in. Then he handed me a towel, small bar of soap, a blanket, a clean pillow, and a lock and key for a locker. He charged me three dollars for the bunk, and a five dollar refundable deposit for the lock and key to make sure he got it back. I ate a great meal at their restaurant and then I made an **INDIANAPOLIS** sign. The letters were squished together due to the name being so long. Lastly I shaved, took a shower, and went to bed. Truckers move early, so I wanted to be up and out in the lot by the time they were ready to roll.

In the morning, I got my things together, turned in my blanket and pillow and got my deposit back for the lock. As it turned out I didn't need my Indianapolis sign, because I walked through the parking lot as the truckers were thumping their tires, and checking their oil prior to departing. I asked in a voice loud enough for several of the driver's to hear... **"Is anyone going to Indianapolis?"** Two fellows spoke up that they were, so I picked the one with the bigger, nicer rig and climbed aboard. Soon we were on our way and by 11:00 a.m. we were in Indianapolis. The driver was friendly, but nothing of note occurred. Unfortunately, his terminal was in the southeastern part of the city and none of the truckers there were going to Peoria or even in that direction. I had to get to the northwest side of town. I made a sign reading **PEORIA** as that was the most recognizable city with the shortest name ahead of me.

Actually, I did quite well getting around the south and west side of Indianapolis. It wasn't too long before I got a ride to Champaign. After a bit of a wait another ride came along that would have taken me to Bloomington, however, I got out at the junction just before LeRoy, where there is a straight shot due west for Havana. For some reason I didn't feel it was necessary to make a Havana sign, however, there wasn't much traffic and I wasn't getting any rides. I had plenty of blank signs so I decided perhaps I had better make one for **HAVANA** and another for **QUINCY**.

The second car that came along stopped and took me to McLean. Rather soon I got a ride that was going on through Havana to Macomb. Actually, that was better because I had to go seven miles beyond Havana to reach US 24 anyway. There, I switched to my **QUINCY** sign. Now all I had to do was head southwest for twenty-seven miles through Summum then Astoria and I'd be home in Rushville.

It was a little after 6:00 p.m. when I walked across the yard. I detected some tantalizingly wonderful smells wafting from the kitchen as I approached the house. I paused at the door before entering, and in a loud voice said... "You better put on another plate, because you're having company tonight!"

On this trip I had traveled through fifteen states and two provinces of Canada, plus I had visited their respective capitols, except one or two I had been to previously. Now the northwest section of the United States was all that remained for me to visit, but that would have to wait another year.

The 48th

Trip #7
* * THE NORTHWEST * *

1947 - August 22nd - September 4th

Age: 19 years, 1 month, 0 days

SOUIX CITY - YANKTON - WALL - RAPID CITY - STURGIS - SHERIDAN - BILLINGS - RED LODGE - YELLOWSTONE - POCATELLO - BOISE - PENDLETON - WALLA WALLA - SPOKANE - MISSOULA - WHITEHALL - BISMARK - MOTLEY - MOLINE and HOME.

This would be a rather special trip. By the time this trip was over... if the course I charted remained as planned, I would have entered my 48th state of the Union. This would be the state of North Dakota.

From Rushville, IL, I headed north to Moline on the banks of the mighty Mississippi. I stopped briefly to say hello to my Aunt Myrt. Uncle Paul wasn't home at the time. Aunt Myrt fixed a great lunch for me and packed another for the road. Then to help me out even more, she drove me across the Mississippi River, over to the west edge of Davenport, IA, which got me out of the Quad City Metropolitan area. Using my destination signs, I soon caught a ride to Des Moines, IA.

Next I made a sign that read **MINNEAPOLIS** and headed north. Actually, I was only going as far as Webster City where I would turn west and head for Fort Dodge, IA. Most people didn't know where Webster City was, but everyone knew Minneapolis, and would be more inclined to give me a ride.   After turning west, the rides became noticeably shorter and farther between, but that was to be expected.   Not long after passing through Fort Dodge I got in a car and apparently misunderstood how far the driver of the vehicle was going.   He meant well, and thought he was doing me a favor, but as it turned out he dropped me off at a cross road in the middle of nowhere.   That is <u>nowhere</u>... as in *not a house insight*.   At least this was better than a similar situation back in North Conway, NH the year before.   That time it was cold, pitch black, raining cats and dogs, and in the middle of nowhere-nowhere.   This evening was dry and promised to be reasonably comfortable.   As I stood there waiting, occasional rides came, but... kept right-on-going.   Now and then one would slow down.   I'd get all enthused, but it would turn off onto the cross road where I was, and would disappear into the abundance of more nowhere.   It soon became rather dishearteningly evident that I might as well make the best of the situation, which had every indication of not getting any better. Therefore I began to review my options.

In the southwest quadrant of the intersection there was a nice rolling grassland pasture with a little stream running through it. I decided to sleep out under the stars that night. I climbed the fence and went a few hundred feet into the pasture and down to the nice, clean looking, babbling brook. While lying down I would be out of sight of the highway. I picked a grassy place on the bank where I would be comfortable. I ate the remains of the generous lunch Aunt Myrt had packed for me, then laid down, and before long was asleep.

The next morning, August 23rd, as I began to rouse, but before I had opened my eyes, I became aware of a wheezing sound, and felt some warm air on my cheek. I opened my eyes and was rather startled to see a big black and white Holstein cow checking me out. She was just curious and wondered what she had found. I was used to cows, so other than being startled at first, I wasn't scared. I looked around and there were maybe eight or ten of her buddies quietly standing in a semicircle, chewing their cud and watching what was going on. No one got excited. I slowly reached up and patted her jowls and scratched her forehead. She just stood there for a bit, and then, with her curiosity having been satisfied, she sauntered off into the field with all her buddies following along. I got up, used the stream to wash up, and then headed back toward the highway.

Nothing else of any particular note took place that morning. I got a ride on into Sioux City, IA, and then soon crossed into South Dakota making my way to Sioux Falls. People must always be getting those two cities mixed up. Going west from Sioux Falls, my next destination was the famous Corn Palace at Mitchell, SD.

It was a huge rectangular shaped building with large Russian onion style cupolas on top. The outside was adorned with murals depicting the history and culture of the area. I learned that the original building was built in 1892 and was called the Corn Belt Exposition. The current building was built in 1921 and was called The Corn Palace. The murals were designed by local artists and were crafted using some 2,000 to 3,000 bushels of corn of all shapes, colors and sizes. Also, incorporated were a great number of bushels of wild oats, wheat, and various grasses such as brome, and straw, etc. to lend color, texture, and depth to the works of art. These colorful displays were the building's primary covering. I was surprised to learn that the exterior is replaced every year. The replacement ears of corn are cut down the center using power saws, then nailed in place by following a corn-by-numbers diagram furnished by the artists. Inside it was larger than one would assume, or than it appeared from the outside. The Corn Palace served as a local multiuse facility for both the local community as well as the general region. They would put on stage shows, exhibits and even hold sporting events there.

From there I continued on west to Wall, South Dakota. No trip through this area would be complete without stopping at the Wall Drugstore. For many years, before and after I visited Wall, this was one of the most highly advertised tourist traps in the nation. There are roadside ads for it all over the country. Technically it is a drug store, though you probably would be hard pressed to find any aspirin. It did have an old-fashioned drug store type of soda fountain tucked away in one corner. The place was huge and seemed as large as today's Super Wal-Mart. All the shelves were loaded with what I considered overpriced junk. Nonetheless people were buying the items like they had more money than they knew what to do with. After satisfying my curiosity, I made the short jaunt to Rapid City, SD. The hour was rather late when I arrived so I located a tourist home, ate supper, and went to bed.

The next day, August 24th, I headed southwest from town, some thirty or so miles, to visit the Mt. Rushmore memorial. You don't go to where the faces are themselves, but to an observation facility east of Mt. Rushmore. I made the mistake of starting to walk up, toward the viewing facility. It was rather steep and kept getting steeper and steeper. People didn't want to stop on a steep grade to pick up a hitchhiker, and I couldn't blame them. So I walked and walked, and walked. It was a bit before noon by the time I reached the top and I was nearly worn out. I sat outside in the cool air, rested, and just looked at the awesome sight of the carved faces of George Washington, Thomas Jefferson, Teddy Roosevelt and Abe Lincoln, cut in the side of Mt. Rushmore. The observation site was a very nice, neat and clean facility. Quite a number of years later, in the movie *North by Northwest* with Cary Grant, Eva Marie Saint and James Mason, a rather long scene was filmed there in the observation facility. The whole facility was run by the U.S. Park Service. Besides the observation area, there was also a cafeteria where I decided to get a bite to eat. A brief glance at the menu indicated that the prices were in line for a tourist stop with no competition, but they were a bit stiff for a hitchhiker's pocketbook. I did eat, but rather selectively and frugally. After being there perhaps an hour, I got a ride down the mountain and back to Rapid City.

I continued northwest and made it to a little place called Sturgis, where I rented a second floor room in a decent tourist home for the evening. In later years, Sturgis would grow much larger, it would also become noted for a highly attended yearly Motorcycle Rodeo gathering, but in 1947 it was a just a sleepy little town in the Black Hills. I was tired and hungry after all that walking, up hill, to see the stone faced carvings. I had money, but just for the heck of it I decided to try my hand at panhandling, or working for my supper in more common terms.

In 1947 there were two restaurants on Main Street. I went to the first of two restaurants and asked for the owner. I told him I didn't have any money and I asked to wash dishes, or mop the floor, for my supper. He was a rather glum and sour faced looking fellow. He flat out told me no, that everything was already done and he didn't need any help. He didn't offer me a chance to do anything else and he didn't offer me any supper either. So I left and went to the second and only other restaurant I saw. I told that owner the same thing, and asked to work for my supper. The owner told me to go out to the counter and tell Rosie that he said I could have whatever I wanted off the menu. I told him, "Don't you think I'd better work first, AND THEN eat because for all you know I might take off after I eat?" He said that was ok, because he didn't have any work for me to do anyway since it was getting late and they were all caught up. I told him, "I thank you kindly, but if I can't work, I can't eat." Then I left.

So now I was in a fix. I was hungry, but yet I had turned down a free meal and I wasn't going to let him know I had lied to him about not having any money and I sure wasn't going back to the first place where they didn't offer me anything at all.

There was a Phillips 66 gas station on the north side of the street, a few hundred feet west and across from the tourist home where I was staying. I went in there and bought two giant Babe Ruth candy bars. They were 25¢ each back in those days. I went back to my room, took my belt off, put it around my stomach and tightened it. I *slowly* ate and savored the two large candy bars, drank five glasses of water to fill me up, got in bed and went to sleep with seemingly a full stomach.

August 25th dawned a bit gloomy. I pushed on down into the Black Hills National Forest on US 14. One of the most interesting places I visited was Deadwood, some ten miles southwest of Sturgis. It is located at the bottom of Deadwood Gulch, and it is so narrow that there is only one street in town. The rest of the town, such as it is, clings to the canyon walls. In the late 1800s the place was haven for all sorts of gunfighters, gamblers, and people with colorful and questionable backgrounds. Wild Bill Hickok, Calamity Jane,

Wyatt Earp, Doc Holliday and countless others were all frequent visitors to town. I visited the saloon where Wild Bill Hickok was gunned down from behind during a poker game on August 2, 1876. After leaving Deadwood, I went to the Homestead Gold Mine outside of Lead. The mine was theoretically still working, but mainly for the benefit of the tourists. It was making more from the visitors than from any gold they were finding.

I followed US 14 southwest, and it eventually swung 180-degrees to the northeast, then along the Spearfish Canyon scenic highway into Spearfish itself. The town got its name from the Sioux and Cheyenne Indians, who many years before speared fish in the creek that currently runs through the center of town. Spearfish Creek itself is unusual in that somehow it freezes from the bottom up.

My next stop was in the colorful little town of Sundance, where Harry Longabaugh, the original Sundance Kid, is said to have gotten his nickname. The story is that he spent an eighteen month residency as a guest in the county jail because of his fondness for a horse that didn't happen to belong to him. I never understood that because I thought back then they just hung a horse thief. Upon leaving town I headed northwest to the Devils Tower, twenty or so miles away, still in the Black Hills National Forest. It was formed by a volcanic intrusion and resembles a very large tree stump with heavily fluted sides. After many years of erosion, it still rises some 867 feet above its base. The top is 1.5 acres and is covered by grasses and sage brush. There was an interesting and informative visitor's center onsite at the base which I enjoyed visiting.

So far I had spent a good portion of the day sightseeing and not much traveling. Though seeing what I could see was what it was all about, I knew I still had a long way to go. Therefore, once again I hit the open road and headed for Sheridan, WY at the eastern edge of the rugged Big Horn Mountain range. The traffic was definitely lighter, but with my sign that read **SHERIDAN** I made it on into the city in about three rides and arrived at a decent hour. I found a tourist home for the evening, settled in, and enjoyed a better supper, at a nearby restaurant, than the two Baby Ruth candy bars and five glasses of water I had the night before in Sturgis.

My first goal for August 26th was to visit the site of Custer's last stand some sixty miles mainly north and a bit west of Sheridan. I left at my usual 7:00 a.m. time with a new sign reading **BILLINGS**. I got a ride fairly soon, crossing into Montana around 8:00, and around 9:00 a.m. I was at my destination; at the site of the Battle of the Little Bighorn. It was fascinating to stand there and imagine what it was like back in June of 1876, when Custer and 210 men of his 7th Calvary were set upon by several thousand Indians of the Lakota, Arapaho, and Northern Cheyenne Indian Nations. After enjoying my look back into history, I headed to Billings arriving around noon in just two rides.

Billings was a good sized city and a major point on the Northern Pacific Railroad. It had an interesting history, as did most of these places, though I didn't spend much time there. I made a new sign reading **YELLOWSTONE** and headed southwest on US 212 for the northeast entrance into the Yellowstone National Park, at Silver Gate just beyond Cooke City. Both the park entrance and Silver Gate were just inside Montana on the north side of the Montana-Wyoming border.

My first ride was to Laurel where dead ahead I could see the rugged Bear Tooth Mountain Range. From Laurel, my next ride took me to Red Lodge, MT where I arrived around

2:00 p.m. By now US 212 was just skirting the Bear Tooth Mountain Range that laid immediately to the west. Red Lodge really wasn't quite as large as my hometown of Rushville, IL, and there was nothing particularly special about it. However, I took a special liking to the place for some reason, and paused there for maybe a half hour before pushing on. It was a nice sunny day, but off to the southwest, the sky looked darker and less hospitable... and that was the direction I was headed.

With my next ride, I began to climb in altitude. Red Lodge was at 5,500 feet and within 25 miles I would nearly double that, to an altitude of 10,900 feet, at the Beartooth Pass. Then the road would gradually drop down in another forty plus miles to something still over 7,300 feet at Silver Gate.

Beartooth Mountain range near Sheridan WY.

Before I even got to Cooke City, which is four miles east of Silver Gate, the car I was riding in passed through a few showers and even a few flits of snow. Arriving in Silver Gate, my ride took me to the front door of a very large and impressive lodge with an exterior covering of varnished logs that gave it a rugged, warm and cozy, up scale look. The lodge was just outside the northeast gate entrance, at the northeast corner of Yellowstone National Park proper. The good news was that it was large, and obviously had many rooms. The bad news was, there were no vacancies, or so I was told. Unfortunately, it was getting rather late in the afternoon and was starting to drizzle. From the look of the sky, it was going to go from bad to worse and there was not a dry spot in sight. I thought about trying to get back to Cooke City, but decided I probably couldn't find anything there either. Besides there was little to no traffic headed east, and everywhere people were shutting down for the night.

On the south side of the road, perhaps a block and a half east of the park entrance, there was a Shell gas station. I hoped it was an all night station, manned by a very kind station attendant who would display some compassion for *a poor shelterless waif*, and let me curl up for the night in an out of the way corner.

Well, I guess one out of two wasn't too bad, considering my unenviable situation at that particular time. I found out that it was not an all night station, and, of course, he couldn't let me stay inside after he closed, however, I lucked out in the compassionate category. My kindhearted station attendant said he did have an old, *reasonably* clean blanket and that there was a junked Model A Ford parked alongside the station. If I wanted I could take the blanket and sleep in the car all night. Any old port in a storm was welcome.

Considering my alternatives, I took him up on his hospitable offer.

Now that night was an interesting experience. I went out to the old Ford, and in the fast fading light I peered inside. Actually, it wasn't as bad as I had expected, and it was even relatively clean. That is, there was a back seat in place, there weren't any chicken nests, raccoons, or clutter, and all the windows were up, except the front passenger window which had been broken out. It was the window facing the wall of the station, so it was fairly well sheltered from the direct wind. I looked around and found an empty cardboard oil case which I dismantled and used to cover the opening. Not having the breeze or elements blowing through made it a tad cozier inside. I crawled in the back seat. It wasn't comfortable, or very warm, but at least it was out of the wind and rain. I curled up using my bag as a pillow and covered myself with the attendant's *reasonably* clean blanket. The light drizzle made a soothing pitter patter on the roof of the old car. Surprisingly, I was soon fast asleep.

Sometime during the night I awoke. At first I had no idea as to where I was or what I was doing there. It was a rather strange feeling until I got my bearings. But then not too many people wake up to find themselves in the back of an old junked car either. I do recall it was pretty cold. It took a bit, but finally I dropped back to sleep until around 5:00 a.m. The drizzle had stopped during the night; however, on the morning of August 27th, when I emerged from my boudoir, I found a light skiff of snow covering the ground. I was chilled through and was stiff from a rather cramped position, but I managed to stumble out of the car. I ran around, beat my arms, and gradually came alive.

Unfortunately, the Shell gas station was not open yet, so I didn't have access to their free facilities. However, there was a little mountain stream maybe twenty feet or so from the old car. I went down there and washed up in the cold water. One of the cardinal rules of hitchhiking is to be as presentable as possible and that included being clean shaven. Even though there was no hot water available, I proceeded to shave anyway. The water was ice cold, the Gillette razor blade was dull, and all I had for shaving cream was Lifebuoy soap. Now that was an interesting experience. It wasn't fun, but I got the job done. I folded the attendant's blanket and, since the station was still locked, I left it in the back seat of the old car. Then I headed out in search of something to eat.

After breakfast I headed over to the northeast gate entrance into the park. I paid my entrance fee and entered the huge 3,472 square mile park that is truly one of America's gems. Yellowstone was wild and beautiful. The weather was on the cool side, but as the sun rose, it warmed, and you could tell it was going to be a nice day. By now the light snow from the night before had all but disappeared except in and around the fringes of the woods. I began to look around for a ride. It wasn't all that easy because most people were there with their families and, after kids and baggage, there was little extra room for a total stranger. Therefore I did quite a bit of walking. It wasn't all that bad because everywhere you looked there was some awesome vista, and when you were walking you saw it longer. There were lots of bears to be seen, lakes, canyons and forests. One didn't want to rush through it, and besides I had allowed an extra day here anyway. Therefore, I just took my sweet time to 'smell the roses' as the saying goes.

The inner park road system is basically in the shape of a

huge figure eight, with roads shooting off to the five official park entrance gates. Now and then I would get a short ride to the next attraction, usually with an older couple who didn't have kids with them. Then my ride and I would part ways because they would be ready to move on before I was, or vice-versa, though once I did get a second ride with the same couple. When I was ready to move on I'd look for another ride, or set out walking and just look at things along the way.

There was certainly plenty to observe. I suppose most people liked to watch "Old Faithful" go off at regular intervals. However, there were various other geysers all over the park, and more than a few involving a group of them in a relative small area. They looked as if they were choreographed as they spouted upward.

Old Faithful Yellowstone National Park.

I also enjoyed watching the area called the Paint Pots, which were large springs filled with hot clay ranging in color from white to pink to black, and there may have been a yellowish one also. There were also the deep gray bubbling ponds, called the Mud Pots, which I found interesting. They made large bubbles, and looked like they had just been waxed and polished. Besides the geological wonders to observe, there were also spectacular wildlife observations to be made. If one stared off into the woods, now and then you would see bears, deer and elk at the edge of the trees; and there were always eagles and other birds circling overhead.

Near nightfall I made my way to a campground where there were others camping out in tents. As I didn't have a tent, I gathered some soft as possible forest material, such as moss and leaves, to lie on and located some small branches to cover myself with as best I could. It wasn't cold, but cool, and would get cooler into the night. I hoped they would keep me a bit warmer though actually, they didn't help at all because every time I'd move the little branches would either fall off, or move to where I didn't want them. I recall wishing I was back in the old Model A Ford back at the Shell station. At least it wasn't drizzling, or snowing, but it was a darn sight colder since I was out under the stars, and didn't have that *reasonably* clean blanket to curl up under. I did sleep some off and on, but this was definitely not one of my better nights.

Yesterday, when I arrived, I had toured the north and west side of the top loop, and the west side of the bottom loop, camping out near the Old Faithful Visitor Center. This morning, the 28th, I picked up the pace a bit. I could see the Grand Tetons to my south, and they were aptly named because they were simply gorgeous. However, unfortunately, I didn't have time to include them in this trip. I swung along the bottom and up the east side of the lower loop, then cut basically due west at Inspiration and Artists Point, on the road between the north and south loops, and headed for the west gate of Yellowstone Park.

I left Yellowstone at the west gate around 2:00 p.m., and three rides later I found myself in Pocatello, ID. I promptly located a tourist home with a genuine bed and shower. This was a giant upgrade from the past two nights of sleeping in a junked car, and then on the floor of a forest. After a great meal at a good restaurant, I showered and hopped into bed. I was asleep before my head hit the pillow.

When I arose on the 29th the weather looked promising. I ate breakfast at a small, nearby Mom & Pop type restaurant. Since I needed a new sign, I opened my roll of sign blanks and using the restaurant's counter for my desk I proceeded to make a sign reading **BOISE**. That created considerable interest with the owners and several customers. They huddled around and curiously wanted to know what I was doing. So I took a little time and explained I was hitchhiking around the country, and that the signs let people know where I was headed.

As far as I was concerned, the land in southern Idaho left a good deal to be desired. It was rather arid and reminded me of going across portions of New Mexico. Just to the north across the Snake River is the National Monument called Craters of the Moon. This covers over 1,000 square miles and consists of lava deposits and numerous cinder cones, due to past volcanic activity in the region. Other than the unusual landscape to the north, nothing of any particular note occurred during my journey from Pocatello, northwest along US 30, toward Boise. The traffic was much less than I was accustomed to and they were shorter rides as well. In Boise I

159

visited the capitol and then located a place to stay the night near the west end of town.

On August 30th I continued northwest on US 30 with my new sign now reading **PENDLETON**. About an hour after leaving Boise I entered the State of Oregon, and arrived in Pendleton shortly after noon. I ate lunch and then I took a tour at one of the factories that made the famous Pendleton sweaters, shirts, and blankets. I didn't buy anything because I had no way to carry it. I also didn't have any extra money to buy something and have it shipped home. It was interesting watching their process. After my brief look around Pendleton, and going on a tour at one of the numerous weaving mills, I switched to a new sign reading **SPOKANE** and made my way to the north edge of town. It was around 2:00 p.m. and Spokane was a good 150 miles or so up the line. This time I got a ride, fairly soon, to Walla Walla. I lingered perhaps a half hour maximum, just looking around, because the name of the town had always intrigued me. Then it was on to Spokane. Unfortunately, after leaving Walla Walla the volume of traffic slowed down, and so did the rides. It soon was evident I wasn't going to make it all the way to Spokane before nightfall. That was ok because with hitchhiking you never knew exactly where you would end up for the night. Before dark I came to the little town of Colfax, WA that was situated in a rather hilly region. It was pretty around there, and about the size of my hometown of Rushville, IL. While I probably could have gotten to Spokane, the way things were going it would have been after dark and harder to find a place to stay. I found a decent tourist home, rather easily, and a place to eat supper. It was a nice evening so I sat on the front porch with the owners, visited with them, and viewed the night life in Colfax as it unfolded along the main street in town. This was about as exciting as watching an uphill turtle race, but admittedly it was rather tranquil and relaxing.

The morning of the 31st was a little overcast as I headed out around 7:00 a.m. The rides were a bit better than the night before, but it took me about two hours to cover the sixty or so miles to get to Spokane. This was the farthest northwest point on my trip and from here I would be headed home. There were a lot of things of interest to see in Spokane, and I probably should have taken an extra day to look around, however, by now I was ready to head east and home. It wasn't a very nice day as I steadily worked my way toward the east edge of town, thumbing as I went. A car stopped, and the driver told me he wasn't going very far, but my chances, where he would drop me off would be better than where I was. That was fine with me because I wanted to get to the east end of the city anyway, to where I could begin some serious eastbound hitchhiking.

Shortly we came upon a brand new multilane highway. Then we ran into some very unusual weather. At first it began to get extremely foggy, then it started to rain lightly, soon turned heavier and developed into a very wet snow. The elevation of Spokane is a little less than 2,000 feet, yet it seemed unseasonably cold. The mixture of rain and snow usually just produces slush, but in this case the temperature took a nose dive, it froze, and the surface of the pavement became an instant ice rink. Due to the fog, snow and ice, coupled with the fact that visibility was next to zero, nobody except a few, less than intelligent individuals were moving. They were slipping and sliding, spinning around, and no doubt wishing they hadn't ventured out on the highway. I saw a couple of minor accidents, but nothing serious.

The driver of the car I was in only had a few blocks left to go when this unexpected storm hit. Where he turned off to go home, there was a large truck stop on the north side of the highway and he let me out there. I went inside the truck stop, got a cup of coffee, and just watched the fog and the limited traffic struggling on the highway. I needed a new sign, so while I was waiting I made one showing **MISSOULA** as my destination.

The fog lifted around 10:00 a.m., but it was still slick. I saw a salt truck go by, but I knew it would take more than one, as well as some time, to loosen up the ice, so I waited. Before long I noticed three more salt trucks going by, so I decided to eat an early lunch and then head out afterwards. By now the fog had lifted completely, it had warmed up some and the ice had been reduced to slush. The traffic was beginning to return and it even looked like it might turn out to be a decent sunny day, though cool. I took my time, making a few stops along the way. The scenery was beautiful. It wasn't long before I entered the stove pipe of Idaho, as the long necked upper portion of the state is called. It was quite mountainous and the views were stunning. The area in and around Coeur d'Alene, ID particularly caught my fancy, and I took more time going through that area than planned. I was beginning to fall behind in my tentative schedule, but it was worth it.

I continued on with a series of short rides, enjoying the scenery along the way. However, it became evident that these short rides were becoming progressively fewer and far between. Also, it was apparent that it was getting colder again. At each little place I came to, I would look for a hotel or tourist home. Either they didn't have any, or I didn't find them, so I kept going. It was dark now. Outside Wallace, ID it started to rain lightly and the chill in the air became quite penetrating. Surprisingly a ride came along sooner than I thought. It was a bright red Monte Carlo with just a driver. He was a young man, probably in his early 20s, and was very expensively dressed. He had a tan, camel hair car coat, and was wearing a scarf, and told me he was going to St. Regis. That was all right with me because it was perhaps forty miles ahead, and at least I'd get warmed up by then. Hopefully I could find a place to stay there. He didn't say much so I kept rather quiet, also. Soon we began to gradually gain altitude. Next the drizzle turned to snow, but was not freezing on the roadway. Then the snow became very heavy and was obviously quite wet because it rapidly coated the trees. There were a lot of pine trees and it looked like a virtual winter wonderland, with the lights of our car reflecting off them as we twisted and snaked our way up the mountain, then down and back up again, all the while getting higher and higher.

I was getting warmed up very nicely now and, as I was rather tired, I slouched back in the corner of the front seat with my back between the seat and the passenger door. I was angled out and was just about to doze off when... I felt the driver's hand on my leg about half way up my thigh. My eyes popped open... he glanced over at me... I glared at him. I never moved, but in a *quiet, very unmistakably clear voice,* I advised him, "The last person that did that found himself on the deck with a mouth full of loose teeth." He quickly withdrew his hand and mumbled "Sorry," and that was that. However, from then on, I decided a more upright position and one to the far right of the seat was perhaps more appropriate. I was no longer even a *little bit sleepy* from there on into St. Regis. The incident was never mentioned again. When we arrived in St. Regis, he told me he knew of a little hotel (I didn't ask him how he knew), and said he would take me there. He was as good as his word. When we arrived, I thanked him. He went on his way and I checked into the hotel and went to bed.

September 1st saw me rolling out of bed earlier than usual because I was running somewhat behind my tentative schedule. I ate breakfast at the hotel and headed out. St. Regis was a rather quaint little town and I was surprised they even had a hotel. Most of the snow from the night before had now melted. I began holding up my **MISSOULA** sign about as soon as I stepped out of the hotel around 7:30 a.m. Normally that is a little early to catch a ride, but they are out there and if you are lucky you can find one. Well, luck was with me because within the fifth or sixth vehicle I scored on a ride all the way to Missoula.

As in Spokane, I probably should have taken more time to look around Missoula because it also is rich in history. Missoula is situated at the mouth of Hell Gate Canyon which was named Porte de L'Enfer (meaning Gate of Hell) by the French Canadians, because here the Blackfoot Indians would often ambush the Salish Indians as they traveled to their hunting grounds on the Great Plains to hunt buffalo. Lumber is a big industry here and the U.S. Forest Service has a large fire research station and training center for smoke jumpers. The University of Montana maintains an experimental research station of over 20,000 acres. According to the local information kiosks, there is also a wide range of recreational activities as well. But I settled for just trying to take note of what I was going past, as compared to any in depth exploration. Though I do not recall any such instance in Missoula, I would often stop here or there, on the spur of the moment, to take something in, such as a local attraction, exhibit, or whatever caught my fancy. I went to a restaurant, got a cup of coffee and used their counter to make a new sign reading **HELENA**. As back in Pocatello, ID, a number of the locals started looking over my shoulder to see what I was doing and asked several questions. I departed Missoula around 10:00 a.m. and reached the capitol at Helena shortly before noon. I ate lunch, looked around the capitol briefly, and then headed south toward Butte, arriving there shortly before 3:00 p.m.

The city first became famous for its gold and silver mines, but it was copper that caused the region to be called 'the richest hill on earth'. According to some records, the area ended up producing nearly 5.5 billion tons of copper. Of course, there were several large mining companies in the beginning, but eventually Marcus Daly's Anaconda Company gained ownership of all the mines and became the primary power in Montana politics, and in just about everything else for that matter.

Basically I have two etched-in-stone memories of Butte. First, I found it depressing. It was a dull day with the sun only sparingly breaking through. I made my way out to the southeast edge of town and then I got a short ride a bit further. We came to a Y in the road. My ride turned to the right, but I needed to go left. At that point there was nothing in sight but these ugly, dark reddish-black, and foreboding slag heaps. This was overburden caused by the open pit mining for copper. It was very similar to the coal slag heaps elsewhere at that time, such as in Illinois and wherever any kind of strip mining took place. Fortunately, in later years mining companies had to restore the land and replenish the nutrients though, of course, the soil was never as good as it was originally, but at least it got rid of those ugly, depressing, piles of earth and shale. There also seemed to be an unpleasant odor in the air that I took to be from traces of sulfur and various mineral deposits in the slag heaps. I especially recall the bilious, cumulous, clouds in the sky at the time. They showed an eerie reddish color. I presume it was from the late afternoon sun shinning on the slag heaps, and then reflecting off the clouds. Secondly, I had a habit of jotting in my diary when I got a ride, anything of note during or about it, and when I got out. At this location I waited two hours and thirty minutes to get my next ride. This was the longest I ever waited for a single ride. This beat, by one minute, my former longest wait of two hours and twenty-nine minutes in front of the Henry J. Kaiser shipyard, at the east edge of New Orleans just over two years before, in August of 1945.

When I finally got a ride it took me to Whitehall, MT. There I hit it big time. If the good Lord hadn't of held me up, back in Butte, I would have been on through Whitehall long before and would have missed out on a huge piece of luck. It was pushing 6:00 p.m., or a little after, when I arrived in Whitehall. At the west edge of town there was a large truck stop and restaurant, on the north side of the road, with a wide parking area on both sides. I was getting a bit hungry so I headed for the restaurant. Then I spotted two large, empty, car-carrying semi trailer rigs, on the south side facing east. Due to the fact that they were car carriers, and because of the direction they were facing, I suspected they were headed for Detroit. Actually, it turned out that they were to pick up new cars in Duluth. I went on in the restaurant and tried to spot who, I at least thought, were the drivers of the two rigs. I spotted two men who I thought were the probable drivers. I noticed they hadn't been served yet. This was good because if

I was lucky I could order light and be through eating by the time they left; because these fellows looked like the 'steak and eggs' type guys to me. But in case they weren't the drivers of those car carriers I sat where I could also keep an eye on the rigs, because I definitely wanted to catch their drivers before they pulled out.

I finished eating before the two fellows did. I paid my bill and then waited on the covered porch for them to come out. They finished, leisurely got up, paid their bill, and headed out. I was right behind them. I was correct; they were indeed the drivers of those two car carriers. As they were about to split up to go to their respective rigs, I called out and asked to speak to them. I sauntered over, greeted them, and told them I was headed for Illinois and if they didn't mind, I'd sure appreciate a ride. We chatted a bit as they sized me up. Pretty soon the younger one said ok, they'd take me in the general direction. Obviously they were keeping their options open as to how far, since they didn't know if they wanted my company for the long haul. As it turned out, I was with them for the next 913 miles, all the way to Motley, MN. This was the longest single ride I had ever gotten, and beat my previous record from Columbia, SC to Memphis, TN by about 200 miles. Though this was the first time I was with them, it would not be the last, as I would repeat the same identical trip one more time, however, that is another story.

The fellow I mainly talked to was the younger of the two, and seemed to be the one in charge. His name was Jim. His partner, who was a bit older, was named Walt. We struck it off real well. I found out later that they were friends who had each bought a car hauler rig with sleeper cabs and formed a partnership. They would drive all day and at night pull into a truck stop, fuel up, eat, shower if available, crawl in their sleepers and sleep. Then they'd go at it again the next morning.

I rode with Jim and we all headed for Bozeman, MT. We passed through Three Forks, and after around sixty miles and an hour and a half east of Whitehall, we were in Bozeman where we stopped for the night on September 1st. They had a routine and usually made it to the same places each night. They knew where all the good places to eat were, the best places to refuel, and the places with amenities for the truckers such as showers and bunks for those who needed them. We pulled to the back of a good sized truck stop. These places often had a hotel for truckers, nothing fancy, but they covered necessities, of beds, washrooms, showers and food, and were very reasonable. I had stayed in one or two before. The last one was the year before on the west side of Frankfort, KY.

They both grabbed a change of clothes, told me to leave my valuables locked up in the truck, and come along with them. We went up and into the shower facilities. Actually, I figured I had one more day's wear left in the clothes I had on before I'd have to change. But since I had a nice shower right there, and as I might not be so lucky the next night, I brought my spare change of clothes along, also. I washed the ones I was wearing, and changed into my clean spare set.

Now I was squeaky clean, wearing fresh clothes and my laundry had been done. On the way out I spotted some discarded newspapers, so I took them along. Back at the truck Jim rustled around in his gear and came up with a blanket. Walt found a spare one also. Jim suggested I crawl under the cab portion of his rig, so I'd be away from the hot motor, and sleep there for the night. He assured me I'd be safe enough, but if for some strange reason someone or something got nosey I should yell and he'd come down with his 'persuader'.

Then he pulled out a short ball bat from under his seat and sort of grinned as he tapped it on his open palm.

I crawled under Jim's truck. As I recall the surface of the parking lot was crushed limestone. It wasn't any featherbed, but thank heavens it wasn't concrete or blacktop which is harder and more unforgiving. At least with crushed limestone, you could squirm around a little and somewhat make a nest. I spread the newspapers out on the surface of the lot directly under the motor, and spread my damp clothes on them. The heat from the still warm motor helped them dry. There was enough vertical clearance under the cab of Jim's truck, that I didn't feel claustrophobic. It had been a good and an interesting day. It was totally dark and had been for some time now, but for some reason I wasn't very tired. Maybe it was because of this ride, these two great guys, and of all the miles I would be able to cover. I just laid there and watched the truck stop, the people moving around, and the trucks coming and going, until I finally drifted off.

The next day, Sept. 2nd, they were up early. Time is money to these fellows, and you can't cover miles lounging around. We all went in and ate breakfast, and then were on the road. Every three to four hours, or as convenient, I rotated riding between Jim and Walt's rig. This helped them each pass the time by having someone to visit with. It also helped me pass the time. I enjoyed every minute that I spent with each of them, and I was covering an awful lot of easy miles at the same time. Both of them were friendly and interesting fellows, who had had a wide variety of experiences, and I felt I learned a good deal from them.

I had ridden with a lot of truckers, but in the last couple of years more and more truckers had a sticker on the lower right corner of their windshield stating 'No Riders'. Mostly these were big company rigs, and it was a company policy. I could understand that because there are a lot of kooks out there with their thumb up in the air looking for a ride. Some were not above robbing drivers or worse. A few, especially those who owned their own rigs, would still give you a ride though. Really, I doubt if Jim or Walt would have given me a ride if they just came across me on the open road. I never thought to ask them if they would have or not and it is probably just as well. However, in my case I had the opportunity to meet them on the ground, by themselves, and ask them for a ride face to face. Usually that kind of an approach is better. We three hit it off real well early on. Also, I had now ridden some distance with each of them, and even slept under their truck, and we bonded more with each mile.

Besides rotating me, they also rotated the lead. Jim would be the lead rig for a while and then Walt would take the lead. About the only difference was, the lead driver was a look out, and a big brother, to the driver behind. But the vehicle in the rear had his job, too. The trailing rig would watch the back for police activity or any problems approaching from the rear.

They each had a two-way CB (citizen's band) radio in their cabs. The normal effective range, that they could hear clear enough to understand one another, varied a good deal depending where you were. Due to a multitude of reasons, their effective radio range varied from perhaps a half to one mile in hilly areas; three to five miles in moderately rolling stretches; and maybe ten to fifteen miles out in flat open prairie. In some very rare instances, for a short time they might get a bounce off the ionosphere, and the distance they could send and receive, usually only for a short time, would be unbelievable. They tried to keep close enough to be within range; hence they were always in communication with each other. This was very important. If the lead truck blew a tire it was no problem because the second vehicle would come upon him. But if the last truck blew a tire, or had some mechanical trouble and if they didn't have radio contact it might be some time before the leader would know something was wrong. That would cause them to lose some valuable time so they either kept each other in sight, or talked to each other fairly often.

If Jim and Walt wanted to discuss something more privately, they'd say something like... 'Let's talk to Gertie', which to them meant to switch to a prearranged channel that usually had a low volume of radio traffic. Of course, no CB channel is ever totally private, but there were some channels where there was less radio traffic than others, hence more private. After that, they'd go back to Channel 9 to keep up on the news of the road.

CBs were not very common back then, so a small town kid like me had never had the opportunity to talk on one. I got my first taste of it on this ride. Jim told me to pick up the mike and give 'Wonder Boy' (Walt) a call. I did and it was sort of fun. Jim asked if I had a handle, or a CB nickname. I told him, "No," so he told me I ought to get one. I thought a bit and came up with Bottle Stopper. Since I was nicknamed Corky, didn't drink, and was a good sized kid, I figured I'd make a heck of a bottle stopper. So from then on my official CB handle was Bottle Stopper, and is to this day, though I seldom have an occasion to use it.

They would always keep their radios on Channel 9 which was called the trucker's channel. This way they could monitor the CBs of other truckers and would know what was going on around them. They would learn of such things as

171

police in the area running speed checks, accidents, drunk or erratic drivers, suspicious activity, or anything else that would be helpful to know about.

During our more than 900 mile trek across the northwest, I remember one of the more interesting CB conversations that we overheard. I don't remember the exact details now, but some trucker was supposed to meet another trucker at a truck stop some 100 miles ahead of us. He had some trouble and was going to be about three hours late, and he wanted to get word of the delay to his friend who was waiting for him. He gave his location, which direction he was going, and his CB handle which was Bushman, then he asked if someone would relay the information eastbound for him.

That was sufficient to give everyone who heard it enough information to know if they could help him or not. If a trucker was going in the opposite direction, he couldn't, so he stayed out of it. Likewise, if someone else was near the end of his run he probably shouldn't get involved either, because the relay could take a while. Neither Jim nor Walt volunteered because the fellow was only a few miles behind us, and he needed a contact farther ahead to start the relay.

Pretty soon we heard a faint, but clear voice from a trucker somewhere well ahead of us calling Bushman. He said he was Sugar Daddy, and he'd give the relay a try, and asked for the message. Again, I don't recall the exact message, but it went something like this: *"This message is for John Agab, known as Little John, at the Carlyle Truck Stop at routes 12 and 59 in Miles City. Tell him Bushman had some trouble, but is now moving east of Billings with the hammer down. My ETA will be about three hours later than planned."* We heard Sugar Daddy say *"Roger that,"* which meant he understood. We faintly picked up the request for the relay broadcast ahead by Sugar Daddy, and that was all we heard, because the relay was now way out of our range. I sort of forgot about it and was surprised about a half hour later when the relay was returned to Bushman that the message had been delivered and acknowledged.

By in large, truckers are a bunch of people who stick pretty close together. If one trucker has a problem, I've seen as many as six big rigs pull over to help in any way they could, whether they knew him or not, and they usually didn't. The message relay I just mentioned is another example. Outwardly, most truckers are big and rough men with dirty fingernails, and a vocabulary that would even make a sailor blush. But inwardly, for the most part, they are just big pussycats.

It was a nice day, but by the time we got east of Billings, as far as I was concerned, the scenery left a good deal to be desired. While the western part of Montana is mountainous and quite beautiful, the eastern part is flat, dull, and not too interesting. By now most of the mountains were behind us. Ahead of us was nothing but wide flat prairie that seemed to stretch forever. It had its own beauty in a way, but it was pretty hard to find. All-in-all it was a rather monotonous drive. This was before there were interstates; there were just two lane roads for the most part. I continued to switch back and forth between Jim and Walt's rigs. The second night, we stopped at a truck stop in Glendive, MT.

Nothing of any particular note took place. We ate supper, the three of us talked for a while and then we hit the hay, figuratively speaking. Again I slept on the parking lot under Jim's cab at the truck stop where they always stayed. However, my bed was a bit harder than any hay, even with Jim and Walt's extra blanket.

The next day was September 3, 1947. This was the day that I would pass into North Dakota, and entering my 48th State. Nothing else of any consequence happened, but I felt that was quite an accomplishment for me. After that it was just miles and miles of nothing. That night we made it into Fargo, ND. They slept in their sleepers, and again I slept on the ground under Jim's rig.

Sept 4th we got an early start as usual. This would be a rather bittersweet type of day. The bad news was that I would be leaving Jim and Walt, but the good (and better) news was that with luck, I would be sleeping the next night in my own bed, at home, rather than on some parking lot. We pulled into Motley, MN before 10:00 a.m. This was where I'd be leaving them. As they came to the junction of 10 and 210, they pulled over, and we all got out.

I thanked them for the ride and for their friendship. Jim and Walt both gave me their home addresses and phone numbers back in Spokane. They both told me they had enjoyed my company and that if I, or any of my friends, *ever* wanted a ride to or from the Spokane area to just give them a call. If our schedules matched... we had a ride! I didn't know it then, but about a year later I would be taking them up on their offer! We said our goodbyes and shook hands all around. Then with a wave, I headed south and they continued east toward Duluth.

From Motley, MN, I skirted Minneapolis heading for Moline to my Uncle Paul and Aunt Myrt's. Rides were no problem as they came often, were fairly long, and were pretty fast. The first two got me south of Minneapolis, and the next took me east of Des Moines. It was early evening when I got to my Aunt and Uncle's. Aunt Myrt had just prepared a late supper, so I was just in time! I called Mom and Dad to let them know where I was. They decided to drive up that night to get me, rather than wait until the next morning.

As we were ready to leave my Aunt and Uncle's, to head for home, my mother was admiring a cloisonné vase that Bud, the younger of my two first cousins', had brought back from China after the war. Jokingly Mom said to me, "If you ever get to China, I'd like you to get me a cloisonné vase." And, just as jokingly, I told her, "Ok, I will!" [*For some reason, I never forgot what she said, and as it turned out, some seven years later... I did just that.*]

It was as great trip... but now I had a dilemma. I had been in all of the 48 States... Canada five times...Mexico once... NOW where would I head next?? Well, my decision wasn't too far into the future.

The Gandy Dancer

Trip #8
* * NORTH TO ALASKA * *

1948 - June 17th - August 19th

Age: 19 years, 10 months, 26 days

DENVER - PROVO - SALT FLATS - RENO - SAN FRANCISCO - COSTAL
HIGHWAY (US 101) - PORT ORFORD - SEATTLE - KETCHIKAN - JUNEAU -
SEWARD - ANCHORAGE - COLORADO SECTION - ANCHORAGE -.YAKUTAT
- SEATTLE - SPOKANE - WHITEHALL - MOTLEY - MOLINE and HOME.

It was now the spring of 1948. My thirst for the open road had not waned in the least. If anything it had waxed because I knew I was fast approaching a phase of my life that required a bit more responsibility, and I couldn't just take off on a whim, and run around the country. I was 19 years old and had been a student at Western Illinois State College in Macomb, IL since graduating from high school in the spring of 1946. Actually, during my first year it was called Western Illinois State Teacher's College, but then the curriculum was broadened, and in 1947 they dropped the name Teachers. Ten years later, in 1957, it would be elevated to a university status.

During the preceding summer, in 1947, I couldn't even buy a job, as there just wasn't any work around. Therefore, I continued going to school during the summer sessions offered at Western, the campus was only about thirty miles north of my home. In the fall of 1948, I would be transferring to the University of Illinois at Urbana Champaign to continue

177

working toward a Civil Engineering degree. So in the interim period, I naturally had to make some serious money. Maybe... just maybe, I could come up with a way to combine both business *and* pleasure.

My youth was fast passing and I wanted to see some more new country before being saddled with responsibilities that come with age. Tales of the Royal Canadian Mounted Police and the stirring poems of Robert Service relating tales of the far north, one of the world's last frontiers, were always favorites of mine. So I figured I'd make my way north to Alaska. With a little luck I might be able to land a job for the summer. I would give myself three weeks and, if I hadn't found some sustaining work by then, I would have to prematurely head for home as a casualty of adventure. I sure didn't want to be stranded, so I would have to make certain that I hoarded enough funds to be able to get back. If things worked out, and I found work, then I would make some money, see new territory, and amass many more experiences. Maybe even enough to someday write a book of my travels.

I wrote to inquire about ship passage out of Seattle. I didn't want to try to hitchhike up the Alcan Highway. Back in 1948 the road was still quite primitive, traffic would be sparse, and what traffic there was would have little extra room for a hitchhiker. School would be out around the first of June, so I planned on leaving then. About the same time I was finalizing my plans, I got a letter from my friend Doug Waugh who I had met up in Canada two years before, and who was still living in New Haven, CT at the time. He said he had been thinking about going to Alaska, and would I want to go along? I contacted him right away. I told him my bags were packed and for him to come on out to Rushville ASAP. Unfortunately, Doug couldn't make it for a couple of weeks, so that delayed our start. Mom and Dad decided that since they had not been out west for a long time, they would take a trip, giving us a ride as far west as they went.

My packed gear consisted of a khaki army surplus down sleeping bag with a pair of work shoes, two pair of socks, a spare shirt and a pair of dungarees, all rolled up in the bottom. Also, I had a canvass zippered bag about fourteen inches wide, 24 inches long and twelve inches high in which I had clean socks, underwear, another shirt, my toiletries kit, diary, etc., and, of course, my sign making kit. I always wore a money belt and carried a switchblade knife, which was legal at that time.

Doug got to Rushville on June 16, 1948 and we all started out on Thursday, the 17th. We took US 24 to Quincy where we picked up US 36 west through St. Joseph, MO to Oberlin, KS in the northwestern part of the state. We stayed overnight in a motel and got an early start the morning of the 18th, continuing on west to Denver.

Doug Waugh and Corky in Rushville, ready to leave for Alaska.

There Doug wanted to go north, then west to Seattle. I had been over that route just the year before and preferred to go west, then north, along the Pacific Coast to Seattle. So we decided to split up and meet in Seattle at the YMCA at 7:00 a.m. on June 26th, the day before we were to catch the ship to Seward. This was an excellent solution since, with respect to each other, both of us preferred to travel alone because it was so much easier to get rides when you didn't have someone with you.

As Doug left the car, there was a big hail storm that made the ground almost white with nickel sized hail. The folks and I continued on west, going by the way of the Berthod Pass which had snow on the ground. We spent a little time there. The car seemed sluggish, but it was due to the altitude since the carburetor was set leaner for lower altitudes. We made it to Hot Sulfur Springs for the night where we got another motel.

We were on US 40 now, took our time, and enjoyed the scenery as we continued west. The evening of June 19th we stayed at a motel in Provo, UT. This was the last night I was with my parents before we parted. Dad and I walked up to the motel office to get a paper, as he always wanted to catch up on the news.

Corky with Mom & Dad
at Berthoud Pass in Colorado.

The headlines read, "DRAFT REENACTED." This was because of increasing world tension. Dad looked up at me and said, "Maybe you weren't so dumb after all," and that was all he said. Now that was not said with any malice, and I knew exactly what he meant. The year before I'd joined the U.S. Naval Reserve, much against his wishes. But that is another story within itself and has nothing to do with this tale. Suffice it to say here, that I always wanted to go to sea, and joining the Naval Reserve was one way to do it. If a war came along, and Korea did a couple of years later, I would already be in the Navy, and not subject to being called by the Army. At least I'd have three squares a day and a clean place to sleep at night, and a chance to see a heck of a lot more than if I was in the Army.

The next morning, Sunday, June 20, 1948, we said goodbye. The folks headed south and I set my course west toward the pacific. I went past Black Rock and Saltaire, where back in 1945 I'd gone swimming in the Salt Lake, and then I headed across the salt flats, through Emigrant Pass and eventually into Reno, NV, where I got a room. I went to the State Line Cafe to eat supper that night. That was an unusual place. There was a broad yellow line painted on the floor. On one side was Nevada and the other side was California. On the Nevada side of the line there were slot machines, but not on the California side. After I paid for my supper, I had a quarter left over. For the heck of it, I put it in a slot machine, pulled the handle, and won around $2.50. I scooped up the coins and walked away a winner, little as it was. I didn't even take the machine off pay. Why should I? They were out to make money on me, but I beat them. The odds were the machine wasn't going to pay me off again on the next pull of the handle, so why should I spend a quarter to help them hide that fact from the next sucker.

On June 21st I left Reno and passed into California. It took me two hours and twenty-seven minutes to get a ride. That then became my third longest wait after my two hour and twenty-nine minutes wait in New Orleans in 1945, and what eventually ended up being my longest wait ever of two hours and thirty minutes to get a ride a little east of Butte, MT, the year before, in 1947. An unusual thing happened when I finally did get my ride out of Reno. The fellow who picked me up had a cream colored 1947 Chevrolet and said he recognized me as the hitchhiker he had seen, and passed up, back in Salt Lake City the day before.

The drive was beautiful. California was a virtual oasis after the bleak and austere Utah and Nevada deserts. I visited the California State Capitol at Sacramento and then pushed on to Oakland where I got a room at the YMCA. Since it was only around 5:00 p.m., I decided to go across the bay and over to San Francisco that evening to look around. It would be somewhat less crowded, and therefore save me some time the next day. As I was waiting for the Oakland Bay train to San Francisco, a fellow drove up and asked if I wanted a ride. I said, "Sure," and got in. I thought that a bit odd, but he seemed stone cold sober and in a real good mood. He told me he was going to pick up his girlfriend that had just gotten in town, and was going to show her around. I thought to myself, 'Then why do you want me tagging along?', but what the heck, I was getting a ride so I'd play it by ear. Well, he picked up his girlfriend, and man was she ever a good looking doll. I popped into the back seat so she could be in front. The fellow introduced us. For some reason she didn't seem to mind that I was along either, and that I was a total stranger besides. They were both very friendly and we drove all over.

We went up Telegraph Hill from where you can see all of San Francisco; visited the Coit Tower overlooking the Golden Gate Bridge; down to the bay across from Alcatraz for an excellent view of the prison; and along Fisherman's Wharf, etc.

San Francisco street car

After a while I got a little embarrassed at being a third wheel, even though they still didn't seem to mind at all. I excused myself, thanked them for a nice evening, wished them well, and asked to be let off where I could get a bus back to Oakland where I was staying.

The next day, Tuesday, June 22nd, was to be a day I would never forget, as it developed into a bit of excitement that I could have done without. I was thumbing for a ride west across the Oakland Bay Bridge. Shortly after 7:30 a.m. a friendly Australian picked me up. We drove past Treasure Island and, as we left the bridge and entered San Francisco proper, we heard a siren from a police car, with lights flashing, directly behind us. The Aussie pulled over to the curb. Immediately there was an officer on the Aussie's side, and he wasn't your Officer Friendly type either. He had a very business like look about him and his hand was on his gun, which was half, if not all the way, out of his holster. I glanced over my left shoulder and saw his squad car which was stopped behind us. It looked like a Christmas tree with all its lights going. The officer's partner was half out of their squad car. He wasn't smiling either. I took particular note of the sawed off shotgun that he was holding, and the fact that it was aimed directly at us.

They definitely had our total and undivided attention. The officer didn't ask, but, in a clear loud voice, ORDERED us out of the car. Naturally we got out right away. The officer with the shotgun approached, keeping us covered. He stopped about ten feet from me. They told us to turn around... put our hands on the top of the car and to spread eagle. They promptly patted us down. The Aussie kept asking, "What's wrong?... what's wrong?," but they were not talking. I didn't say anything, but wondered who it was that I had gotten a ride with and what he might be wanted for. Then they asked each of us for our license, name, where we were from, what we were doing, where we were going, etc. When it was my turn to answer, I told them I was just a hitchhiker that had gotten aboard in Oakland. They continued to ask the Aussie all sorts of questions. Finally they got around to why they stopped us. They asked the Aussie where he had gotten the license plates. I couldn't believe it when he quite frankly told them... "I made them." I thought to myself, he will be lucky if he doesn't end up where he will be making a lot of them. The officers were also obviously rather taken back by his ready admission. They asked him, "Don't you know that is illegal?" The Aussie told them he thought it was illegal to drive a car without one and that he had just bought the car from such and such a dealer, so he made a plate so he could drive it. The officers were even more astonished at his explanation. They asked him if he ordered plates when he bought the car, and if they had given him a receipt. He said, "Oh yes, but it is not the same as a plate, it's only paper." Then he opened his billfold, and sure enough he had the receipt and it was totally legal. The officers gave a sort of shallow, bewildered laugh and said, "Fellow, you put that piece of paper in the back window and take your homemade plates off." One of the officers came up with some scotch tape, from their squad car, and a screw driver. The officers had the Aussie scotch tape the receipt to the inside of the back glass, then remove the plates, and hand them over to them.

Then they told us that they had spotted the bogus plate, and that it was actually quite good, which made them even more suspicious. They said they didn't know if we had just come *from* or if we were on our way *to* a bank robbery. By now they were convinced the Aussie was an over zealous, law abiding, foreign citizen, who wasn't familiar with the way we did things here, and that I was just a hitchhiker who now had a new experience to log.

When I left San Francisco, I caught a ride, headed north, across the Golden Gate Bridge. I kept on US 101 through Santa Rosa. When I reached Eureka, I was at the coast itself. I really enjoyed the ride up along that twisting, rugged, coastline road skirting the Pacific Ocean, and I enjoyed watching the surf and breakers coming in. The traffic was light, and I was perfectly willing to slow my pace some by taking more time between rides to enjoy the many beautiful views as I progressed northward.

After another fifty miles north I was in the middle of

the Redwood National Forest. By now it was getting late in the afternoon, so I stopped at a Ranger Station and asked if I could pitch my sleeping bag out in the woods. They told me OK, but warned me... "No Fires." So I spent that night in a different and interesting setting among some of the world's tallest trees. Being in a down sleeping bag was much more comfortable than the night I slept on the ground without one, in a forest back in Yellowstone, the year before. It wasn't long before the soothing night sounds of the forest, and the distant hoot of an owl lulled me to sleep.

The next morning, June 23rd, I exited my sleeping bag, rolled it up, and then went to the visitor's shelter at the ranger station to wash up. For some reason I left my gear outside, only taking my toilet kit in with me. There were a lot of people in the visitor's shelter. Pretty soon a ranger came in the washroom and asked in a loud voice, "Who does the khaki bag with the Western College sticker belonged to." I told him it was mine. Then he asked me to step into the office when I was done washing up. I wondered what I might have done, but finished my morning ritual of shaving, etc. When I finished I went to his office. He introduced himself as Ranger so and so and asked if I wanted a job with the Park Service, guarding and answering visitor's questions about the, then known, World's Tallest Tree which was on that site. I told him no, that I was headed for Alaska, but I thanked him for his offer and asked why he sought me out when he didn't even know me. He said they needed a responsible person, and when he saw the college sticker he figured I couldn't be too bad a risk, so he asked.

I stayed on US 101, the road hugging the ocean, all the way up the coast. To me, this stretch of US 101, in the northern part of California and Oregon, is the prettiest of all the roads in the United States. The general area of Maine, Vermont and New Hampshire runs a close second.

That night, Wednesday the 23rd of June, I had a rather unique experience. A little before dusk I got out of a ride that had taken me to Port Orford, OR, at a point across the street from a U.S. Naval Reserve base. I went over and told them I belonged to a Naval Reserve unit back in Illinois, and asked if they minded if I pitched my bedroll and slept on the base that night. The Officer of the Deck said it was ok, but if I wanted to do something a little different he'd have the messenger take me in the jeep out to The Point. "There" he said, "You will be the westerly most person in the continental limits of the United States tonight."

I told him, "Thanks, I would appreciate that." So the messenger drove me in their jeep a short distance out to the edge of the cliff. If I had rolled over twice that night, instead of being the most westerly person in the continental U.S., I might have been the most easterly person in the Pacific Ocean!

The most western point in the continental United States.

June 24th would be a memorable day, also. I hadn't much more than gotten back on the road before a fellow stopped and picked me up in a brand new station wagon made by Jeep. I had never seen one before. His name was Walt Mendel. He was going *somewhere*, but had no plans, just wherever the Jeep took him. Walt was a bachelor who had stayed home and had always taken care of his ailing mother. She had recently passed away, so he bought the Jeep and decided to take a trip. He asked where I was headed. I said "Seattle," and he thought that would be a nice place for him to go to, also. I could see *right then* that Walt and I were going to get along great! He mentioned he didn't particularly care to drive, so I volunteered, and Walt was glad to let me take over. We were into the logging country. We stopped at some logging mills and saw how they handled the logs. Also, they had been having a good deal of rain in the area, so we drove around Astoria, OR looking at the flooded areas.

The water was so high that we had to wait while they raised the bridge over the Columbia River to literally allow an outboard motorboat to pass under. We had plenty of time. My ship wasn't to leave until the morning of June 26th, and this was only the 24th, so we could just take our sweet time and do as much sight seeing as we wished.

Walt Mendal and his new Jeep station wagon.

When we crossed the Columbia River, we were in Washington State. We drove on north, still on US 101, past the large army base at Ft. Lewis, WA, and on into Seattle proper. Then we drove to the YMCA and booked a room for that night and for the 25th as well, since Doug and I were to leave for Alaska the morning of the 26th. I checked at the desk and found that Doug had already arrived, but was not in his room. It had been a rather full day, so we found something to eat and went to bed.

On the morning of the 25th we made another attempt to contact Doug, but he was already gone. So after a leisurely breakfast, Walt and I spent the day driving around just sightseeing all over the Seattle area. In the evening we had a great seafood supper down on Seattle's Fisherman's Wharf. We ate shrimp, clams, scallops, white fish, etc. till we nearly burst. After eating we decided to check out the range of Walt's car radio. Seattle is pretty hilly, so we drove to a high point to get better radio reception. As we were going through the radio's range and trying to figure out where each broadcast was coming from, we stumbled across the World's Heavyweight Boxing Championship prize fight between Joe Lewis and Jersey Joe Walcott which was being held in Yankee Stadium in New York. I always liked Joe Lewis, and even though the reception wasn't too clear we listened to the entire fight. Joe Lewis won with a knockout in the 12th round using a flurry of combination punches. Joe Lewis later retired from the ring on March 1, 1949.

Saturday, June 26, 1948, Walt and I went to the dining room of the Y and, as planned, there was Doug. I introduced them to each other and we ate breakfast. Walt drove us down to the docks where we boarded the SS Aleutian at 9:15 a.m.

In good time we cast off and waved goodbye to Walt standing on the pier. The ship headed north past Vancouver and into the Inland Passage. We were in a sea passage nestled between the Canadian coast and a line of offshore islands. The trip up the Inland Passage was quite nice.

Ready to board the SS Aleutian.

We were very close to land on both sides, most of the way up, and we passed many places where there were people living right on the shore line. Once or twice we would be close enough to yell over and talk to the people on shore. The islands sheltered the waterway from any violent pacific storms, but since it is fairly shallow there is a good deal of a wallowing motion that one doesn't experience in the open sea. Some people actually find the wallowing, which is a slow pitch and roll, to be more disagreeable than the determined and perhaps somewhat jerkier motion one gets in a storm on the open sea, when you are often being slapped by large waves.

Doug and I had each booked Steerage Class for our one-way passage to Seward, AK at a cost of $35. That was from Seattle, WA all the way to Seward, AK. Now, that was reasonable even for those times, but then one has to understand what *Steerage Passage* is. It is one passage higher than letting you swim in the ship's wake. Basically it's the same as if we were cargo. The only difference between us and a box of Caterpillar tractor parts is that we got to eat, and the parts didn't. Our quarters were, of course, below deck with the cargo. My bunk was so far forward on the starboard (right) side that once, just for the heck of it, I literally swung out with my feet still in my bunk, and holding on to the bunk above me I stretched as much as I could, and I was actually able to touch the port (left) side of the hull also.

Topside, in the open air, we were restricted to the first deck, or work deck as they called it. That is where the anchor capstans and winches and other various equipment was. The regular passengers were not allowed down there because of the machinery, and so that they didn't have to mingle with the *riff-raff* as many of the steerage passengers were considered to be.

Updating my diary on the work deck.

The steamship company had good reasons for their rules. Out of the maybe 50 steerage passengers, probably ten percent were decent Alaskans who were headed home as cheaply as they could; fifteen percent were some college kids out for a little adventure, like Doug and myself; and the remaining seventy-five percent of them you wouldn't want to claim. They included a combination of pickpockets, thugs and some on the run from the law, as we would soon find out when we arrived in Juneau. On the ship Doug and I got fairly well acquainted with two fellows in particular, with whom we seemed to have more in common. One was Bob Haven from upstate New York. The other was a fellow, who looked like a young Abraham Lincoln, by the name of Stewart Meffenin from somewhere in New Hampshire. We would later team up with them. We also became more or less friends with a half dozen other fellows. Little Doug, as we called him to differentiate him from Doug Waugh, was from Alaska and

Hoag, Mosser, Sanders, Radford and Corky in the ship's bow.

was going home. The others, Hoag, Mosser, Sanders, and Radford, plus a few more, were just out for some adventure. We never saw them again after arriving at Seward. But most of the remaining steerage passengers were pretty much undesirables. They stayed to themselves and we stayed to ourselves... thusly we coexisted, and no one seemed to bother the other.

In the hole where our bunks were, in the steerage area, was a table perhaps fifty feet long stretching down the middle of the ship. We would use it to play cards on, write letters, etc. Also, this was where we ate. The ship's mess staff would bring down food in large covered pots. As I recall the food was good and there was plenty of it, at least I do not remember anyone complaining.

Our first stop was Ketchikan, AK. We were locked below deck until all the regular passengers had an opportunity to disembark, and then we were allowed to go ashore. They told us what time the ship would leave, with or without us, so if we were to continue on we had better be back.

Ketchikan, AK

193

Ketchikan was a bit of a different world. There were several totem poles to be seen, for decoration I am sure, but it was also indigenous to the culture of the area.

It was a rather bleak day, and there was not really much to see. We just looked around at the trading stores, went to what they called The Federal Building, and then went back to the ship.

It wasn't long before we pulled out and headed north again, this time for Juneau. As we pulled into Juneau we saw the cruiser Atlanta which was in port. I was up on deck on the starboard side near the bow. Our ship made its approach at about a 20-degree angle to the wharf.

Approaching Juneau

Then she was to put her port engine slightly in reverse, cut her starboard engine so her bow would swing counterclockwise a bit until the ship was parallel to the pier, then she would cut her port engine. That way she could moor (tie up to the dock) on the starboard side. We were getting pretty close and I thought they had better back the port engine down pretty quick. All of a sudden, I heard a lot of shouting going on up on the bridge. It seems they couldn't get the port engine to reverse, so we plowed right into the pier at about the same 20-degree angle. People who were there to watch the ship dock began to run as the piling and planks began to snap like match sticks. Water lines, suspended beneath the pier, broke and shot water everywhere, which added to the confusion. We drove about eight feet into the pier before the ship finally stopped.

Among the people waiting for the ship to dock were three U.S. Marshals, and they were on a mission. The ship's officers ordered all steerage hands below and they locked us in. Eventually the hatch opened, and the three Marshals and a few of the ship's officers came in. Then they relocked the hatch behind them. It seemed that three of our steerage brothers had committed an armed robbery back in Ketchikan. The Marshals had a good description of the three and were quite sure they were on board. They had us all line up and then they went down the line. Pretty soon they grabbed three guys. Though it wasn't unusual, all of them had a large Bowie knife. They made a search and found the items they had stolen, and then they led them off handcuffed. After that, the rest of us were let out to go ashore. Both of these events were certainly colorful additions to our already memorable sea passage.

The weather in Juneau was about the same as it was in Ketchikan. It was overcast, bleak, and cool. We saw some fish processing plants along the water, visited the capitol, looked about town and returned to the ship.

From Juneau, the SS Aleutian backtracked a little down a neighboring channel, then headed west at first, then northwest as we cleared the outer islands, and finally we were headed out across the north Pacific for Seward. Here I saw my first large blue whales about a quarter mile off to port.

Corky & Doug in the bow of the SS Aleutian.

There were two of them that kept station with the ship, for maybe an hour or so. They would rise to the surface and spout a jet of water, maybe ten feet high, out of their blowhole that was located in the middle top of their head and then they would dip below the surface. Pretty soon they'd be back up and repeat the routine all over again. It was if they were acting as an escort.

That night I had an interesting experience. We, the steerage passengers, had a head (that is a toilet), but no shower facilities. That was unfortunate, because I personally felt I needed a shower, and besides I had some laundry I needed to do. HOWEVER, by nosing around a little, I found out where one of the crew's showers was, though it was definitely off limits to steerage passengers. I knew the mid-watch would come on duty at 2345 (11:45 p.m.), get their orders... then relieve the watch at 2400 (midnight). Those going off watch would probably be out of the showers by 0020, or 0030 after midnight, by the latest. So I decided to wait until around 0040, which is twenty minutes till 1:00 a.m., before I 'got lost'... and ended up in their shower.

I hadn't done any laundry since Seattle, so I got all my dirty clothes together. Leaving my shoes, billfold, money belt and wrist watch on the shower room counter, I walked into the shower with all my clothes on and my dirty laundry in my hands. I first washed all the loose items I had brought with me, and then I soaped the clothes I was wearing, took them off, rinsed, and rung them out. There were steam pipes that ran through the compartment where the showers were, so I laid all my damp clothes on them while I took a nice shower myself, getting out once to turn my clothes. They were drying nicely on the pipes. After I was all spic and span, I got out, dressed in some clean clothes I had brought along, gathered up all the clothes I had laundered, and returned to my bunk in the forward hole. Fortunately, I had gotten my laundry done, and bathed, without getting caught. Most everything was dry by now except the heavier dungarees, and maybe a shirt or two. I rolled my mattress back, folded my clothes neatly, placed them under the mattress, put the mattress back, and hit the sack. In the morning my clothes were both dry and pressed.

It was around 1430 (2:30 p.m.) when we disembarked at Seward on June 29, 1948. Seward was named after William H. Seward who was the Secretary of State in

President Andrew Johnson's Administration. It was he who negotiated the purchase of Alaska from Russia for $7.2 million in 1867. At the time people referred to the purchase as Seward's Folly, but certainly history has proven them wrong. Incidentally it was in 1896, just twenty-nine years later, that the big Alaska Gold Rush took place.

On the beach there were pill boxes that had been built to help protect Seward from the Japanese if they had ever made an attempt to land during World War II. A pill box was a concrete bunker, or fortification, from which those inside could fire on anyone invading. However, though the Japanese never did attempt to land there, the pill boxes were still in place. Again it was a cool, bleak and overcast day. There wasn't much to Seward that we saw, and we made our way to the train station.

In 1948 the Alaskan Railroad was owned by the U.S. Government and run by the Department of the Interior. Alaska did not enter the Union as our 49th State until Jan. 3, 1959, so in 1948 it was merely a Territory of the United States. The railroad begins at Seward at Mile Post 0.0, and runs north to Fairbanks. Anchorage was mile 114.3, and for now that was our immediate destination. The railroad ended in Fairbanks at mile post 470.3. I never got that far north back in 1948. For me, Fairbanks would have to wait another 50 years.

The train was waiting the ship's arrival, so it wasn't long before we were on our way north to Anchorage. The train was made up of a mix of freight and a few passenger cars; however, there was no caboose at the end. Doug and I were in the last car which was one of the regular passenger cars. It was around 3:00 p.m. when we pulled out, and Doug and I soon became acquainted with the conductor who was named Dick. He growled, and appeared to be a real grouch with the people, but he sort of took a liking to Doug and me for some reason. He told us a good deal about the country and pointed out wild game, at the edge of the wilderness that otherwise our novice eyes would never have seen.

As we approached mile post 23.3, the train's whistle let out a long rapid series of "Toot.. toot.. toot.. toot.. toot". I asked Dick what that was all about. He grinned, and said that we were approaching "Alaska Nellie's". With that, he got up and went out onto the platform at the rear of our car, apparently to wave to this Alaska Nellie as we passed.

The old time steam engine we took to Anchorage.

In another minute or so we heard the engineer whistle a fast "Toot... tooty-toot-toot... toot-toot!"

In looking out the rail car window, I soon saw a tall, lanky, erect woman with stone gray hair pulled tightly back into a large bun. She was wearing a gray flannel dress with a white half apron down to her knees, standing near a fairly good sized log cabin. She was smiling and waving for all she was worth. On impulse I snatched my camera and squeezed off a couple of shots... one of her, and one of the cabin.

Milepost 23.3 and the famous Alaska Nellie at Lawing, AK.

When Dick came back in I asked him, "Who is this Alaska Nellie?" As I recall, Dick said, "Oh, she is one of us." He went on to tell us she was a pioneer woman who had been a railroad employee when the railroad was built. At any rate, she obviously was a very unusual type of woman and, according to Dick, all the railroad people apparently had a lot of respect for her. She was retired by then, but yet when the trains would go by we were told the engineer would announce the trains impending arrival by rapidly tooting, then give her a whistle salute as the train passed.

NOTE: In April 1995 I wrote to the Governor of Alaska, inquiring about any available information regarding Alaska Nellie. The Alaska State Library responded on April 24th informing me that:

Alaska Nellie was born July 25, 1872 near Weston, MO. In 1915 she came to the Alaska territory after hearing about the beginning of the construction of the Alaskan Railroad. At first she cooked for a family at a mine. Later she got a contract to feed and house railroad workers for 50¢ a meal and a $1 per night. Once she operated two such bunkhouses simultaneously. Her last railroad bunkhouse contract was at Dead Horse Hill, later renamed Curry.

Alaska Nellie also had many personal achievements. She was quite a big game hunter, with all types of trophies, and also an author. She was held in high regard by those who knew her, and especially by the entire railroad community. Whether they knew her personally, or not, all considered her as... 'one of theirs'. Newspaper articles referred to her as a female Davy Crockett. She died on May 10, 1956 at age 83, and is buried in Seward.

At one point, around mile 50.7, we were going downgrade around a long curve to the right. Dick told us to go out on the rear platform and look up. We saw that we were passing under ourselves so to speak, though, of course, the train wasn't that long. The railroad alignment was designed in this fashion to lose a good deal of elevation in a fairly short distance. To do so, they built a trestle bridge with a long downgrade curving to the right. It kept curving right and eventually actually passed under itself. They called this place The Loop. [*The Loop was replaced with a tunnel and a new alignment on November 6, 1951 to save costly bridge repairs.*]

At mile post 64 we passed through Portage where a spur track ran southeast to Whittier. [During the 1964 earthquake the town of Portage was totally destroyed.]

It was about a three hour ride from Seward to Anchorage. So by the time we got to Anchorage it was around 6:00 p.m. on Tuesday, the 29th of June.

I never will forget pulling into Anchorage. What a bummer! It was bleak, cold and raining; I hadn't seen the sun since we had gotten to Alaska; the train station was at least a good half mile from

Arrival in Anchorage.

what looked like the town; there were no paved roads, just mud; outside of Doug, I didn't know a soul; I didn't have a job; I had very little money; night was coming on and I didn't know where I'd sleep that night; I was tired and hungry; I was several thousand miles away from home; and I had a splitting headache that you wouldn't believe. That was my first impression of Anchorage, AK.

But then things took a few turns for the better. I always figured the reason they did was that they couldn't have gotten much worse. As we got off the train Dick, the conductor, told us he had a car and would drive us up into town so we wouldn't have to trudge through the mud. We sort of felt bad to see all the other passengers slipping and sliding, and lugging their suitcases and packages through all that muck. I was a bit surprised they didn't have a bus, or even a wagon, to haul the people and their baggage, but if they did, it wasn't running that day. On the way up the hill to town, all of a sudden Doug recalled that when he had stopped in Yellowstone on his way to Seattle he, quite by chance, had become acquainted with a Reverend F.H. Griffin from Anchorage who was a Baptist preacher. He checked his diary and found his address. Dick drove us to where the preacher lived at 426 6th Ave. We thanked him and he bid us goodbye.

R-504 Anchorage from the Air

Aerial view of Anchorage. Rev. Griffin's house in circle.

The preacher and his family had been on their way home to Anchorage at the time he and Doug met. While the good preacher probably never expected the situation would ever arise, Rev. Griffin had told Doug if he needed any help when he got to Anchorage to look him up. Well, that preacher was about to have company. Fortunately, for us the preacher had gotten home that very day. He was *more* than a bit surprised to see Doug again so soon, and in the company of a stranger at that. Doug asked the minister if he knew of some place we could stay that was reasonable because we didn't have much money. Reverend Griffin was as good as his word. He paused and then offered us his garage... and at no charge. Since it wasn't in use during the week, he said we could bunk there as long as we picked up after ourselves, swept up, and had our gear out of the way for Sunday Services. Though it was just a garage, he had remodeled it, put in a floor, and turned it into a place for Sunday worship and Sunday school. It was clean and dry. It didn't have any running water or indoor plumbing (only an old-fashion outhouse), but it did have electricity and a stove that we could use to get warm. So things were definitely looking up for us. By now it was around 6:30 p.m. on June 29th, but up there at that time of year, which was only about a week past the summer equinox, it didn't get dark until around midnight, and even then it wasn't pitch black. So after we stowed our gear in Rev. Griffin's garage, we headed up town, which was only a couple or so blocks away, to find something to eat and look around. Doug and I split the cost of a copy of the *Anchorage News* to see if we could find any job leads. I recall the paper's headlines stating that the population of Anchorage and it's suburbs, which took in a good deal of territory but excluded Elmendorf Air Force Base, was 19,000. Anchorage was the largest population center in the Territory, and has been ever since.

Eating was another exercise in frugality. We found a restaurant and the cheapest thing that even resembled a meal was a hot beef sandwich consisting of two slices of bread, sliced beef between, a scoop of mashed potatoes on top and covered with gravy. It cost 80¢. That was exactly double the price of what you had to pay back in Illinois at that time. A glass of milk was 50¢, so we felt we would stick with water instead. After we ate my headache gradually went away, and we looked around our new surroundings some more before returning to the preacher's to sleep.

This was a real frontier town, like you see in the Wild West movies, only this was no movie. There were numerous residential streets and several business blocks in Anchorage. We became the most familiar with what seemed to be the main street, called E Street. Surprisingly there were actually quite a few cars around, but they still had hitching posts as well. From an aerial photo on a postcard, the tallest building I saw was three floors, and it appeared there were about fifteen two story buildings, the rest were singles. I am sure there were others not in the photo. Most of the single story stores had the high wooden western style false fronts that they mostly used for sign space. The shops all had a raised wooden sidewalk across the front, at least a foot or two above street level. This came in handy to keep people out of the mud, and from tracking it into the stores. Often the shops had a porch roof over the sidewalks.

Supposedly in 1948, Anchorage sported three paved streets in town. Now I was in the middle of what was considered downtown and, if they even had one, they must have hid it. The only streets I recall at the time were dirt, not even gravel, actually more precisely MUD, since it had been raining ever since we got there. Several of the muddy streets had a plank across them. If you met someone while crossing on the plank, one of you had to step off into the mud or back up. Many of the locals here wore six shooters and the bewhiskered ones, in from the bush, all normally toted 30.06 rifles in addition. Now, I always figured discretion was the better part of valor so whenever I met one of those old sourdoughs, crossing on the same plank I happened to be on, I would step off into the mud, smile, and say, "Howdy, have a nice day." Finally the rains stopped and it gradually began to dry up.

In Anchorage the streets ran north and south, and the avenues ran east and west. Now the Anchorage Hotel, located at 330 E Street, between 3rd and 4th Avenues, near the north

Anchorage Hotel - Anchorage AK

end of the street, was the best of any of the accommodations around. It had been built in 1936, so was only 12 years old at the time. It was three stories high; had about 50 guest rooms; and overlooked a valley and the railroad depot where we had arrived on the 29th of June. There was a portico over the entrance and inside the lobby, while rather old-fashioned, was quite POSH. At the right rear was a massive dark wood counter which served as the hotel's guest desk. The lobby was furnished with large overstuffed chairs and couches, as well as heavy wood furniture including tables, lamps, straight-backed chairs, and writing desks, which were well stocked with pens, stationery and envelopes for the hotel's guests comfort and convenience. There were even brass spittoons. This looked promising as a place to relax, when we weren't looking for a job, so we definitely planned to go back.

The next day, Wednesday, June 30th, we went looking for a job. The paper we had bought the night before wasn't too helpful. Actually, this was a bad time to be looking because nearly all big construction up there was government connected. President Harry Truman, who filled out FDR's term when he died, was running against the NYC District Attorney, Thomas E. Dewey, for the presidency. Since 1948 was an election year, appropriations had been cut to near nothing to make it look to the voters back home that the politicians were doing a good job of keeping costs under control. Therefore jobs that paid much at all were nearly non-existent. There were even soup lines for the unemployed, sponsored by different organizations. For the next few days Doug and I sure were part of the unemployed scene and we stood in a soup line or two.

Late afternoon of June 30th, after a disappointing day full of rejections in our search for any kind of work, we went back to the Anchorage Hotel. It was soon obvious that if you were well dressed, such as in anything that resembled a business suit, you would look out of place, but you would command respect among the hotel staff. The normal attire was more of a blue-collared look, such as a mackinaw, or heavy jacket, a slouch hat, and a flannel shirt. Many men were bewhiskered, wearing dungarees or heavier pants, along with boots, mukluks, or heavy work type shoes. Carrying a six shooter or a 30.06 rifle, or both, was not considered out of place, in fact a good number of the hotel's clientele fell into that category. Then there was the derelict, broke and down on their luck type. While their *appearance* was much the same as the above, they were dirtier, their clothes were more tattered and worn, they would definitely be in need of a bath, and they were not armed. Also, most of the derelict types usually had a dejected, forlorn, distant look in their bloodshot eyes, with no particular sense of purpose. While we sure didn't have a business suit, rifle, or a six shooter, we weren't at the bottom of the local creature scale either.

The room clerks were very familiar with all of the above. They took special note of anyone who appeared to be derelicts or moochers, so they could ferret out those who were not bona fide guests, and who would try to take advantage of their facilities. We soon noticed that we were discreetly beginning to draw the attention of the clerks. The best way to defuse any suspicion, that heaven forbid we *might* appear to be moochers who would take advantage of their facilities, was to have a friendly personality, behave as if we had the right to be there, and act boldly. So we did.

A little quiet observation, plus some reconnoitering, revealed a room with several real flush type toilets and lavatories at the end of a hall. Also, we noticed a rather wide staircase leading down, just to the right of the far end of the hotel desk. For some reason we both felt that down those stairs we might find something of interest, so we decided to investigate. We did not ask the clerk what was downstairs, because that would be a dead giveaway. If we were guests there, we no doubt already knew. So, Doug and I walked over to the staircase, walked right by the guest desk, waved and spoke some pleasantry to the clerk... and kept right on going down the stairs.

What we found nearly made us feel we had struck gold. Back in those days, at least in any hotels I had ever stayed in; very few of the hotel rooms had toilet and/or lavatory facilities in the rooms themselves. They would often be down at the end of the hall, or in some other more central location, and shared by the guests. Of course, I had never stayed in any Edgewater Beach, Biltmore, or Waldorf Astoria premium class hotels either. We had already located the communal toilets up stairs and now, down here, we found where the showers were.

Doug and I went back upstairs and adjourned to some overstuffed chairs at the rear of the lobby, opposite the desk, to consider our next plan of action.

Both Doug and I had been accustomed to a higher quality of life than we were able to enjoy at the good preacher's place. The preacher's contribution to our living arrangements was certainly much appreciated, and adequate, so far as it went. But it was somewhat lacking in the area of relaxation after looking for work all day. Also, it definitely provided *nothing* in the area of personal hygiene or laundry. We decided we had to so something *innovative* about that in order to satisfy our needs, and in as inexpensive a way as possible. The Anchorage Hotel appeared to be able to fulfill all of these major gaps in our present lifestyle. In view of our limited finances we felt we could go up to a top price of *FREE,* which was about all we could afford. However, we had a problem. We noticed the clerk kept glancing over at us, now and then, as if he was wondering if we were guests or not. We knew it was only a matter of time before we would be approached and challenged, and subsequently get thrown out because, of course, we were not paying guests. Therefore, it was imperative that somehow we rearrange our apparent guest status creditability in the clerk's mind, from *questionable at best* to a solid no question that we were *indeed* guests of the hotel. If we didn't, and soon, our chances of ever continuing to enjoy the relaxation, toilets, and writing privileges, let alone any hope of getting a shower, would be doomed. So remembering the old adage that the best defense is a good offense, Doug and I hit upon a plan to thwart that inevitable eviction before it happened.

Doug was one of those fellows who could charm the skin off a snake. We decided he would go to the other side of the clerk and engage him in conversation. That way the clerk would turn to talk with him, and away from me. As Doug struck up a conversation with the clerk, I approached the desk from the clerk's blind side. I spun his guest book around on its lazy susan so I could read the names. I randomly picked and jotted down two names, along with their room numbers, and where the individual was from. I just hoped the clerk didn't know them personally. Then I returned the register to its normal position, and went back to my seat. Shortly after that, Doug concluded his friendly chat with the clerk and joined me.

Doug assumed one name, and the corresponding room number, and I the other. So now we had a plan of how we would handle our bogus residency if we should ever be questioned. As it turned out this was none too soon, because in the afternoon of the next day, July 1st, the first of two different clerks did politely ask if we were guests of the hotel. In a rather *hurt tone* we replied something like, "Well yes, of course. We are *so and so* from *here and there*, and our room numbers are *this and that*. Please feel free to verify them on your register." In both instances the clerks seemed a bit surprised that we gave those names and room numbers for, until then, they were fairly certain that we were free loaders. However, when they went back and checked their register... sure enough our names were opposite the respective room numbers. They looked up, smiled rather sheepishly as if they were ashamed they had *ever* doubted us in the first place, and gave us a small friendly wave. We gave them a forgiving smile and nod in return. However, if one of them had happened to know Mr. *so and so*, then we would have had a problem... but that didn't happen. After that, when we would come in we'd give the duty clerk a friendly wave and, if they weren't busy, we'd call out a greeting. They would just smile and wave back at us, and we never did have any trouble. Later, one of the two clerks even came over and apologized for suspecting us. While biting our tongue we told him, "There is no need to apologize... we realize there is a lot of riff-raff around who would try to con the hotel and take advantage of your excellent facilities." There were other duty clerks, but only those two ever challenged us. Perhaps the first two clerks clued the others in that we were ok... or else they could have cared less. At any rate, if any others had gotten nosey, we were ready for them, too. So things went pretty smoothly after that. When we weren't out looking for a job, we'd sit around, relax, play cards, and write letters using their stationery, naturally. Their indoor plumbing facilities at the end of the hall meant we didn't have to rely on the out-house and the Sears Roebuck catalog back at the preacher's and, of course, there were the showers. We kept trying to find work, but to no avail, and our limited finances were trickling away at the rate of at least 80¢ a day for our daily hot roast beef sandwich supper.

The day before, on the afternoon of the 30th after solidifying how we would handle the situation if questioned about our residency, we moved our priority of getting a shower up to just under finding a job. Since I hadn't had a shower since June 28th, when I had slipped into the crew's quarters on the SS Aleutian, I sure could use one, and Doug was getting a little raunchy, too. We felt it would certainly be more convenient for us, and a nice gesture on the part of the hotel, if the hotel also provided us with free towels and soap as well. But we could hardly ask the clerk because they would just tell us to use the ones out of our room which, of course, we didn't have. Therefore, we developed a plan of convenience, and implemented it the morning of July 1st. We arranged to be back at the hotel early in the morning, when the maid was servicing the rooms, just off the lobby. We each brought in a change of clothing in an inconspicuous sack we had found, and we watched the maid with her cart as she was servicing the rooms. With Doug as a look out, I got up and headed toward the maid when she came out of the room she had just serviced and was on her way to the next. I timed it so by the time I reached her she had arrived at the next un-serviced room, picked up her items, and had entered the room. If the coast was clear, I'd help myself to two towels and two bars of soap from the cart, head directly toward the stairs to go below to the shower area, and then Doug would follow me down. However, if for example the clerk was looking around or there was some other problem, Doug would clear his throat, I'd just walk on by, and we would recycle our attempt later. Walking by the desk with towels would not cause any suspicion because that was what all guests did when they wanted a shower. However, they brought their towels from their rooms... not liberated them from the maid's service cart as we had done.

Down in the shower room, the routine went pretty much as on the SS Aleutian. Since this time there were two of us, one would stand guard over our belongings and the other would prepare to shower. Off came the shoes, belt, watch, billfold, we emptied our pockets, and walked into the shower. First we washed any dirty loose clothes we had brought with us, and then we'd soap down with our clothes on, take them off, rinse them, and finally take a shower ourselves. When one finished he'd get dressed in the clean clothes out of his bag and then stand watch, while the other washed his clothes and got himself squeaky clean, also. After that we left the hotel towels there, put our damp clothes in our sacks, and headed south on E Street to Rev. Griffin's garage where we hung our clothes up to dry. The Reverend lived only about two and a half blocks south of the hotel, and then east of E Street approximately two houses on the south side. Once our clothes were taken care of we went job hunting again. That day the noon soup line was sponsored by the Kiwanis Club. Unfortunately, no jobs were to be had that day either. So again it was another 80¢ hot beef sandwich, a few hands of cards, a letter or two, and watching the people come and go at the hotel, before retiring to Rev. Griffin's garage.

Friday, July 2nd, again we were out looking for a job. Still no luck. Around noon, we stood in another soup line that was sponsored by some church this time. There were quite a few in the line. We'd talk to the people to see where all they had looked, and if they knew of anyone who was hiring. Other than telling us where they had been, and who *wasn't* hiring, that was about all we found out. After we had a bowl of soup and some corn bread, that somewhat filled the void, we'd head out again to see if we could find something where we could make a few dollars, until we could find something better.

Later in the day we ran across Bob Haven and Stewart Meffenin, who we had gotten to know on the ship coming up to Seward. They were real excited because they had found a job working on the railroad as Gandy Dancers. That is a fancy name for section hands, who are nothing more than common dirt laborers. But what the heck, at least it was a job. They were assigned to the railroad maintenance section, at milepost 215.3, 101 miles north of Anchorage, with the unusual name of Sunshine. We asked if the railroad had any more jobs and they seemed to think they did, so all four of us went to the railroad hiring office and inquired. They had an opening for one more man at Sunshine, but there were two of us and we didn't want to split up. However, the railroad agent said that they had an opening for four men on the Colorado Section #35, which at that time, ran from mile post 300 to 308. [Years later, after the 1964 devastating earthquake, the replacing of The Loop, and some other realignment, the Colorado Section was measured starting at MP 297.1.] That was twelve railroad maintenance sections, and some eighty-two miles, north of the Sunshine Section. Bob and Stew asked to be switched to Colorado, so we could all be together.

So on Friday, July 2, 1948, Doug and I signed up to work on the Alaskan Railroad and Bob and Stew transferred to the Colorado section. Since the 4th of July was coming up, and it was a paid holiday, they wouldn't let us go to work until July 5th, but what the heck at least we had a job. We felt GREAT! Now we were employed, and we wouldn't have to return home in disgrace as a casualty of adventure. We would make $1.41 per hour with time and a half over forty hours, and we would work nine hours a day, six days a week. That came to $86.01 per week. That doesn't sound like much today, especially for in Alaska, but remember that was back in 1948 when our steerage passage only cost us $35 one-way. Even then, by Alaskan standards, it was not top dollar, but it wasn't bad and it sure beat nothing at all. Also, it was more than the same job would have paid in the Lower 48, as the Alaskans referred to the continental U.S., giving us more money to spend back home. Out of that a nominal sum was withheld for our room and board, and we were to be paid once a month. There was one catch though... there was absolutely no place to go, or anything to spend it on. I suppose one could use it to gamble, but none of us were into that. So we told them just to leave it on the books, and we'd pick it up when we came out and were ready to head for home.

We asked Bob and Stew where they were staying and they told us that they had been sleeping under buildings. Up there most of the buildings were propped up a few feet on wood cribbing due to the permafrost. So they merely crawled under a building to sleep. By being on a wood cribbing, the buildings sort of floated on the surface of the ground since it was not rigidly attached. If the buildings had conventional footings, as we had in the Lower 48, the uneven heaving of the permafrost would destroy the building. Since Bob and Stew had been sleeping under buildings, I guess you could call them homeless by today's terminology. We told them of our good fortune at the preacher's and said we'd ask if they could stay there, too. We talked to the preacher and his wife. I don't think either of them, especially the preacher, were overly delighted with our request and we couldn't blame them. However, Doug and I had not given them even the slightest concern or trouble and finally they said ok. So Bob and Stew moved in with us until we all left to go up to our Section on July 5th.

I don't know when Bob or Stew had an opportunity to bathe last, but it sure hadn't been for a while because they were down right grubby. So we explained the ploy Doug and I had used at the Hotel. It didn't take them long to work that into their schedule. While they were showering, Doug and I picked up a couple of identities for them. However, since they were always seen with us, and the clerks had already checked Doug and me out, I don't recall the clerks ever asking Stew or Bob if they were guests.

Though we hadn't previously seen them, we found that Bob and Stew had also taken some liberties with the hotel's free facilities. However, they didn't know about the showers. Actually, none of us had spent a lot of time at the hotel before we got our jobs because we were always job hunting. However, now that we were at least theoretically gainfully employed, we could rest on our laurels in the comfort of the hotel's overstuffed chairs and write letters home, using the Anchorage Hotel's stationery, of course.

Bob and Stew had also researched the local culinary establishments and had ferreted out the best cuisine available that would fit their budget. It happened to be the same place that we had been eating and the same thing as well. So after they had gotten cleaned up, we retired to our favorite restaurant for our usual evening repast. However, we felt like celebrating this evening so we decided on having a glass of milk *in addition* to our usual glass of plain water. At the restaurant we knew the milk was 50¢ a glass. However, we also knew you could buy a quart of milk at the grocery store down the street for $1.00, plus a 10¢ bottle deposit. Before, when there was just Doug and me, we didn't want to spend the money for a whole quart of milk because it was something we could do without. But now that we had Bob and Stew to split the cost with us, and considering the auspicious occasion we were celebrating, we simply threw caution and financial restraint to the wind. We each kicked in our share, then I went to the grocery, bought a quart of milk, gave the grocer the deposit, and returned to the restaurant. Since there are four glasses to a quart, and there were now four of us, it would only cost us 25¢ per glass. We ordered our usual, and a glass of water. We drank the water, opened the bottle of milk, and poured each of us a glass. After eating we rinsed out the bottle, took it back to the grocery store, and got our dime deposit back.

July 3rd and 4th, we mostly sat around the hotel, played a lot of pinochle and wrote letters. At noon we'd search out where the soup lines were and usually there were two. I guess we were getting a little picky because we'd check to see what kind of soup they were having; however, the soup of the day always met our approval. That would tide us over until evening and our usual dining routine. In the afternoon we would look at some of the stores to see what they had and how much it cost; most of which we didn't need and couldn't afford anyway.

On the night of the 4th of July, there was a prize fight for the boxing championship of Alaska. It was held outside in a large open air enclosure, formed by a series of eight foot high tarps. Doug was working on his diary so Bob, Stew and I went. It was held at 10:30 p.m., but no extra lighting was needed as it was plenty light up there, even at that hour.

It cost $3.00 to get in at the front opening. Since we didn't have money to spare for that sort of thing, we looked around and found a loose area under the tarp in the rear that was <u>exactly</u> $3 less than at the regular entrance.

Prizefight arena for boxing championship of Alaska.

On Monday, July 5, 1948, all four of us went up to Mr. and Mrs. Griffin's back door, knocked, and expressed our gratitude for their kindness in letting us sleep in their garage; then we headed down to the depot. We showed our new railroad pass, which was basically our employee card, to the conductor and boarded the train to head north. Unlike the day we arrived, today was clear and you could see Mt. McKinley off to the north-northwest. We rolled by fast moving streams and dense timber, clattered over bridges, across rocky gorges and broad flood plains of gravel and rock. Now and then one could spot an elk, or sometimes even a bear, and there was usually an eagle circling around in the sky. The air was cool and invigorating, and it felt good to be alive and heading into what, for us, was the unknown. We were excited because we were on the trail of adventure, and a whole new experience, that few would ever have the opportunity to taste.

A.R.R. No. 722

DEPARTMENT OF THE INTERIOR ①
THE ALASKA RAILROAD

EMPLOYEE Ralph D. Sutherland   No. 33937

SIGNATURE *Ralph D Sutherland*

WITNESS *M. Irene Robinson*

PLACE AND DATE Anchorage, Alaska   7-2-48

P.S.N.S. 11-14-47 10M

railroad identification

We arrived at Colorado, AK some four hours later. This was to be my home for the rest of the summer, until it was time for me to pack up and head back to college.

Arriving at Colorado, AK on July 5, 1948.

We were met by a Mrs. Collins, who was the cook. She was a short, plain, and rather plump woman with graying blondish hair, who appeared to be in her mid-fifties. She was rather surprised at our arrival because for some reason Anchorage had not told them of our coming. The section crew had not returned yet so while we waited we helped Mrs. Collins set the table for supper, and brought in some more wood for the cook stove, while she was busy preparing some additional food.

When the section crew came in after work, Jim, the foreman, greeted us in a quiet business like way, and introduced us to each member of the section. I never knew his last name or anything about him. Jim wasn't one to socialize; he was a loner, but not unfriendly; I never heard him laugh or ever saw him smile. He looked out for his men and was always fair. No one ever challenged his authority or whatever he said. He knew exactly what had to be done, and how to do it, and he would not ask anyone to do anything that he wouldn't do himself. Jim was all business, no nonsense, and had the respect of everyone on the crew. He was a good foreman.

We then introduced ourselves. The population of Colorado, AK, before we arrived, was eight people. There was Jim, the foreman, who was possibly in his early 50s. Later we would come to know him as a stern man who saw to it that every man put in a full day's work. There was Slim, Tex, and Smokey, all in their late 30s to early 40s. These fellows were pretty much what I would call drifters. They were friendly and we always got along. Tex played the guitar and sang quite well. Once or twice I got the impression that they either were currently, or had been, on the wrong side of the law. Then there were three Eskimos that rounded out the regular work force, Alec Melik, Henry Tuffolna, and Mike Yakasoff. They were 32, 40, and 22 years old respectively, though Mike seemed much younger. The eighth person on the section was the cook, Mrs. Collins. She was the only woman, not much of a conversationalist, never joked or smiled, but was not mad or unpleasant. She apparently didn't hold any allure for anyone, or at least not that I noticed.

Stewart Meffenin, Corky, Bob Haven and Doug Waugh.

Colorado, AK consisted of the section house, a twenty foot by forty foot warehouse with a platform on the north side and located maybe 100 feet to the south, and an outdoor privy. All of which were on the west side of the tracks. There was a small shed for our gas powered section car. It was not much more than a lean to, and it sat adjacent to the tracks on the east side. There was a pole near the house with a dozen numbered, twelve inch wide, red and white rings painted on it, each ring a foot apart. This was to measure the snow depth in the winter. I never really figured out what purpose it served. After the snow got over six foot deep, you couldn't see it anyway, and by then, who cared?

The section house was comprised of a kitchen, dining room, a small room for Jim, another for Mrs. Collins, and there was a bunk room where the work crew slept. None of the rooms were very large, and while I suppose the four of us could have squeezed into the bunk room it would really have been crowded.

Jim told us to sleep over in the warehouse which was a storage area for odds and ends. One partitioned off section had plenty of room, as well as iron cots where we could pitch our sleeping bags. It also had a pot bellied stove that came in real handy. Since we were more or less of the same age and general background, we found this arrangement more to our liking. I presume the rest of the workers felt that way as well.

Inside our warehouse was our 'all important' stove.

Corky, Haven & Stew

222

The warehouse where the four of us lived.

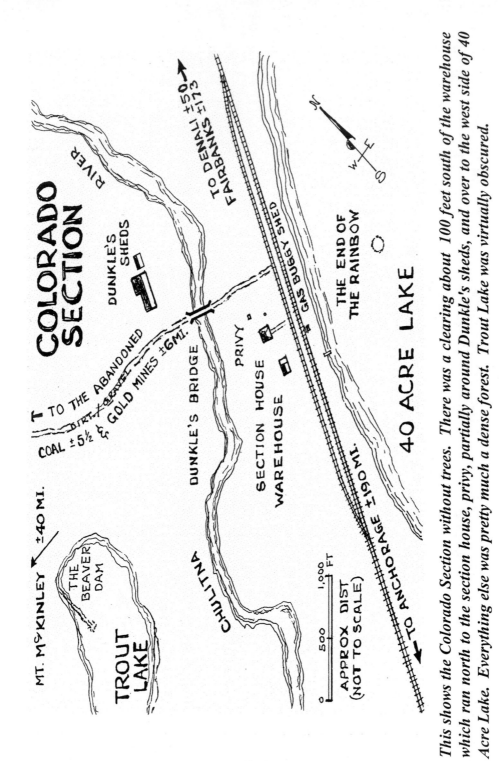

COLORADO SECTION

RIVER

DUNKLE'S SHEDS

TO DENALI ±50
FAIRBANKS ±173

↑ TO THE ABANDONED
DIRT / GRAVEL
COAL ±5½ & GOLD MINES ±6MI.

DUNKLE'S BRIDGE

PRIVY

SECTION HOUSE

WAREHOUSE

GAS BUGGY SHED

THE END OF
THE RAINBOW

40 ACRE LAKE

MT. McKINLEY ±40 MI.

THE
BEAVER
DAM

TROUT
LAKE

CHULITNA

1,000 FT

500

APPROX DIST
(NOT TO SCALE)

0

TO ANCHORAGE ±190 MI.

N
W — E
S

*This shows the Colorado Section without trees. There was a clearing about 100 feet south of the warehouse
which ran north to the section house, privy, partially around Dunkle's sheds, and over to the west side of 40
Acre Lake. Everything else was pretty much a dense forest. Trout Lake was virtually obscured.*

Our water system in the section house consisted of a well with a hand pump, where we drew our water. To take a shower we drew water, heated it on the stove, and then poured it in a big holding tank located above the shower. Everyone was responsible to draw and heat his own water. There was no regular electricity, but they did have lights for the winter which were powered by a gasoline generator. In the summer it was generally light enough so you didn't need lights anyway. If one did, we had coal oil lanterns. The only modern convenience we had was the railroad telephone that Jim used to communicate with Broad Pass, which was our Division Headquarters and was the next section north of us. Each morning Jim would call to get the train schedules, and to find out when the trains were due through our section. He would call in when we came in for dinner, again when we went back out on the tracks, and the last call of the day was after we had returned in the evening for supper. That way Broad Pass knew we were all safe. You couldn't call home, or home couldn't call you; it was strictly a closed circuit railroad phone with no outside access.

There were five sections that made up our division. From south to north they were: Hurricane, Honolulu, Colorado, Broad Pass, and Summit. The northern most section in our Division was Summit, at 2,363 feet elevation and on the continental divide. Our section house was located roughly in the middle of our track responsibility, which was the eight mile section from Mile Post 300 to 308, as measured from Seward. We were approximately fifty miles south of Denali National Park and we could see Mt. McKinley in Denali Park quite easily. It was some forty miles pretty much west of us.

To the east of our section, some distance away, was the

Susitna River. It angled south-west and passed under the railroad some five sections south of Colorado at Gold Creek. Also, immediately on the east side of the tracks, across from our section house, was a lake that was perhaps a good three quarters of a mile long and a half mile wide. We referred to it as Forty Acre Lake. To the west side of our section house was the Chulitna River, which was less than an eighth of a mile from our section. We would often go down there to bring up water. The elevation of the area was not high by some standards, still, as compared to the 640 foot elevation of Peoria, IL, we were fairly high up in the mountains at an elevation of roughly 2,000 feet. I would estimate the daytime temperature averaged in the high 50s. At night it would drop to an average of the low 40s to upper 30s. We were far enough north that you could read the finest print in a newspaper around the clock. Since we were below the Arctic Circle the sun still set, but didn't get very far below the horizon, and because we were well up in the mountains one didn't really know where the horizon was. However, by the time I left Alaska the days and nights were getting fairly even. We were fortunate to have seen several dramatic displays of the northern lights. They were more noticeable later in the evening when the sky was darker.

There wasn't a town, a village, or even a trapper's shack close by, and at that time the nearest highway was fifty miles across a range of mountains with no reasonable way of getting there. With the exception of the railroad, this was the out back of the Out Back. It wasn't the end of the world... but you could see it from there. Actually, its remoteness was responsible for it being quite beautiful, in a quiet, lonely, untamed, and rather pristine sort of way. Beyond you, in any direction, the woods, streams and lakes were alive with all sorts of wild game. Here there were no neighbors and you certainly didn't have to lock your doors at night.

When Bob Haven, Stewart Meffenin, Doug Waugh, and I arrived, we increased the population of Colorado, AK by fifty percent! Smokey left the section maybe a week or so after we arrived, so that reduced our inhabitants to eleven. I was a bit surprised that we greenhorns were accepted as well as we were. I don't think it was because there were four of us, young, and all fairly good sized. Their welcome and acceptance always seemed genuine. Of course, up there on a work section, many miles from anyone or anything, life is a bit different. Everyone had to depend on everyone else, but at any rate we got along surprisingly well for the entire time we were there. There was no quarter expected, or asked, and no quarter was offered, or given. We had a job to do and everyone pulled their own weight. When necessary, no one minded helping the other fellow. Also, to my knowledge, no one ever tried to take advantage of anyone either, so as a result there was a mutual respect that built up between all hands.

My first week working on the railroad is painfully memorable. It has been indelibly etched in my memory forever. In the summer of 1947, the year before I went to Alaska, I could not find a job so I went back to college, at Western, for the entire summer. Then, with a full school year on either end, that meant that when I went to Alaska the following summer the heaviest thing I had lifted for two and a half years was a pencil. When I arrived at Colorado, I was 230 pounds of pure unadulterated blubber... with no muscle in sight. Now, all of a sudden, I was expected to wrestle these creosoted railroad ties and to help manhandle ninety pounds per foot of steel railroad rail for nine hours a day, six days a week. I found muscles I never knew I had before. Every one of them was *screaming* from my pain racked, soft and supple body. During the first week I ate breakfast, I probably ate some dinner at noon, but I don't recall eating any supper at night. I just collapsed on my rack, completely exhausted, until it was time to get up the next morning and go at it again. I don't recall how long Doug, Bob or Stew missed supper, I wasn't counting, but at least all of them missed a few. Not one of the old timers ever made fun of us, or let on that they had missed us at the supper table the night before. We showed up and we did our work. No one complained and apparently we gained their respect. That is perhaps one reason why we all got along as well as we did. Anyway, I don't think they would have tolerated any 'cry babies'. Strange as it might sound, I was not actually stiff one day. No, I am not kidding, I'd gone far BEYOND that point. It is called total exhaustion. I can't speak for the others, but we were all pretty much in the same boat. By the end of the first week all of us greenhorns were beginning to get in shape. By the time I came out, that 230 pounds of pure blubber had turned into 185 pounds of hardened muscle.

I decided to grow a beard, not a big, woodsy, bushy type, but a shorter respectable one that ran from one ear to the corner of my mouth, dipped, then up to the center of my lower lip, and likewise on the other side, up to my other ear. It grew until I could even comb and part it if I wanted. I don't know why, but for some reason I didn't even try to grow a moustache. I had always wanted to grow a beard, but didn't really care about showing it off in public. I figured now would be the time, as this would be about as un-public a place as I'd ever find myself in.

As an employee of the Alaskan Railroad you worked

for the U.S. Department of the Interior. The section ordered their groceries out of the government commissary once a month and you had best not forget anything because there was no running back to the store. That was it until the next month. It was sent up on the railroad and the cost was split among the employees. Well, guess what! They didn't know we were coming until we arrived and they had already ordered all of their provisions for July! So technically, since we'd increased the population by fifty percent, our food would run out two-thirds of the way through the month. Well the main staples got pretty short, but we didn't go hungry. We simply ate off the land. It was there I had my first blueberries, succulently fresh, hand picked off the bushes and I have loved them ever since.

We also speared salmon right out of the Chulitna. We never took more than we would eat, and we would save the eggs to use for bait to fish for trout. The smallest salmon we took was 15#, and the largest was 25#. I ate so much salmon I couldn't look at another salmon steak for many years after, and even to this day it is not all that high on my list of food choices.

Mike Yakasoff and our foreman, Jim, with a salmon catch.

Mrs. Collins cooked all of our meals and she could bake bread *almost* as good as my mother, and Mom was second to none. mmmm it was good! *But,* unfortunately, baking bread was the *only* culinary art she ever mastered. Other than that, she was a lousy cook. That is, lousy as in *terrible.* She didn't have much use for salt or pepper either. However, it was there that I developed a keen taste for blueberry pie. In a way that's surprising because Mrs. Collins made a perfectly awful pie. She never thought to mix the ingredients. For an example, and I am not kidding, she put a thick layer of pie dough in the bottom, next a thick layer of blueberries, then a layer of sugar on that, and finally she covered it with another thick layer of pie dough like the one on the bottom. Apparently she had not exposed either crust to any more than a minimum number of passes of a rolling pin. Then she proceeded to *under* cook it. As you passed your fork down through a piece, and popped it in your mouth, you got the following sensation. There was the raw chewy upper crust, pure sugar, sour berries, and then the soggy lower crust that wasn't much more than raw dough. Now I am not fussy when it comes to eating, but what that woman would do to a blueberry pie was almost criminal. However, I rose to the occasion and made the best of a bad situation. I added a little salt, which she had no use for, then stirred my pie to mix it thoroughly. And only then did I eat it. After you mixed the berries and sugar together, all you had to do was to ignore the under baked crust. That wasn't too easy to do though, because that doughy crust wanted to stick to the roof of your mouth like peanut butter.

If she opened an industrial sized can of green beans, or corn, or applesauce, and just placed in on the table as it came out of the can, heating if appropriate, then that was ok. *But,* if she tried to use them to make something such as scalloped corn, or if she tried to cream the beans, or who knows what, if she ever attempted to do *anything* like that, then we all were in trouble. At least for me, I ate an awful lot of bread.

No one said a word about her cooking. Certainly none of us new kids on the block felt like we could complain. That would be looked on as whining. I think the *real* reason was, if we complained she would walk out and cooks on a section, like we were on, were hard to get.

Jim decided, that with us additional mouths to feed, the four of us new fellows would rotate doing KP with Mrs. Collins. Maybe he secretly hoped the food would improve. I had KP only once. I was real glad when my turn was over and I could get back on the tracks. Then Doug's turn came, and he sort of enjoyed it, so he volunteered to do it all the time which was fine with Bob, Stew and me. He had to get up early, and had dishes to do late, but then he had time off in the middle of the day to work on his diary and to explore around. So he was happy and so were the rest of us.

Our primary railroad job was to replace ties. We also replaced a few rails and both aligned and adjusted the tracks to make a better ride, with less sway and undulations. To start off with, Jim would walk the track while the rest of us were busy with our jobs. He would use a large yellow keel (crayon) to mark the ties that he wanted replaced with a big X. Also, he was always squatting and squinting along the rails to look for places where the track had shifted. Those shifts were where the track needed aligning, and he would use a red keel to denote the limits of the wobble.

Looking west across the tracks at our section house.

View southeast of back of the section house, and the warehouse.

Our gas buggy.

As we were ready to go to work, we'd load as many ties as we could carry on the flat car, which we often pulled behind our gas powered section car. We'd pull out onto the main line, from the siding at our section, and head toward the work area. As we came to the first tie that Jim had marked with a yellow X, Jim would yell, "Humph," and a couple of us would heave a tie off as we rolled along.

Putting the gas buggy on the tracks.

If he came to three close together, we heard "Humph," "Humph," "Humph," and three ties got pitched off. After all our ties had been pitched one man would get off with his tools to replace the last three ties.

Gauging the rails to check the distance apart.

Jim would reverse the gas car and start back up the line. At each third tie another of us would get off with our tools, until all had dismounted. We would replace our three ties and then walk through the gang to the next three ties beyond the crew, for a bit of a change. That way no one was getting in the other fellow's way as they worked, everyone knew which ties were theirs to replace, and we were all in the same general area. It was a pretty good arrangement, fair, and worked well. I recall once that my last two ties were maybe 200 feet or so from where they were needed. That happened because there were several ties to throw off at the same time, as we were rolling along, and we couldn't pitch them off fast enough. So I went to get the ties to bring them back to where I was to install them. I recall thinking I'd have to take one back and return for the other one, which would be two trips. I said 'to heck with it', so I put the ties side by side, picked up one end of both of them, then let one fall down across my left shoulder and the other one across my right knee where I hooked my arm around it, and walked off with both ties. All told, I was probably packing in the neighborhood of at least 300 pounds. I chuckled as I walked along, recalling how I had been struggling with even one tie when we first arrived on the section. Packing two ties, now that *was* a load, and I only remember that happening once.

The ties we were replacing were ninety-nine percent original, from when the railroad was first built. There were a few attempts at building the railroad back in 1904, but they were not successful. In 1914 President Woodrow Wilson was given the authority to build the Alaskan Railroad.

Pulling a tie spike.

Construction began in 1915 and completed on July 15, 1923, in Warren Harding's presidency. So all of those ties we were replacing in our location were older than we were, as they had been in use for around twenty five years or so. Now, those were not your regular standard railroad ties as we know them today.

Preparing to insert a custom tie to replace an old hand hewn one.

Back then, they simply cut a tree out of the wilderness. They usually chose a tree that was in front of them, because they would have to clear it out anyway. They cut it in about nine or ten foot lengths, took an adze to flatten one side, slid it in place, packed some rock under and around the tie, spiked the rail to it, then they went on to the next. We were to remove the spikes using a five foot long spike bar, one end of which was like the claw end of a hammer. We would stick the claw end under the spike head and push down to pry the spike up and out. It usually worked quite well, but sometimes the spikes were pretty tough to pull and we would have to get on top of the bar and sort of bounce to break the spike loose. Next we would dig a trench in the ballast, leading to the ditch, on whichever side we were going to slide the tie out. Then we'd take our heavy tie tongs that looked like the ice tongs the icemen would use to deliver block ice. We'd slam them into the end of the tie and _P U L L_ for all we were worth, sometimes wiggling the tie back and forth to slide it out from under the rails. More often than not, the old original ties were crooked and we would have to enlarge the trench along the length of the old tie to conform to the widest part of tie being moved. Many times this made the trench quite wide.

We replaced the ties with the custom factory made ones. These new ones all had a uniform cross-section and length, and they were a lot lighter than the original tree ties. I don't know what the new ties actually weighed, but a seven inch by nine inch by eight foot white oak tie weighs around 185 pounds. These, however, might have been cedar since they didn't seem to weigh that much. If so, they were maybe only 150 pounds each. Someone told us the ones we were using were lighter than the ones used in the Lower 48. Anyway, handling these ties was actually the easy part! Digging out the ballast and removing the large old tree trunk ties was the hard part. Putting the new tie in place was easy, but then we had to force ballast under the tie to get the tie up snug against the rail so we could drive in the spikes. After driving the spikes, we'd have to go back and tamp the ballast to firm it up more, and then give the spikes a last pound or two to be sure they were tight and the ballast was firm. Since the old tie was larger, that meant we had to work more ballast under the smaller tie to raise it up. The original ballast for the most part was native rock that had been broken up. Since the custom ties were smaller, it often took more ballast, than was available at the location. That meant we had to haul in more ballast from our supply.

Another important job we performed was aligning the rails. Often as we were working replacing ties, Jim would wander off up the track. Soon he'd squat and sight down the rail, then walk a bit farther and squat and sight again, and so on. If he was on a curve, he wanted to be sure it was a *smooth* curve from one end to the other. If he was on a straight away section of track, he wanted it as *straight as an arrow*. Any wobble in the alignment was unacceptable to Jim. That meant the track had shifted, which was probably caused by a soft spot in the ballast, allowing the ties to shift both horizontally as well as vertically. Also, a train going over the track would wobble, which in turn would make the track shift ever so slightly more. It was like a cavity in your tooth, once it started it never got better by itself until you took care of it. When Jim saw something he wanted to adjust, he got out his red keel crayon and marked the wobble boundaries. After a while, he would get us all together and tell us where to stand. We would take our long track (spike) bars and jam them into the ballast at maybe a 60-degree angle under the outside of the rail that we wanted to move in the opposite direction. Then on the count of "One, Two, Three, HEAVE" we would push our bar hard against the rail, and actually shift the track over a tad. Jim would squat down again and sight along the rail. Then he might say give me one more "RCH." At first he might want three or four RCHs, but when he got down to just one that meant we just needed a smidgen more. I never knew what RCH meant, and felt a little stupid asking something I probably should have known, but one day my curiosity got the better of me so I asked one of the older fellows. He just grinned and gave me the definition of one of Jim's rather off color expressions. Ok, I didn't know the origin of that one, and I wasn't about to ask. Whenever we realigned the rails we would go over the area and tighten up the ballast under all the ties, which was the cause of the problem in the first place. We aligned the tracks fairly often because the freights would find soft spots in the ballast easier than we could.

Now and then we would find a broken rail, and that was a priority to replace. All the rails that we had up there were of a standard length, and weighed ninety pounds per foot. The ones in the Lower 48 were normally heavier at 120 pounds per foot to 150 pounds per foot, and perhaps some even heavier than that. This was because the trains in the Lower 48 were generally bigger, and heavier. They often used welded rails at that time in the Lower 48, but we didn't. Ours were the standard length and bolted together using splice plates. We stocked rails in our section yard, as well as a large supply of ties and extra ballast.

The Colorado Section was roughly eight miles long and I personally liked the southern end the best. There was a high arched bridge over a deep gorge that carried the east fork of the Chulitna River, flowing in from the east, over to the Chulitna River which was the same river that flowed about an eighth of a mile west of our section house. The view from there was awesome. It gave one an observation point from which we had an unobstructed view of the vast expanse of the forests and mountains. On clear days we also had a great view of the 20,320 foot Mt. McKinley which was over forty miles west of us. Of course, we didn't have time to stand around and admire the vista; however, we did look as time permitted. On our breaks we would watch the edge of the woods down by the water for wildlife. Now and then we would spot some, including bear, elk and moose, and there always seemed to be eagles circling high above us anytime we looked up.

A passenger train would run from Anchorage north to Fairbanks one day, and then it would turn around and come back the next. There were numerous freights that were going along all the time, too. As we were up in the mountains, most of the freight trains had what they called a light engine. It was nothing more than an extra locomotive, occasionally two, that helped get a train through the mountains. Then after they got to Summit, the section beyond Broad Pass, they weren't needed any more, so they would turn the light engines around and send them back south to pick up another train.

Every morning, before we'd go out on the tracks, Jim would call Broad Pass and write down the train movements for the day. The last thing we wanted to do was to be caught on the tracks and find ourselves looking a train in the face. If it was a northbound that wasn't so bad because it was usually going upgrade which meant it wasn't closing on you real fast, but if it was southbound most of the time it would be going downgrade which meant it was traveling faster. Then if it was a light engine, which was traveling by itself and not pulling a train, they would often travel even faster. At noon we would take an hour off, but that included travel time, to and from where we were working, in to the section house to eat. One day, around noon, we were headed in for lunch from the south end of the section. As we began rounding a curve on a mountain, all of a sudden we were staring straight at a light engine coming southbound, without a load, running flat out toward us. No one said a word. There was a set out maybe 500 feet or so ahead. It is a supported pair of ties, at right angles to the rail, where you can park the gas buggy while you are working on the tracks so it will be out of the way when trains go by. Well, Jim gave our gas buggy full throttle and we raced for the set out. This was scary because that meant we were also heading directly toward the fast approaching locomotive. Just before we got there, Jim cut the engine and pulled the brake lever all the way back. He couldn't have done it any better. That gas buggy literally slid, with wheels locked tight, right up to the set out. Everyone jumped off. We grabbed the buggy, picked it up, turned it 90-degrees, and swung it over and onto the set out. Immediately after that, the light engine went thundering by. I remember seeing the engineer with a look of horror and disbelief on his face. Obviously he had not been looking out of his cab, as he should have, and hadn't seen us until he passed us; hence he did not have time to react.

No one spoke until after the train had gone by. We knew what Jim was doing, and what we had to do, when we got to the set out. So there wasn't anything to be said. However, after it was over, Jim vented what was on his mind and it wasn't pretty. I do not recall *exactly* what Jim said, and that is just as well. If we had been on the straight away, that would have been bad enough, however, we could have seen the engine coming a lot sooner. Even if we weren't near a set out, we could have stopped, picked the car up, and pushed it into a ditch, or at least jumped. Not so in our case. We were on a curve, which meant we had very little advance warning, and we were on the side of a mountain. On our left was the mountain itself, which gave us precious little clearance and the gas buggy would have been lost. On our right was a very deep drop off, down the mountain.

We sat the car back on the tracks and proceeded back to

the section house where Jim immediately went to the phone and called Broad Pass. He had a few words with the dispatcher who admitted he had forgotten to mention the light engine that would be coming through about noon. Jim's dissertation could have gotten him a job with Mr. Webster, as a word consultant, for an obscene language edition. My gracious, I never heard such words, language and phrases before. Personally I seriously doubt if the dispatcher, or anyone, could have done half the things Jim suggested. He didn't chew that dispatcher's 'you know what out'; he just chomped all the way around and let it fall out all by itself.

I recall one other instance where Jim was looking out for us, and when Jim spoke everyone instinctively obeyed... no discussion, or questions asked. We had come back to our yard for some more ties. We loaded them on our flat car and were ready to go, but Jim said, "There's a northbound freight due any minute now, so we'll just sit on the siding and wait until it passes." Pretty soon to the south we could hear the labored "chug-chug-chug-chug" of the approaching train. I was sitting on the outboard side of the gas buggy, facing the woods and watching a bald eagle sitting high up in a pine tree. The locomotives (there were usually two hooked together) rolled by pulling a long mix of rolling stock, however, since I was facing away from the tracks I wasn't really paying any particular attention to them. You could hear the creaking of the rail cars, the squeal of their wheels against the rails, and the "clickity-clack"... "clickity-clack" of the railroad car's dual trucks as they passed over the rail joints.

All of a sudden Jim yelled... "JUMP BOYS JUMP... GET THE HELL OUT OF HERE!" No one argued, no one asked why, and for sure no one dawdled. I dove head first off the buggy, ducked my head, grabbed my knees tucking into a ball, and ended up maybe fifteen feet or so away in a shallow ditch alongside the siding. The rest of the guys were right behind me. I rolled over on my back, and looked at the train to see what the problem was. Only a few people would have ever noticed and sensed the danger that Jim had. There was a flat car of cut lumber coming toward us. Apparently a strap, holding one of the bundles of lumber together, had broken, and a long one by twelve, or two by ten, or something, had worked its way out of the bundle and between a couple of the vertical stays, which held the bundled lumber on the flat car. It was sticking out like a scythe, and undulating up and down as the car swayed going along the track. As it passed us, the board happened to be at the apogee, or highest point, of its undulation, and as such passed over the top of our gas buggy. But, of course, there was no way of knowing that at the time. If it had been at its perigee, lowest point, and if Jim had not been watching out for us, it would have wiped out the entire crew.

Jim told us afterward that on some other section a few years earlier the same situation occurred. However, unfortunately, there were two differences: 1] No one noticed the board, and 2] the board was at its perigee when it got to where the fellows were sitting on their car. It decapitated the entire crew. Every night, when the crews come in off the track, the foreman is required to call the Division Head to advise them that their crew was in safe. That section never called in that night. So Division sent out a search party and found the grizzly sight. Later they located the train that had passed through the section and noticed it had a flat car of sawed lumber with one of the boards sticking out, with blood all over it.

Though personally Jim was a loner, and always seemed

243

aloof, he was like a mother hen. Whether we knew it or not, he looked out for us constantly. From the experience of the loose undulating board, it was apparent we needed a mother hen like Jim. He was always watchful, cool and level headed. He knew his business, and we knew he knew it.

Mosquitoes! I have NEVER in all my life seen them as big and vicious as they were up there. They are considered the State Bird of Alaska. There were quite a few rather marshy areas in the tundra where we were, even though we were in the mountains. Unfortunately, this terrain was conducive to their breeding because I never saw mosquitoes actually swarm before, until I went to Alaska. One night in our warehouse I cornered one and beat him to death with my track shovel. I stuffed him in an envelope to mail home so my parents could actually see how big those critters got. Would you believe it took extra postage just to mail the letter? Another time, I was lying in my sack and two mosquitoes were circling over my head. Besides their buzzing I overheard them talking. The first one said, "Shall we eat him here, or take him down by the river?" The other one rationalized that they'd better eat me there, because if they took me down by the river the big boys would take me away from them. Wellllll... *maybe* those two stories are a bit exaggerated, but it seemed pretty realistic at the time.

Fortunately, I had brought along some mosquito repellant, that I rubbed around my wrists and on the back of my neck, or any other exposed areas. On the track we always wore heavy leather work gloves and, of course, a hat. I had one with an attachable mosquito net that I could let down and tie it under my shirt collar. If the wind was blowing the mosquitoes didn't bother us, but if it was still, or a light breeze, then we had all sorts of company.

244

Besides the mosquitoes, there were what the Eskimos called moose flies. Back home we called them horse flies. They were more or less the same thing, but BIGGER! I think the biggest one I saw could carry three passengers. Now that too is a bit of an exaggeration, but they were quite large, and they would bite. We would have a ten minute break about every hour and often we would engage in, what now seems a rather sadistic pastime. Some of us would take a piece of wild grass that looked like a thin wheat straw and would clip them so they were all the same size. Then we'd catch the biggest moose fly we could find, stick the straw up his you know what, and bet as to whose could fly the farthest before crashing. We didn't have any money so our bet would be, if we lost then we would carry the other fellow's next tie from where it got dumped off the dolly to where he was to put it in. Yes, I know that it was not very nice or humane, but we all had been bitten by those darn moose flies so many times that we didn't really think, or care about any moose fly rights.

There was another nasty little beastie called white socks. They were nearly as annoying, but actually quite small, like a fat fruit fly. Normally you often didn't notice them until it was too late. They didn't sting you like a mosquito, instead they actually took a chunk of skin out. Man did they get your attention! If you looked closely at their legs, they were white from what appeared to be the knees, down hence, the nickname of white socks.

We managed to have a little fun, and do a little exploring on our downtime. Have you ever been to the end of the rainbow? Well I have, and though it pains me, I will tell you that the old story, about there being a pot of gold there, is a bunch of bunk. I mentioned we had a fair sized lake across the tracks, on the east side from our section house.

The Eskimos had built a johnboat, which is a flat bottomed dinghy. It wasn't bad, and we would use it to paddle around the lake for fun. On this particular day, there was a little shower as we got off work. Bob Haven and I walked across the tracks, and were looking at the Forty Acre Lake, when before our eyes there appeared a large rainbow that came right out of the lake and went off to the south.

The Eskimos had built a
'johnboat' we used for recreation.

Of course, a rainbow is only the refraction of sunlight suspended off of moisture droplets. As you get closer you can't see it anymore, because it just sort of disappears in the mist. However, from a distance you can see all the different colors. Knowing it wouldn't last long, I told Bob, let's go the end of the rainbow, but we had to triangulate where it came out of the water first. We picked out two trees on one side of the lake, and a large rock and tree on the other side. The intersection point of a line between these points would be where the north end of the rainbow came out of the lake.

Then we jumped in the johnboat and rowed out to… *the end of the rainbow*. As we approached, the colors began to fade, but it was sort of misty so we knew it was still there. As we got at the point where these two lines intersected, I looked down, over the side of the boat.

A rainbow coming out of Forty-Acre Lake that Haven and I <u>literally</u> went to the end of.

The water was as clear as could be and you could see all the way to the bottom, which I guessed was probably around fifteen to twenty feet at that point. No gold, not even an empty pot. HOWEVER, less some skeptic should challenge my story; I kicked off my shoes, dropped my pants, and went over the side. I swam down to the bottom. I picked up what was there and brought it up to show Bob. It was nothing but rock and mud, and not a *trace* of gold! But, *I had literally* been to the end of the rainbow!

Often we would go swimming in the lake, but not for long. About ten minutes was as long as one could stand to stay in before turning blue. The water was real cold, but that was not surprising because you could look off and see the glacier that was the lake's source.

A mining engineer/prospector, by the name of Dunkle, had a coal mine and gold mine some five and a half and six miles, respectively, west of the section. He called the gold mine, "The Golden Zone" mine. He went broke before he ever hit the mother load of gold, abandoned both his operations, and everyone left.

Dunkle's mess hall and supply shed destroyed by winter snows.

As I recall, Jim told us that was about five or so years before. I don't know how many people he had working for him at one time or another, but there may have been perhaps twenty to twenty-five, or more. The reason I say that is, there was a combination mess hall/bunk house type of building,

248

down by and across the Chulitna River, which would easily sit about that many at one time. There was a kitchen in there, as well as a pantry which had been pretty well picked over by the railroad workers over the years. Yet there was still a goodly amount of large, institutional sized tins of applesauce and a few other items, plus plenty of coffee which we liberated along with what else we could use as we had need. The building wasn't really very substantially built and a good portion of it had collapsed from, apparently, past snow loads. It had been rather hastily built with regular lumber, and celotex lining mostly on the outside and some inside. If they had ever intended to finish it, they hadn't.

I looked up at the southeast corner of the building, and by reaching as high as I could, some seven and a half feet, I could *just barely* touch the bottom of a huge paw print that was imprinted into the outside of the building. Apparently, some big Alaskan Brown Bear had strolled up, stood on his hind feet, and 'ker-POW', hauled off and smacked the building with his forepaw, leaving his mark.

An undamaged section of the building with the shorter of the two bear paw marks.

249

I saw another such paw mark on the side of the building around six feet off the ground. Maybe that was his missus. In the south end of the building there was an office of some sort, in this long and rather narrow structure. I could never figure out why someone at one time had placed a sack of flour on the desk in the office. When you walked in you could see that the place was a shambles, but all one had to do was to just look around and you knew exactly what had taken place. Obviously a bear had strolled in, saw the sack of flour and because he probably had nothing else to do at the time, he hauled off and slapped it. When he hit it, the sack virtually EXPLODED in his face. With that, the bear probably panicked. He literally went right through the side of the building, still in an upright position. There was flour ALL OVER that office and a hole through the west wall that very closely resembled the vertical silhouette of a rather large bear. I still get a chuckle thinking about what that poor bear must have thought, and how the scene would have looked unfolding.

Dunkle's base included an equipment repair shop completely outfitted with tools, of every imaginable kind, that their mining operations would need. I saw surveying instruments, assaying scales, chemicals, dynamite, all sorts of supporting supplies such as boots, clothing, canned goods, and equipment worth thousands upon thousands of dollars. I asked Jim why Dunkle hadn't taken it out when he left. He said Dunkle wanted to come back if he could get refinanced and the items were safe enough there because the only way into the place was by the railroad. Also, it would have cost a lot of money to have taken it out and stored it. If he did come back, then it was already there and in the meantime his storage was free. So I guess it made good sense just to leave it.

There were five dump trucks that I saw. Three of the five were in working order when we got there. Somehow the three Eskimos got a friend to smuggle some booze into them via the train. Then, one night they got stone drunk. Before Jim found out, they decided to take the trucks for a spin and have a game of chicken. I don't know for sure which one did what, but at least two of them weren't chicken because they wrecked two of the trucks in a head on collision. Luckily no one got hurt because I didn't know where the nearest doctor was located. Also, somehow the other dump truck got driven off a cliff. I didn't know anything about any of it until the next morning and it was just as well because Jim was *r-e-a-l-l-y* bent out of shape about it. In the first place, it was against the rules to have booze on the section. I suppose it was Jim's rules, but at any rate it was a No-No! Then there was the little matter of the destruction of personal property. Even though they were theoretically abandoned, the trucks still belonged to someone. I guess the same could be said for all the coffee, applesauce, etc. that we liberated for that matter. But wrecking the trucks in drunken horseplay, was just a senseless act in which someone could have been killed or seriously hurt. Out there in the middle of nowhere, a bad accident could drastically curtail one's personal longevity. We couldn't afford ANY accidents of any kind, particularly the avoidable variety. That was another reason why we only had one gun. It was a 30.06. It belonged to Jim, and *no one* ever borrowed it.

Well, Jim held court after the wrecking of the dump trucks. We understood he gave the three Eskimos a choice. They could either take the next train out and he would request three replacements... or they could perform some extra duty. They took the latter. The rest of us were not involved, and were not present at the hearing. I don't remember now, for sure, what the punishment was, but as I recall it was more than a slap on the hand.

Dunkle also had a Caterpillar road grader (it survived). They used it to work on the road they constructed, which lead about six miles into the wilderness to their operation. Dunkle's men had also built a substantial bridge over the Chulitna River, at a point where the river was perhaps only fifty feet wide. The river was quite shallow, being maybe three feet or so deep at the deepest, and basically had a rock bed. It was a good salmon river, and that is where we gigged our salmon during the run. We took some half inch dowel reinforcing rods we had found among Dunkle's supplies. We used Dunkle's blacksmith's forge to heat one end red hot. Then we used our track hammers to flatten it, doused it in water, then with one of Dunkle's hack saws we barbed the flattened end. Using an old foot operated stone grinder we put an edge on the barbed end. Then with the aid of a steel hand drill, we *laboriously* drilled a hole through the other end and put a piece of raw hide through, making a loop to which we fastened a line. Then we had ourselves a harpoon. We would stand on Dunkle's bridge, over the Chulitna, and harpoon the salmon as they swam upstream to spawn.

Now and then, at night after supper we would all get together over at the section house. Tex had a guitar and would play for us. He was a pretty decent singer, too. Mostly he played softly and sang by himself, but sometimes one, or two, or more would join in. They were usually the typical, lonesome, forlorn, cowboy type songs. Jim also had a guitar, but he didn't play it too often. However, now and then he and Tex would get together with a little guitar harmony. They made a pretty good duo.

Usually the four of us, Bob, Stew, Doug and I, would spend the evenings by ourselves in the warehouse where we slept. We'd play cards using wood matches for money. More often than not, we had a pot of coffee on the pot bellied stove. It was 'Dunkle's Special Blend', brewed in 'Dunkle's Pot' that we had also liberated. The pot didn't have any inside components so we just put the raw coffee in the pot, added water, and boiled it. Then we added some cold water which more-or-less settled the grounds out, before we poured it into our 'Dunkle mugs'. I've related how we got the coffee pot, coffee, and mugs from Dunkle's pantry, but there is a little story as to how we got the other ingredient... the water.

For the life of me I don't know why we didn't just go to the well near the section house to get our water... or to the lake across the tracks. Both were closer, more accessible, and definitely far less hazardous than how we attained it, but therein lies the basis for this little story.

We had a special matchbox in which we kept four matchsticks. There were two long ones, one medium, and one short stick. One of us would take them out and hold them in one hand so the tops stuck up the same height. Then the other three each drew one. If you drew a long match, you didn't have to go get water. If you drew the medium or short one, then you were one of the ones who had to go. The one that got the short match had to carry the water, which was usually two buckets. The fellow that got the medium length match went as the shotgun. Of course, no one had a shotgun, but that merely meant he went along armed with a big club. We would sing, shout, yell, beat the trees and brush with the club, and in general we made as much noise as we could to announce our impending arrival. Why? Well, a lot of the time, but especially during the salmon season, there would be a bunch of bears down at the Chulitna batting out salmon for their young to eat; and that was where we went to get our water. You knew they were there because you could hear a lot of splashing, growling and squealing going on. However, we hoped that if the bears heard us coming they would graciously get out of our way. At least that was the theory we were fervently depending on. But it would be immensely unwise; I mean a *huge* mistake, ever to surprise a mother bear with cubs. Apparently our theory was valid.

The day we went on our unsuccessful caribou hunt was another day I will not soon forget. It was a Sunday and our only day off during the week. It was also drab, overcast and misty. Most of us went on the hunt, but one or two may have remained at the section. Jim had a high powered 30.06 rifle, and though primarily we were looking for caribou, we'd have taken anything to help supplement our larder. The section foreman could, and usually did, own a weapon for protection from bears, and to shoot game for the crew. But the average Gandy Dancer usually had more brawn than brains and certainly didn't have any business having a gun. Fortunately, all the fellows on our section got along unusually well. I can only recall one actual fight and maybe a half dozen shouting matches, but nothing I would term as really serious. I am sure most sections could not claim that degree of congeniality.

On our hunt, we saw plenty of fresh caribou tracks in the muddy areas and later in the snow as we rose above the snow line, but we never caught even a glimpse of a caribou. I'm sure it was because we were jabbering and in general making too much noise. I expect one could probably have compared our stalking to something like a herd of elephants trying to sneak up on a spooked goose.

We walked across Dunkle's bridge and along the road,

which was more a trail than a road as we think of a road today. Four miles west of the section, Jim pointed off to the south across a broad stream to a long narrow clearing, maybe 1,500 feet away. I could hardly believe my eyes. There, nosed over, was a P-51 Mustang fighter plane. Jim told us that during the war there were little narrow strips like that all over Alaska which always housed at least two planes. If the Japs had ever tried to fly over on their way to bomb us, these fighters were supposed to come up out of the wilderness and shoot them down. As far as he knew, that never happened. Anyway, when they closed the strip and headed for home the first plane crashed on takeoff. According to Jim, the other pilot flew out ok. From what I understood Jim to say there apparently were just the two planes and two pilots at that strip. Of course, they had to have had some support crew, who no doubt came in and out by the railroad. At any rate, it certainly was an austere post.

About five and a half miles west of our section we came to Dunkle's coal mine. We walked back into the mine a short distance using some crudely constructed torches we had made. The tunnel was shored up with timbers, but some didn't appear in the best of condition, so we didn't spend much time inside. There was plenty of coal lying about. They had built a tipple for unloading the coal cars brought out of the mine. They apparently had quite an operation at one time. At first I didn't understand why he had a coal mine, and actually mined coal, unless he was really looking for gold and found coal there instead. However, there was certainly a need for coal especially in Anchorage and Fairbanks, and all he had to do was to transport it to the railroad after it was mined.

Dunkle's abandoned coal mine.

Then we went to the end of the road, which is where the Golden Zone gold mine was located. The gold mine was somewhat more primitive than the coal mine. Basically it was a fairly large opening in the side of a big hill that the miners had dug a tunnel into. Again we made torches and went in to see what, if anything, there was to see. We could see definite traces of what appeared to be gold in the tunnel walls, but just traces. We didn't expect to find anything worthwhile because Dunkle hadn't, and he knew what he was looking for.

Near the mouth of the cave there were perhaps five traditional log cabins. They were about twenty by twenty feet in size, and made of approximately eight inch logs. Doug and

I noticed the door to the cabin nearest to us was open, so we walked in. I never will forget the feeling. It was *eerie*. It was as if the people had just stepped out and would be back any second to find us standing in their house. Inside there was just one room separated by a partially drawn sheet, which was supported by a wire. On the east side of the cabin was a homemade bed and a baby crib with a dirty diaper draped over the side. There was a pair of overalls and a woman's dress on a peg pounded into the log wall. Neatly aligned up against the north wall was a pair of mukluks and a pair of slippers. There was a table in the corner with some personal items, eyeglasses etc. lying about, and there was a window in the south wall. On the west side was what passed for the living room and kitchen, so to speak. There were two windows, one each on the west, and south walls. In the corner was a cooking/heating stove, some pots and pans, a bucket, drinking glasses, etc. There was a homemade table and three chairs. Over one of the chairs was draped a woman's apron. On the table there was a bowl with dried batter and a spoon sticking out of it. Beside the bowl was an open can of Hershey's cocoa. It was obvious that the woman had been in the process of baking a chocolate cake, when everyone... apparently just disappeared. That was over five years before and obviously the people had not returned. However, standing there gave me a very uncomfortable feeling that they had just temporarily stepped out and would likely return before we left. I knew it was ridiculous, but it was still spooky.

After leaving the gold mine we climbed on, up to well above the snow line, still following the fresh caribou tracks, but since we still had about a six mile hike to get back we soon headed for the section empty handed.

I always had a picture of me taken on my birthday. This year, 1948, would be special because I would leave my teens and enter my twenties. Well, I almost forgot this time. The four of us, Doug, Bob, Stew and I were sitting in the warehouse playing cards. All of a sudden I remembered I hadn't had my picture taken. So Doug and I stepped out on the platform that was along the north side of the warehouse.

I gave Doug my camera and he took a picture of me. It was at 11:30 p.m., with no flash, yet there was plenty of light to give me a decent picture. This prompted me to recall some seven years prior when I was detasseling corn in a field north of Rushville.

My 20th birthday picture taken at 11:30 p.m. without a flash.

I thought, 'Ok, I am entering my teens here in this corn field north of Rushville. Now, I wonder where I will be when I leave my teens.' Little did I know I would be several thousand miles from there. Another little oddity occurred that

258

day that I would never have imagined back in that cornfield, when I passed into my teens. I watched one heck-gee-gosh of a snow storm, above the snow line a few hundred feet higher in the mountains from where we were. It is not often a kid from Illinois sees a blizzard on his birthday, especially when his birthday is on July 22nd.

Lakes abounded in the area, however, Forty Acre Lake, the one across the tracks by the section house, was the only one we ever went swimming in. We would do our fishing out of an oversized pond a little west of the section, on the other side of Dunkle's bridge. Mike used a modified safety pin as his hook. I had brought a line and some hooks and made my own bobble, but I didn't really need one. The trout would not bite on a bare hook, but just stick a salmon egg or two on it and they lined up waiting for you to throw it in.

With our trout catch: Stew (4) - Mike Yakasoff (22) – Corky (7).

One day Stew, Mike Yakasoff and I went to what we called Trout Lake because that was all you caught there. Mike walked out on a beaver dam while Stew and I were on the shore. We were pulling out trout right and left. We were there about a half hour and between us we had thirty-three nice trout. Stew got four, I got seven, and Mike caught twenty-two. Our fishing expedition came to an abrupt halt when I looked up and noticed a cow moose, with her calf, wandering down to get a drink of water. Now a female moose is no small animal and can have a very nasty disposition at any time, especially when she has a calf with her. She was perhaps only fifteen feet from where Mike was standing. Fortunately, he didn't have a bite at that time and was standing perfectly still. I held my forefinger to my lips and urgently whispered ... *"M i k e."* Mike looked up and I pointed to his right. He slowly turned his head. Noticing some movement, the cow moose turned to her left and she and Mike were looking at each other eyeball to eyeball. Mike took off down that beaver dam in the opposite direction. The moose looked at his rapid departure as if a little surprised. She apparently was unalarmed because she went back to drinking. I suppose she was up wind from him and hadn't detected his scent. Also, she didn't notice him at first because he wasn't moving. Even if she had, she might not have known WHAT it was she was looking at. I imagine it is highly unlikely that she had ever seen a human being before. Well, we had enough fish anyway so we went back to the section to clean them. Though it was still fish it was a break from all the salmon we had been eating.

Our days in the Alaska bush were numbered now and the last memorable event would be the Gandy Dancer's Ball up at our Division Head, in Broad Pass. Now that was a real blast and I wouldn't have missed the experience for the world. Years later it reminded me of the once popular TV show called the Twilight Zone where one would find himself in the past and present, both at the same time. But before proceeding, I should define just what a Gandy Dancer... and a Gandy Dancer's Ball really is. Earlier, when I said we got a job on the railroad, I mentioned it was as a Gandy Dancer and alluded to the fact that it was a fancy term for a common dirt laborer on the railroad. That is true and can be found in most dictionaries, but it doesn't explain the actual origin of the term. I'm not totally sure where the term Gandy comes from, but I suspect that *Gandy* may be a derivation of the term Gander. According to one of the definitions out of Webster's New World Dictionary, it defines a Gander as a stupid or silly fellow. The common concept of a railroad track laborer, at least back in those days, was that he was not much more than an employed hobo, tramp, vagabond, or drifter. He often had a low IQ; was somewhat unkempt; more interested in the pleasures of the moment than taking any responsibility for planning his future; and on top of that, he often had a rough and tumble disposition. So I believe that description, and Mr. Webster's definition, is a reasonable basis for the word Gandy. However, I honestly feel the men on our section were much better than this very general description. We had become friends who would do anything for each other and were sort of a family.

Now the term *Dancer* comes from the fact that when a track laborer is tamping the rock ballast under the ties with his shovel, he stands on one foot, has his other foot on his shovel, and repeatedly jams the ballast under the tie. During this process he is raising and thrusting the shovel tip up and down, up and down, up and down, to get the ballast packed tight so it will firm up the bedding support for the ties that holds the rails. From a distance, it looks like this unlikely individual, or *silly fellow,* is doing a dance... hence the term: ... Gandy Dancer.

Now, as to what a Gandy Dancer's BALL is... it is rather like payback time, or an expression of appreciation, to all those men scattered out over hundreds of miles of track who work a hard nine hour back breaking work day, six days a week. These fellows are isolated under rather primitive conditions and are deprived of many of life's basic comforts. They have no home or family and are all alone except for their fellow workers. Even while surrounded by boundless beauty it can, by some, be considered a rather dull, drab, even depressing existence. This type of job does not draw out the cream of society, but more often the dregs and adventurers. Indeed, the turnover was probably pretty high because it was not considered by most to be their life's ambition, or profession. So the Gandy Dancer's Ball was the government's way to say thank you, and an attempt to keep the men happy. It was an event that the men would talk about for months and look forward to attending the next time. I don't know for sure how often they had them, but I believe it was probably twice a year, once in the spring and in the fall.

Going to a Gandy Dancer's Ball is like nothing you've ever seen before, and probably will ever see again. That night was like living a saga from the past. Up in Alaska, in 1948, life was rather austere even in Anchorage, but on the section it was really a step back in time. This was a long time before television was available to the average person, even in the Lower 48, and there weren't even any regular radios up there because there was no commercial radio broadcasting stations.

Let me draw a mental picture of what going to a Gandy Dancer's Ball was like, by giving you some comparisons. Today, when one is going to a Grand Ball, we have our own visions of what we could probably expect to encounter. However, up there, back in 1948, this ball, while containing all the same elements... was a *little bit different*.

A modern ball might be held in a mansion situated on a plush and well appointed estate, with doormen; beautiful women in formals; men in tuxedos; waiters; fancy chandeliers; elegant furniture; an orchestra playing Mozart; champagne fountains; clever professional entertainment; and people arriving in limos.

On the other hand, the old-fashioned Gandy Dancer's Ball that we went to had a counterpart to all of the above. For example... our *mansion* was approximately a fifty foot by one hundred foot log hall with open beam rafters, and our well appointed estate was out in the middle of the wilderness. There were no beautiful women... or women at all. If one or two guys wanted to dance, one had to agree that he'd follow for one dance, but you can bet he was going to lead on the next one. As for formal attire, the Gandies wore their cleanest work clothes, and as far as waiters were concerned... you waited on yourself. Our chandeliers were coal oil lamps, and the most elegant furniture I saw was homemade tables, split log benches and a few obviously homemade chairs. Our orchestra varied from time to time with up to three foot stomping guitar players; two guys with violins who produced some snappy, old-fashioned, hoedowns; one fellow played a six foot two-man saw, and he really could make it sing; another was keeping time rubbing on a washboard; and a piano player. They didn't all play at the same time, but just wandered in and out as they felt like it. Instead of a champagne fountain there was a line of beer kegs that had been brought in for the occasion. Our entertainment wasn't exactly professional and the choices were rather limited. There were all sorts of card games going on and several blankets on the floor where one could get into a crap game. Often there was at least one loud and heated argument or a full blown knock-down, drag-out, fight going on at any point in time. Everyone arrived via the railroad in their version of a limo, which was their section's gas buggy towing their flat car. The fellows sat on the gas buggy or flat car coming in, but going home those who were in no condition to sit were stacked on the flat car for the return trip. So you see, we had all the elements of a regular ball. But yet as you can also see... it was *a little bit different* than the normal concept.

All of us looked forward to the event. Mrs. Collins did not go. While she had nothing to be alarmed about from our crew, she might have looked a bit more interesting to some of the bozos from one of the other less sophisticated sections. We really dressed up for the occasion. We mended any rips or tears, and sewed missing buttons on our best work clothes. We even washed them, put on clean socks, and trimmed or shaved as suited us. Personally I trimmed because I still had my beard. I remember Alec Melik greased his hair down with Vaseline, and he and one of the other Eskimos, Henry Tuffolna, had gotten some toilet water from somewhere. They must have taken a bath in the stuff because they smelled like a couple of French whores on Sunday morning. We kidded them saying they had better watch out because by wearing all that stink juice they just might get some of the Gandies overly excited.

Alec Melik was one of our good natured Eskimos.

The date of the scheduled Gandy Dancer's Ball finally arrived. By now the days and nights were getting about like back home. After supper Jim checked with Broad Pass for the latest train schedule so we wouldn't have a surprise on the way up and meet a train head on. We wore our jackets because the nights were getting a bit cool now. It was starting to get dark as we pulled out and headed north for Broad Pass. It took us around forty-five minutes or so to get there on the gas buggy and it was maybe 7:00 or 7:30 p.m. by the time we arrived. There were perhaps four or five buildings at the site, including the fifty by hundred foot log building where the party was being held. In addition to being a regular section like ours, it was the Division Head; and had some offices and a minor repair facility there, also. When we arrived, the party

265

was already in full swing, but it didn't take us long to join in. As we approached the door we were met by two of the establishment's doormen. They were pretty good sized fellows, well over six feet, in the 200 plus pound range and with an authoritative ring to their voices. Both looked like they probably wrestled a bear or two each morning before breakfast just to keep in shape. They were non-smiling, all business, and I seriously doubt if either of them had a nickname of Chuckles. We were asked politely, yet firmly and with all the sincerity of prison cell block guards, if we had any guns or knives, and if so, to check them before we went inside. There was a table beside them where there was quite an assortment of hardware already tagged. I thought about jokingly asking them if those guns and knives were going to be the door prizes, but thinking perhaps, they might not share my sense of humor; I just let the opportunity pass. They didn't frisk us and, since none of our group had either guns or knives anyway, they just passed us on through. These guys and a few of their buddies were railroad detectives who were the law and order element for the otherwise rather ragtag motley crew that had assembled.

All the beer, sandwiches, peanuts and pretzels you wanted were free. They also had some soft drinks, but I don't recall what kinds they had. Obviously, it was all provided free of charge by the Department of the Interior, for whom we worked, because we were never asked to buy a ticket. In the first place a lot of us didn't have any money. You had nothing to spend it on, so most of us left our wages on the books until we left. Also, that way you couldn't gamble it away. Of course, you could have the Purser in Anchorage send you some of it if you wanted. I feel confident some of the regular section hands had some money sent to them so they could gamble at the ball, but that was not a matter one discussed. Certainly a lot of guys, from many of the sections did have money since there were plenty of card and crap games going on... and they weren't just playing for nickels and dimes. There was some real serious money floating around.

The fellows playing the guitars, violins and piano were pretty good. Now and then one would drop out to quench his thirst and someone out of the crowd would step up and play along. Then, after a while, all of them would take a well deserved break. Of course, the piece that got played the most was the song, *The Gandy Dancer's Ball*. Actually, it isn't a song you hear very often, but it does have a rather nice active tune and catchy words as well. Once in a great while you might hear it on the radio today. There is a part in the song where they talk about dancing around the demijohn. A demijohn is a very large wine bottle, either earthen or made of glass with a long skinny neck, and is usually in a wicker basket. Some of them hold upwards of five gallons, sometimes more. The one they had at the ball was made of glass, and was for show. Anyway, several of the boys danced a jig around it, as is told in the fabled song.

There were several large kegs of beer. I don't recall seeing any whiskey, but I suppose there was at least a limited amount. The Department of the Interior normally frowned on both booze and firearms being accessible to the run of the mill railroader working on the sections. There were many good, sensible, logical and obvious reasons why it wasn't allowed. However, at the ball the bar was not only open... it was free! This officially sponsored party was different and prohibition was suspended. They knew most would get a snoot full, but it was a Saturday night, Sunday they didn't work, and by Monday most would be sober or at least reasonably so.

Anyway, it gave the boys a chance to blow off a little steam and loosen up a bit, which was good for morale. The Gandies spent weeks talking about the ball coming up and when it was over they would spend weeks talking about what a time they had, who saw who get the drunkest, and who got the sickest. That may sound a wee bit gross... but that was how it was among a lot of them.

For the four of us, Bob, Stew, Doug and myself, this was, of course, our first (and only) time there and naturally we didn't know any of the fellows from any of the other sections. We just walked around to see what there was to see... scattered a few smiles, nods, and 'Howdys' here and there. There was quite a line at the beer kegs, and old friends who hadn't seen each other since the last ball, were laughing and slapping each other on the back. There was plenty of loud talk, mostly good natured. Guys were swapping lies and telling jokes and stories. Once or twice we'd come across an individual who'd been overcome by some unhappy event out of his past, real or imagined due perhaps to too many beers, and he'd be sobbing his eyes out. Another fellow or two might be there trying to console the poor, despondent wretch... or even joining him in his sorrow. You didn't want to give the appearance of being nosey, but if you walked close and slow enough past the distraught individual you often could pick up a few phrases or words from which you could fairly accurately figure out how the guy ended up on the railroad in the first place. Often times the fellow blamed some woman who didn't understand him as the source of his problems. Sometimes the local constabulary back home, wherever that was, had been picking on him. At any rate, the more booze he consumed the worse his problems seemed.

If you didn't know better, one might think we had wandered into an opium den. The heavy smoke, with a yellowish-brown tinge to it, was suspended in layers all around, stratified you might say. It got worse as the evening wore on. As the men walked around, the smoke would swirl and sort of remind me of ships slipping in and out of the fog.

Now and then loud shouting and shoving would break out a few tables away. We usually were poised, ready to duck, in case a beer stein might accidentally come flying in our general direction... which happened once or twice. The ruckus didn't usually last but a minute or so, and was almost always at a card game where one felt someone was cheating, or trying to. During the course of the evening, two such instances stand out rather vividly in my memory. One was a good old-fashioned knock-down, drag-out, brawl... which fortunately, was limited to just the two irritated lads in question. A few tables were rapidly scooted back to make room for them to express themselves. Most of the fellows in the immediate area merely stood by and watched. Both of the fellows were pretty well matched and didn't appear to need or want any outside help or interference. And no one offered. They went at it bare-knuckled for several minutes until one was finally proven to be the more durable of the two. Then of all things, the victor went over and helped his fallen fellow combatant up, and they went off arm in arm to get another beer. No one seemed to know what the dispute was about and for that matter we aren't too sure they did either.

The other vivid instance could have been a tad more nasty, but fortunately wasn't. It occurred at a table less than fifteen feet from where Doug and I were moseying through the crowd. Suddenly, a pretty good sized fellow came up out of his chair, pulled out an impressive looking Bowie type knife from under his coat, which he had failed to check at the door, and lunged across the table with apparently every intention of whittling on the player opposite him. About as quick, a fellow on each side of the armed man grabbed him in midair, dropped him on the table, then off onto the floor. They took his knife away before anyone got stabbed or otherwise disfigured. I don't know if he thought the other fellow was cheating, or if it was something that had been said, and for sure we didn't ask. The railroad detectives quickly came over and took the knife. The fellow had calmed down so they let things return to normal. As a rather humorous aside, similar to the outcome between the two fellows that were fist fighting shortly before, we later saw these same two characters, the fellow who had pulled the knife and his intended target, behaving as if nothing ever happened. Now they were both buddy-buddy, laughing and slapping each other on the back. Of course, this was a few more beers later.

At least once for sure, possibly twice, a spirited situation arose when someone pulled out an unchecked gun and fired a round or two through the overhead. It wasn't fired in the heat of anger. Some Gandy had smuggled the gun inside and, no doubt after a few too many beers he decided to celebrate *something*, which he probably didn't remember himself. He thought of the gun and let off a couple of rounds. He was immediately disarmed and promptly invited to check it at the door by the railroad detectives. They couldn't really throw anyone out because there was no where to go. If the detectives found they had an unrepentant, mean, fighting type of customer on their hands, they simply removed him to another building where he was detained until he got control of himself, or was forced to stay for the rest of the evening if he didn't. I don't recall any situation where that was necessary.

As the evening drew on, it was not uncommon to see someone who got sleepy and had decided to take a snooze. It might be in a corner somewhere, in a chair with his face down on a table, or even flat out laying in the middle of the floor. No one seemed to mind; the crowd would merely step over or move around them. I recall a fellow sitting in a chair, leaning back on the rear two legs, and propped against a wall of the room. He was sound asleep. I just happened to be looking at him when he gave a loud SNORT and jumped at the same time. His chair slipped out and down he went, still in a sitting position in the chair, but now lying flat on his back... and he STILL remained sound asleep.

After a while Bob and Stew got in the beer line, and then went off roaming around by themselves. As the party and the evening wore on, the revelry built up until the festivities peaked around 10:30 p.m. After that things began to deteriorate somewhat. Now and then you heard someone, somewhere, get sick. Then someone else who should have taken a walk outside to relieve himself either thought he had, or didn't care. The disagreements seemed to pick up both in number and intensity and there was not as much brotherly love or frivolity by then, as there had been earlier. Several were getting sullen, some a bit testy, as well as a few were getting a tad on the mean side.

Doug and I spent perhaps the last half hour, or forty-five minutes, over in a corner where we had a good view of the hall. That seemed like the safest place to be. We sat there watching the drama of this genuine old-fashioned Gandy Dancer's Ball pass in review before us. In a way it was a little sad. Both of us were aware that this was a vanishing breed of men, in a vanishing society and a vanishing era. Times would soon be changing. There would be automatic rail layers, tie retrievers and loaders, as well as pneumatic tie tampers. The sections as we knew them would cease to exist and there would be work trains that would go back to a central point on the weekends where the men could have homes, families and lead a normal life. They would probably be a little higher class of individuals than we had now. This change was already beginning, to some extent, down on some of the bigger railroads in the Lower 48, but that technology had not yet spread this far north. Everything here was done the old-fashioned hard way. Yet this history and heritage was passing before our eyes as we watched. We were both grateful that we were smart enough to have recognized it and privileged enough to have been a little part of it; to have seen it the way it really was before this chapter of Americana forever faded from the scene.

The party was to be over at midnight, but around 11:30 p.m. Jim appeared from somewhere and asked us if we were ready to head back. I suppose Jim had a few drinks, but if so you couldn't tell it. He checked with the office just to be sure there wasn't going to be any freights or light engines on the track between us and Colorado. We helped him round up the rest of the gang and we mounted either the gas buggy or flat car. It was kind of cool so I rode on the gas buggy which had a shield in front and back, and a top on it and open sides. We laid Tex, Slim, Alec, and Henry on the flat car and Mike sat back there with them to be sure no one fell off. Doug and I were both in good shape and so were Bob and Stew, but they may have had a bit of a headache the next morning. A couple of the others didn't really rejoin the world of the living until Sunday afternoon.

The return trip to Colorado was beautiful. It was a clear night and the moon was at its fullest. Other than that, the trip was uneventful and we pulled in around midnight. It was a great night and one that I would never forget. I still couldn't believe that no one at the ball had gotten much more than a fat lip, maybe a few teeth loosened and a minor cut, scrape or sprain. No one we knew, or heard of, had gotten stabbed, shot, or any broken bones.

I worked a few more days and then it was time for me to depart. Doug was going to stay on for a bit more, and then wanted to go on north to Fairbanks before returning. Stew decided he would stay a while longer, too. As for me, I had worked until the last minute and now had to hurry home so I could get to Champaign and enroll at the University of Illinois. Bob Haven decided to leave at the same time I did. Three days before our departure the passenger train stopped and who got off, but Mr. Dunkle! We avoided him like the plague. He was less than happy to find out that all five of his trucks were out of commission. As I said, two of them didn't work when we got there, but the Eskimos had driven one off a cliff and wrecked the other two with a head on collision. Also, Dunkle didn't have as many supplies then as he had when he left, but that didn't amount to all that much, like the trucks did. He had several talks with Jim. I don't know what all was said and Jim never discussed it with us. It sufficed to say, he was not a happy camper. The rumor was he was about to get additional financial backing to reopen the mines. Therefore, he had come up to see exactly what was left and what was still useable.

.....Finally Friday, August 13th arrived. This was the day that Haven and I were to leave the section. We bid everyone goodbye and I think we were all a little sad... at least I know I was. It was good to be going home, but by now these people were sort of like family.

Corky shortly before leaving the railroad.

As I said goodbye to Doug, we both promised to keep in touch, and to see each other again, which we did. I said goodbye to Stew, Tex, Slim, Alec, Henry, Mike, and Mrs. Collins. Lastly, when I came to Jim, he shook my hand, looked me straight in the eye and said, "You were a good worker and I will miss you." That was like Jim, straight to the point, very matter of fact, no frills, but I knew he meant it. I appreciated that and considered it a true compliment, especially coming from him.

The passenger train would reach the Colorado Section, headed south for Anchorage, around mid-morning. We set our semaphore signal that was alongside the track, to the straight up position. That let the engineer know that he was to stop for freight or passengers. If we only had mail to go out the train would not have to stop. We would attach a gray canvas mail pouch to a hoop, and hang it on a peg on the far side of the semaphore. Then we'd set the semaphore to point at 3 o'clock. This way the train engineer knew we only had mail. As the train sped by, one of the crew would stick their arm out and through the hoop, thus snatching the pouch off the peg on the semaphore. Also, they'd throw us a spare hoop and bag to use the next time. But *this* day the semaphore went straight up, to signal the engineer to stop, because this day there would be passengers!

Besides packing my gear in my sleeping bag, packing my small hand bag and taking a package to mail for one of the fellows, I had one more chore to perform. That was to shave off my beard. In 1948, down in the Lower 48, wearing a beard was unconventional. The only people who wore beards were a few old men; those who generally didn't care what anyone thought; and the young rebel type who were trying to make a statement. I wasn't particularly fond of my beard anyway. I always kept it trimmed and never really let it bush out, but I was glad I grew it while I was up there. At any rate, I was going to be hitchhiking across the northwestern part of the United States and I didn't want it to detract from my chances of getting a ride. My first move was to take scissors and cut it as close as I could. I was out of shaving cream so I heated some water and used my lifebuoy soap to make a lather to soften the whiskers. Then I used my safety razor, which by now was quite dull. Shaving the beard off was not a real pleasant experience.

Now that the crew was dwindling, Doug was back

working on the tracks with the regular crew instead of helping Mrs. Collins with KP. Regardless of what I thought of Mrs. Collins' cooking, I certainly didn't have anything against her. I never really got to know much about her though. For the most part everyone was very private about their background. Apparently that was how they wanted it and we all respected it.

So when the train came, Mrs. Collins was the only one left at the section. Bob and I bid her goodbye and climbed aboard. Mr. Dunkle was also going out on the same train and I'll be darned if he didn't pick a seat directly behind us. He was still ticked off at everyone connected with the section and I couldn't say I blamed him.

Bob Haven and I board the train for Anchorage.

He never said a word to us and we didn't strike up a conversation with him either. Bob and I moved around on the train some and managed to end up at the opposite end of the car from him. Our crew was working at the south end of the section that day and we had a chance to wave to them as we went by. They were expecting us to be out on the platform because they were also looking for us.

As we passed south through this beautiful land, we looked out at the wilderness and had more appreciation for it now than when we first arrived. Now we had tasted it firsthand and would take a little of it away with us... and we'd leave a little of ourselves there, too.

A few hours later we arrived in Anchorage. By now it had become overcast. We went to the railroad office and picked up a little cash, but had them send the bulk of our summer's pay home. I don't remember how much we had on the books, but at that time it amounted to quite a nice sum. We bought a few small souvenirs with some of the money we had picked up and then headed for the airport to catch a plane to Seattle.

We found a nonscheduled airline company called, Pacific Alaska, which was planning a flight to Seattle as soon as their plane got in from Dutch Harbor. A nonscheduled airline is one that, obviously, doesn't have a fixed schedule. They fly to wherever whenever they have enough freight, people, or combination thereof, to make it worth their while. If you can arrange your schedule to meet their flight plan, it is usually a lot less costly than buying a ticket on a regular scheduled flight. The airfare from Anchorage to Seattle was $70 + $10.50 tax for a total of $80.50. Excluding the tax, the fare was exactly twice what it cost us to get up to Alaska aboard the SS Aleutian, but a heck of a lot faster. We found our flight on Pacific Alaska would be a lot *less plush* than a regular flight. In fact, you could go a step further and say it would be plushless. But we weren't accustomed to anything fancy anyway. Besides, it was a different experience and a side of life that most people never see, so I'm glad I had the opportunity.

Well, the plane never arrived when it was supposed to. It seems they had an engine go out on them over Dutch Harbor, so they had to wing it onto Anchorage on the other one. Then, of course, they had to replace it. After the delay in getting to Anchorage on one engine, changing the engine, loading the plane with the freight to ship to Seattle and getting us boarded, we were six hours late getting off.

Boarding a nonscheduled flight for Seattle aboard a DC-3.

The plane was a twin engine DC-3 which, back in 1948, was not exactly considered old and was one of the most durable planes ever built. They had loaded it with a lot of crates of freight, which were lashed down along the center axis of the plane. Passengers sat in metal bucket seats along either side, with our backs to the side of the plane, as if we were World War II paratroopers.

The ports (windows) all had a thick plastic plug in the center; maybe six inches in diameter, yellowed with age, with a short thin rope and wood toggle. I asked someone what the plugs were for and was told that this plane previously flew the Hump (across the Himalayas) in China during World War II. If the Japs attacked, the passengers could pull the plugs out, stick out a machine gun, rifle, Colt .45, etc. to help defend themselves. I'm glad I was not bothered by the myth of Friday the 13th for it was Friday, August 13, 1948, that Haven and I flew out of Anchorage. We did note that a bit of fog had set in; there was a light drizzle; we were in a plane that had just had an engine replaced; and as we gained speed to lift off, we passed nine wrecked planes that had been pushed off to the side of the airstrip. They weren't new wrecks, and no doubt had been there for quite awhile, but they were wrecked aircraft just the same. As we gained altitude we were soon completely enveloped in a heavy cloud blanket for some time. It was interesting to note that, especially when we were flying through some turbulence in the air, the wings would noticeably flex up and down as we flew along. I knew that was not unusual, so it didn't bother me.

The flight was quite informal and after we got to our cruising altitude a few people started milling around. Some even went up and stood in the hatch to the cockpit and talked with the pilot and copilot. When no one was there, I decided to go up and have a look myself. As I was there talking to them, all of a sudden, we popped out of the clouds. We were maybe five miles off shore. The Pacific was a deep royal blue. Off to the east there was a large glacier which had surrounded a few snowcapped mountain peaks, then, as it reached the coast, it dropped off into the Pacific in a near vertical drop of perhaps 300 to 500 feet. The pilot told me it was called the Taku Glacier. The sun was at such an angle that it sent out laser like flashes of near blinding blue-white light as it reflected off of the sheer vertical cliff of ice, making it look like a huge diamond. It was, and has ever since remained, one of the most breath taking sights I've ever seen.

We landed at Yakutat Island where they delivered some freight and topped off the fuel tanks. However, the weather had deteriorated and was generally lousy, so the pilot decided we would hole up there for the night. It was around 10:00 p.m. and there was no hotel, just a small crummy waiting room with a filthy linoleum floor and a few very hard uncomfortable folding chairs. It was a miserable night, but at least we were inside rather than outside in a cold drizzle.

The next morning, the 14th, we piled our cold stiff bones back in the plane and flew onto Seattle. From there Bob and I hitchhiked east, and by nightfall we had finally made our way to Spokane. We hadn't made very good time, but then there were two of us and the second man always cuts your chances of getting a ride. We found a YMCA and got a room. It was around 9:00 p.m. when we checked in and we were both beat. We had worked on the railroad all day on the 12th and due to the excitement of heading for home, we didn't get a lot of sleep that night; then we had been up all day the 13th waiting, or flying, and then spent the night in the cold dingy waiting room at the Yakutat airport; and finally we were on the road all day the 14th hitchhiking. We were now ready for some real sack time and for the first time since early June in a real bed instead of a sleeping bag. Bob popped in the shower while I put in a call to Jim, my trucker friend in Spokane. He and his partner Walt were the ones that hauled cars out of Duluth to Spokane, with whom I had ridden with the year before. They had told me if I, or any of my friends, wanted a ride to let them know and we could check to see if it would work out. Jim wasn't home, but I talked to his wife. I had never met her, but she knew who I was. She told me that they had bought a third truck and hired two drivers, so one of them was off every fourth trip. This happened to be Jim's trip off, but she had sent him to the grocery store to pick up something. She informed me that the trucks had left that morning, but they had a tire problem in Missoula, MT. They had sent a repair truck out, but since they all had the sleepers she felt there was a good chance they would stay there for the night. She told me it was at a Shell station at the intersection of Montana Route 263 and US 93. For some reason I happened to remember that station, and knew exactly where it was. It was a little after 9:00 p.m. then, so the only way to get there was to catch a bus. I called the bus company and found out a bus had just left and that it would be going by the YMCA in about fifteen minutes. Haven just got out of the shower. I told him we had a ride clear across the northwest into Minnesota if we could make it to Missoula, but we'd have to be in front of the YMCA to flag the bus in fifteen minutes. Haven said he didn't care if they drove the bus up to the room to pick us up; he was too tired and wasn't going anywhere, but to bed. I hadn't unpacked yet so I tossed some money on the bed for my half of the room, said goodbye, and then I was out the door. Nothing personal, but I didn't want to hitchhike with him or anyone for that matter, so here was a good chance for me to break off gracefully.

About five minutes later, I spotted the bus coming. I stepped out in the street and flagged him down, got on, and paid my fare to Missoula. I told the driver I wanted to get off at the Shell station at 263 and 93 in Missoula, and asked if he'd be good enough to drop me there, BUT that I was going to be asleep so he'd have to give me a shake. He said he would and he was as good as his word. The next thing I knew it was pushing 2:00 a.m. on Sunday, August 15th, I was in Missoula, and there was the Shell station, BUT my heart sank as there were no trucks in sight! Fortunately, it was an all night station and the station attendant said they had gotten fixed up sooner than they had expected and had left, however, he added, "I thought I heard'em say something about going onto Whitehall." Beautiful! I knew exactly where that was too, and probably even where they would be parked because that was where I had met them the year before. I told the attendant there was no point in my trying to hitchhike at 2 o'clock in the morning. I asked if he minded if I curled up in a corner of the station to get a little sleep, and I told him I sure would appreciate it if he'd be kind enough to ask anyone stopping for gas if they'd give me a ride. If I was ever going to catch the trucks, I had to get to Whitehall before 6:00 a.m. That meant I had to cover around 150 miles in the next four hours. He was a young kid, and probably trying to get a ride for me was the most exciting thing that had happened to him that night. He told me to go curl up in one of the chairs and he'd do his best for me. I went in the station and sat down. I think I was asleep by the time I hit the seat. The next thing I heard was ... "HEY, I GOT YOU A RIDE!" I think he was as excited as I was. The ride was with three college guys going back to the University of Montana at Helena. They were a friendly bunch and about my age. My short nap had given me a second wind and I was excited by the fact that it looked more and more like I would finally catch up with Walt and the other drivers. Also, there is something rather exciting about rushing through the middle of the night on a mission. All three of the fellows were forestry majors and I enjoyed their explanation of the forestry vocation and their conversation in general, as we hurried ahead through the darkness.

They let me out at a rural intersection in the middle of the woods, in the middle of nowhere, but I was used to a lot of nowhere. This was somewhere a little east of Butte, where they were going to take a shortcut up to Helena to where the University of Montana was located. By now it was around 5:00 a.m. and beginning to get a little light. It was pretty nippy as you could see your breath. I was still about thirty miles short of my ambitious night's goal.

In fifteen or so minutes a pickup truck came by from the north and turned east, which was the direction I was headed. He stopped and gave me a ride, and YES he was going to Whitehall!

As we arrived in Whitehall, there were those three, big, beautiful car hauling rigs, all lined up on the south side of the road headed east, just where they had been parked the year before.

The car carriers at Whitehall, MT.

I went into the truckers' restaurant and ordered a big breakfast, sitting where I could keep an eye on the trucks. I was on my third cup of coffee when I saw Walt crawl out of the lead truck, which I had figured was his. He walked back and banged on the sleeper of the other two rigs, then got out his wash pan, filled it from his jerry can of water, put it on the fender and started to wash up. I finished my coffee, paid my bill, picked up my gear and started walking slowly toward him. He glanced in my direction as I came out of the restaurant, but didn't pay any attention to me. I kept heading straight for him, which soon got his attention. He was still half asleep, but he hunched over and squinted at me as I walked up. He said, "I should know you," to which I replied, "You sure should. We met very close to a year ago and in this very same spot." Walt let out a WHOOP and yelled at the other drivers to... "COME HERE … I've got a guy I want you to meet!"

The two new drivers were a sandy haired fellow named Pat and a shorter dark haired fellow named Pee Wee. They were real friendly, but I always rode with Walt and slept under his truck at night. I told Walt of my all night race from Spokane to Whitehall thinking I would catch them in Missoula. He said that since they had completed their repairs sooner than expected he decided to push it a little so they could get back closer to their schedule.

The day I teamed up with them, Sunday, August 15th, they made it to Glendive, MT, which was where we stayed on Sept. 2nd the year before, so this was about two weeks short of a year since I was with them last. The next day we followed our old trail on east, passing into and across North Dakota to Fargo, arriving on the 16th and stopping for the night at the same truck stop they always stayed at.

The next day, August 17, 1948, I left them at Motley, MN at the same location I had left them the year before. I made my way on south, but things were slow and I wasn't able to get to Moline, to Uncle Paul & Aunt Myrt's, until late on the 18th.

The two new drivers, Pee Wee and Pat plus Walt from my 1947 trip.

I stayed overnight with them. My parents arrived at 10:30 a.m. the next morning to get me, and after lunch we returned home to Rushville, arriving by mid-afternoon of August 19, 1948.

The close of my 8th trip also marked the end of an era in my life. Now I would be entering a different phase. Of course, my thirst for travel never ceased, or even slackened, but change was in the wind. There would be a lot more travel in store for me, with many new adventures, but of a different kind. From here on out I would never be traveling alone.

It had been an interesting and maturing time. I am thankful to the Lord for having kept me safe from harm during my travels. I shall never forget the trust my parents exhibited to have officially allowed me to travel about the country on my quest of visiting all the states of the Union, plus Alaska, Canada and Mexico, as well. It was a different world back then and I am glad I lived it.

EPILOGUE

With the exception of Doug Waugh, I gradually lost contact with those I had become acquainted with during my travels.

After Alaska, Doug moved to New York City into an apartment in Upper Manhattan overlooking Central Park. He lived there for thirty plus years until moving to Columbus, OH. Doug wore several hats during the nearly forty-eight years I knew him, but none of them was marriage. He worked for a major map making company, eventually becoming one of their senior cartographers. He also was a commercial artist and illustrator working for major power companies in New York, and later in Ohio. In addition, he was an excellent cartoonist and an accomplished photographer. He continued to take vacations to the far flung reaches of the world; any one of which would seem like a trip of a lifetime to most of us. Doug took at least one such trip a year, then in the 1960s it was up to two. Some destinations and routings were definitely not in your usual tourist brochures.

However, Doug wore another hat that few knew about. He was a spy and had been one since 1958. That went a long way to explain how he financed his numerous vacations and how he managed to get the necessary papers and clearances. During a visit in 1987 he told me that, of the 140 then considered legitimate countries in world, he had been in 108; I might add many of them more than once. The last time I saw Doug, it was at my home in Peoria, IL in June of 1993. He died in Tibet on May 29, 1994. He was friendly, intelligent, charming and beyond a doubt the most interesting, unusual and mysterious man I ever met. Doug had literally hundreds of acquaintances all over the world, but actually he was a bit of a loner and only had a limited number of inner circle friends. I feel I was one of the latter.

As for me, upon leaving Alaska I transferred to the University of Illinois and graduated with a Bachelor of Science degree in Civil Engineering, in early 1951. I went to work for the Illinois Department of Transportation (IDOT) until my retirement in December, 1986. During that time I was granted a leave of absence for a tour of duty in the U.S. Navy during the early 1950s. I was very fortunate to have been able to serve in the 2nd, 6th, 7th, 5th, and 1st Fleets, mostly on an aircraft carrier in the Navigation Division. This took me completely around the world and to five of the seven continents. Soon after discharge I met and married Marilou Lopeman. Together we have three children. Fortunately, she also loves to travel and by 2003 we have both visited all seven continents.

Besides this book, I have two other books in progress. *Sea Tales* is a compilation of short stories of incidents from my Navy days, many of which are humorous. At this time, over twenty of these individual stories have been published elsewhere in a somewhat edited form. I intend to call my third book *Remembrances*. It relates amusing and interesting events that I have experienced from an early age to present.

I am happy to state that all of my writings are non-fiction.

Ralph D"*Corky*" Sutherland...   2004